ANCIENT ETHICS AND THE NATURAL WORLD

This book explores a distinctive feature of ancient philosophy: the close relation between ancient ethics and the study of the natural world. Human beings are in some sense part of the natural world, and they live their lives within a larger cosmos, but their actions are governed by norms whose relation to the natural world is up for debate. The essays in this volume, written by leading specialists in ancient philosophy, discuss how these facts about our relation to the world bear both upon ancient accounts of human goodness and also upon ancient accounts of the natural world itself. The volume includes discussion not only of Plato and Aristotle, but also of earlier and later thinkers, with an essay on the Presocratics and two essays that discuss later Epicurean, Stoic, and Neoplatonist philosophers.

BARBARA M. SATTLER is Professor of Ancient and Medieval Philosophy at Ruhr-Universität Bochum. She is author of The Concept of Motion in Ancient Greek Thought (Cambridge, 2020) and editor of One Book, the Whole Universe: Plato's Timaeus Today (with Richard D. Mohr, 2010). Her research has appeared in dozens of edited collections and journals.

URSULA COOPE is Professor of Ancient Philosophy at the University of Oxford. She is author of Time for Aristotle: Physics IV. 20–14 (2005) and Freedom and Responsibility in Neoplatonist Thought (2020), and has published numerous book chapters and journal articles on ancient philosophy.

T0384708

ANCIENT ETHICS
AND THE NATURAL WORLD

EDITED BY

BARBARA M. SATTLER

Ruhr-Universität Bochum, Germany

URSULA COOPE

University of Oxford

CAMBRIDGE
UNIVERSITY PRESS

Shaftesbury Road, Cambridge CB2 8EA, United Kingdom

One Liberty Plaza, 20th Floor, New York, NY 10006, USA

477 Williamstown Road, Port Melbourne, VIC 3207, Australia

314–321, 3rd Floor, Plot 3, Splendor Forum, Jasola District Centre, New Delhi – 110025, India

103 Penang Road, #05–06/07, Visioncrest Commercial, Singapore 238467

Cambridge University Press is part of Cambridge University Press & Assessment, a department of the University of Cambridge.

We share the University's mission to contribute to society through the pursuit of education, learning and research at the highest international levels of excellence.

www.cambridge.org
Information on this title: www.cambridge.org/9781108813723

DOI: 10.1017/9781108885133

First published 2021
First paperback edition 2023

A catalogue record for this publication is available from the British Library

ISBN 978-1-108-83978-5 Hardback
ISBN 978-1-108-81372-3 Paperback

Cambridge University Press & Assessment has no responsibility for the persistence or accuracy of URLs for external or third-party internet websites referred to in this publication and does not guarantee that any content on such websites is, or will remain, accurate or appropriate.

To Sarah Broadie, whose scholarship and humanity have inspired generations of scholars, on the occasion of her eightieth birthday

Contents

vii

Contributors

JOACHIM AUFDERHEIDE, King's College London

URSULA COOPE, University of Oxford

JAMIE DOW, University of Leeds

LI FAN, Tongji University

DOROTHEA FREDE, University of Hamburg

A. A. LONG, University of California at Berkeley

ALEX LONG, University of St Andrews

ALEXANDER P. D. MOURELATOS, University of Texas at Austin

CHRISTOPHER ROWE, Durham University

BARBARA M. SATTLER, Ruhr-Universität Bochum

THOMAS TUOZZO, University of Kansas

Note on the Editors

The two editors made equal contributions to the volume. The order of their names was determined by a coin toss.

Introduction

Ursula Coope and Barbara M. Sattler

1 General Introduction

In contemporary discussions, ethics and inquiry into the natural world are often treated as two completely independent fields of study. By contrast, many ancient thinkers took them to be intimately connected. This volume aims to shed light on the various ways in which ancient thinkers drew connections between these two fields. We human beings are in some sense part of the natural world and we live our lives within a larger cosmos, but yet our actions are governed by norms whose relation to the natural world is up for debate. The chapters in this volume discuss how these facts about our relation to the world bear upon both ancient accounts of human goodness and also ancient accounts of the natural world itself. The chapters focus primarily on Plato and Aristotle. But we have also included some discussion of earlier and later thinkers, with a chapter on the Presocratics and a couple of chapters that in part point ahead to later Epicurean, Stoic, and Neoplatonist philosophers.

Prima facie, there are at least two ways in which we may think ethics and the study of nature (or physics) are related. First, while ethics is the study of what it is to be a good human being, human beings inhabit a region of the natural world. Arguably, one cannot understand a living thing, and hence have an account of that living thing's good, without understanding something about the workings of its environment. And one cannot understand the functioning of the natural world without understanding the functioning of its inhabitants (including those inhabitants that are human beings). Both of these thoughts suggest that the study of what it is to be a good human being will be importantly related to the study of the natural world.

Secondly, physics and ethics are both interested in the ways in which changing things are subject to laws and regularities. And so it is natural to ask whether the laws and regularities at work in both fields are of the same or a similar kind, and how ethical norms relate to physical laws. Whether ethical value judgements are also applicable to the natural world, or can in fact be reduced to naturalistic factual statements, depends on how the relationship between ethics and physics is understood.

If we do not simply assume that ethics and physics are two unrelated fields, then three principal models are possible to describe their relationship:

(1) The natural world is itself understood in ethical terms. On such a view, ethical norms are applied to the natural world itself (or to aspects of it), so that it can itself be seen as a good or bad place, or the natural world is anthropomorphised. Those philosophers who anthropomorphise aspects of the natural world might thus even be inclined to regard the study of the natural world as a part of ethics.

(2) Human beings are understood as, in some important sense, grounded in and a part of the natural world. This second view leaves open two alternatives. First, one might think that human beings and their actions are just an aspect of nature. On such an account, human actions, emotions, and pleasures are naturalised, in the sense that the rules or norms guiding them are no different, in principle, from those of other realms of nature. When, in the course of ethical inquiry, we ask what it is for a human being to be good, we are not asking a question that differs *in kind* from the questions a natural scientist asks when she enquires into what is involved in the well-functioning of an oak tree or a shark. Alternatively, one might think that the distinctive feature of human beings that makes them subject to ethical norms is itself something that develops out of their animal nature, but that this development cannot be understood simply in naturalistic terms. Human beings are by nature responsive to habituation; the resulting character state is like a kind of 'second nature'. On such an account, human beings, because they possess reason, are subject to norms that differ in principle from those that apply in other realms of nature, and human actions, emotions, and pleasures cannot be understood in wholly naturalistic terms.

(3) There is a structural similarity between the two realms, so that we find the same or similar regularities and values in both and have to ask similar questions about them, but these questions and this structure are not specific to either one of the two realms. Such an idea may arguably be seen in Aristotle's account of teleology, which claims that there is a teleological structure at work not only in human actions but

also in the natural realm, without presupposing that a natural process must arise from an intention.

The choice between these three options raises questions about the distinctiveness of human beings, the origin of value, and the characteristics of the natural world. Is the development of a human being, like the development of a plant or an animal, something that occurs as it does 'by nature'? Should human actions and emotions be understood naturalistically? And if not, how should we understand their relation to the natural world within which they occur? How far are human emotions tied to something that is the exclusive preserve of human beings (namely, reason) and to what extent are they shared with other animals? (For some discussion of these questions, see the chapters in Part III.)

Does ethics differ from natural science in that it studies the good and the bad (not only the true and the false), or should the natural scientist also be concerned with questions about goodness and badness? What is the relationship between nature and goodness? Is goodness to be found in the wider natural world, or is it only a feature of (certain) human beings? Are human beings good by nature? And if so, how should this fact inform our account of what it is to be a good human being? (On these questions, see the chapters in Part V.)

How do ethical norms relate to natural laws? Are the laws and regularities at work in the two fields the same? Do the rules we observe in the natural world also apply to the human world? How does human legislation relate to laws of nature? And how should the fact that human beings are located within a natural world over which they often have little control affect ethical reasoning about the human good? What kind of human reaction should natural occurrences evoke? (These questions are discussed in Part I.)

We should also bear in mind that in some discussions of their relationship, ethics and physics are not immediately connected. Rather, sometimes, their relationship is clarified by linking either or both to the realm of the divine. In this case, usually, either the human or the natural realm is identified with the divine, or seen as assimilable to the divine. We are then faced with questions such as: whether, and to what degree, human beings resemble gods, whether human beings can become more godlike, or whether gods can be cast in human terms. (We find some discussion of these kinds of connection between physics and ethics in Part II.)

One concept central for both realms is causation. Depending on how the relationship between ethics and physics is cast, the notion of a cause can look rather different. Should we follow the first model, so that causation in nature may be understood as some form of intentional action? Or rather the second model, and if we do so, can we give an account of the way in which human actions are related to natural causal chains that allows us to make sense of the fact that human beings are responsible for their actions? Or, following the third model, should human action and natural causation be seen as simply displaying a similar structure of relations of cause and effect? (We will see some discussion of causation in Part IV.)

Any attempt to address questions such as these must be grounded in an understanding of ancient discussions of ethics and of natural science. In recent years, no one has done more to illuminate these fields than Sarah Broadie. Her work has ranged over Aristotle's natural philosophy (*Nature, Change and Agency*, 1982; *Passage and Possibility*, 1982), Aristotle's ethics (*Ethics with Aristotle*, 1991; *Aristotle Nicomachean Ethics*, with Christopher Rowe, 2002) as well as Plato's natural philosophy (*Nature and Divinity in Plato's* Timaeus, 2012) and his account of the good (*Plato's Sun-Like Good: Dialectic in the* Republic, 2021). She has written papers on Aristotle's accounts of causation, teleology, and fate, and on his distinctive view of the good. (See, for instance, the papers collected in *Aristotle and Beyond: Essays on Metaphysics and Ethics*, 2007.) In these writings, she has pursued questions about the relations between the natural and the human worlds and about the distinctive rational nature of human beings. For instance, in her book on Plato's *Timaeus*, she says:

> No doubt it is due to our common natural endowment that we can choose better and worse; but how we do choose on a given occasion is not just a working out of our common natural endowment. Plato is scientific about nature, and like any scientist he assumes that, barring external interferences, nature necessarily works in the same way. But ethically we do not necessarily work in the same way under the same natural circumstances. (Broadie, 2012, 105)

This raises precisely the questions about the relation between the natural and the ethical realms that we discuss in this volume. Broadie's most recent book approaches these questions in a new way, arguing that for Plato the very same principle of value is responsible for both the nature of the cosmos and a well-governed human life. Sarah Broadie's work thus sets the stage for our investigations here.

All the contributors to this volume have learnt a lot from Sarah Broadie's body of work. As importantly, we owe a debt to Sarah as her students, friends, collaborators, and colleagues. All of us have been inspired by

Sarah's combination of imagination and rigour. Many of us have been spurred on by her penetrating questions and by her constructive criticisms of our work. Those of us who were her students are not the only ones to have benefitted from her kind encouragement, her enthusiasm, and her generosity with her time. This volume is dedicated to Sarah Broadie, as a mark of our profound gratitude and admiration.

2 Individual Parts and Chapters

Part I: Humans in Nature: Nature and Law, Humans and Natural Catastrophes

One central question for human comprehension of the natural world is what kinds of occurrences in nature are perceived as following regular patterns and how these regularities in nature relate to the regularities we can perceive in the human realm. We find frequent attempts from the very beginning of philosophy onwards to explain not only seeming irregularities of the heavenly bodies as following a regular pattern, but also natural catastrophes as being part of recurring repetitions.

The way in which such regularities are explained differs in important respects from modern accounts, however: what we today call 'laws of nature' were originally not necessarily seen as behaving according to a mathematical understanding of laws, but closer to what we may think of as social laws, which leaves open the possibility of overstepping them. The relationship between these two kinds of regularities is also a central part of what is discussed in the so-called *nomos-phusis* debate of the fifth and fourth centuries BCE,[1] where *nomos* refers to the regulations human beings give to themselves, while *phusis* is what is given to human beings in some way.

In 'Legislating in Accordance with Nature in Plato's *Laws*', Alex Long looks at Plato's particular take on the *nomos-phusis* antithesis in his *Laws*. Long argues that the goal of the *Laws*, of legislating in accordance with nature, should be distinguished from the much-studied idea of 'natural law' in two ways. First, the focus of the *Laws* is primarily the right way to conduct an activity, legislation, rather than its product (laws or law). It is this activity of legislating that is said to be natural, not the law. Secondly, the discussion in the *Laws* draws a comparison with other specialised or technical activities that can be performed well or badly, such as medicine or

---

[1] Cf. Heinimann 1945 and McKirahan 2011, ch. 19.

building: we can learn how to legislate 'in accordance with nature' by considering analogous activities in these other fields. Legislation is natural, among other things, when it is undertaken in a certain 'natural' order, from the starting point of life to death. This order ensures that no stage of life is ignored during the legislative process and thus guarantees the comprehensiveness of legislation. Plato's comparison of the legislator with other craftsmen presents a view of natural procedure within an art or profession: the craftsman is not subjected to constraints that are external to his domain and he is able to give his full attention to the objectives and questions that belong to his craft. Finally, this account of legislation provides the basis for a political proposal that is not underpinned by theology.

Barbara Sattler's 'Astronomy and Moral History in Plato's *Timaeus*' addresses the puzzling question of why, in his *Timaeus*, Plato combines two very different topics: a cosmogony and account of the universe on the one hand, and a story about the moral actions of ancient Athens, Atlantis, and Egypt on the other. She argues that the key to understanding the relation between these two parts is the recognition that, in Plato's view, they confront us with a structurally similar problem: how we are to account for the intelligibility of processes in the phenomenal world. She shows that Plato no longer chooses to solve this problem by tying intelligibility to complete uniformity, as he did in the *Republic*, but by tying intelligibility to a rule – to norms and laws for actions in the human cultural realm; and to ratios and descriptive rules for the motions of the heavenly bodies in the natural realm. While Plato also accounts for the concerns specific to ethics and physics, the attempt to understand processes raises similar problems for him in both realms. Recurring natural catastrophes, such as floods and fires, appear as one kind of natural regularity in this Platonic account.

In his chapter 'Natural Catastrophe in Greek and Roman Philosophy', Anthony Long shows that theories of natural catastrophes in Greek and Roman literature in general presuppose the repetition of devastating events rather than their singularity, but that the ancient evaluations of natural catastrophes differ widely. Long shows that Plato and Aristotle tend to be detached and dispassionate in their accounts of such natural catastrophes by treating them simply as inevitable phases in the natural world's cyclical history. By contrast, the Epicurean Lucretius and the Stoic Seneca clearly acknowledge human fragility in the face of catastrophes. Both Roman philosophers register the dangers of presuming mastery over the natural environment and are sensitive to the human toll that nature can extort from exceeding such limits.

*Part II: Humans as Godlike, Gods as Humanlike: Presocratics
and Platonists*

Part II of the volume looks at accounts in which the relationship between ethics and physics is established via some connection to the divine. We find cases of understanding the natural world as itself being divine or as being made up of divinities. If these divinities are understood as behaving in a human way, then this raises the question of whether human ethics should not also be applicable to them. On the other hand, we find the idea that human beings, while by nature different from gods, in their highest form should become similar to divinities, so that our common idea of human virtues does not seem to be the right way to think about ethics in these cases.

In 'Anthropomorphism and Epistemic *Anthropo-Philautia*: The Early Critiques by Xenophanes and Heraclitus', Alexander Mourelatos investigates the critique of anthropomorphism that we find in Xenophanes of Colophon and Heraclitus of Ephesus. Hesiod's *Theogony* is assumed as background and as paradigm for the tendency to treat the world's components or gods generally as humanlike. With Xenophanes of Colophon we have the first and one of the fiercest attacks on this kind of anthropomorphism, inasmuch as Xenophanes not only challenges anthropomorphism in traditional religion and myth but also intimates that at the root of religious beliefs and practices, among his fellow Greeks as well as among foreigners, is a motive of *philautia*, of self-love. Another strong early critique of anthropomorphism is found in Heraclitus of Ephesus, who curtly dismisses the idea of world-making by a god and stridently attacks certain traditional forms of religious worship. And yet neither thinker can avoid sliding into a particular kind of anthropomorphism, namely into what Mourelatos calls 'epistemic *anthropo-philautia*' – *philautia* understood not as the 'self-love' or 'vanity' an individual may show, but rather as the *species-philautia* we indulge in when we project upon the cosmos structures and forms that cognitively afford special intuitive appeal to us human beings.

Li Fan, in his chapter 'Nature and Divinity in the Notion of Godlikeness', investigates the apparent tension arising from the fact that Plato presents two seemingly rather different things – both fulfilling human nature and godlikeness – as the human *telos*. Fan argues that these two accounts are in fact compatible, if we understand the fulfilment of human nature as making the divine part in us flourish. If virtue is understood as a disposition to cope with evils that exist in the human condition but are absent in the divine life, it is hard to see how our becoming virtuous fits with our becoming godlike. In the *Theaetetus*, however, Plato understands becoming virtuous as a flight from the world. This has traditionally been understood as engaging in theory as opposed to praxis. However, such an understanding faces the problem that in the *Theaetetus* and in the *Republic*, justice, and thus the virtue concerned with treating other people appropriately, is presented as a central virtue. This speaks against understanding the flight idea merely in theoretical terms. Fan argues that instead of identifying the idea of fleeing from the world with withdrawing from practical affairs and engaging in theoretical activity, we should understand it as a kind of self-transformation, in such a way that as a result we are no longer rooted in the natural world, but in divine, transcendent reality.

Part III: Emotions, Reason, and the Natural World (Aristotle)

The chapters in Part III consider Aristotle's views on the emotions and on their place in the natural world. They discuss how human and animal emotions differ from each other, what they have in common, and what is distinctive about human emotions. Human emotions are distinctive in that they are reason-responsive, that is, they are such that they can be guided by reason (which is not, of course, to say that they are always so guided). Ethical virtue is defined in relation to human emotion: to be virtuous is to have emotions that are guided by right reason. Thus, we can shed light on Aristotle's ethics by coming to understand precisely how, on his view, human emotions are such as to be guided by reason. These chapters discuss the ways in which human emotions differ both from the activities of the strictly rational part of the human soul and also from the non-reason-responsive emotions that can be experienced by other animals.

In 'Human and Animal Emotions in Aristotle', Jamie Dow argues that, for Aristotle, human emotions are both different from, and also importantly continuous with, the emotions experienced by non-human animals. On the one hand, the repertoire of emotions experienced by human beings differs significantly from that experienced by non-human animals. The difference stems from the fact that only human beings have reason. Some human emotions (for example, shame) require the possession of reason and hence cannot be experienced by non-human animals. Other human emotions have counterparts in non-human animals, but they differ from these counterparts because, when functioning correctly, they are guided by reason. For instance, the disposition to feel fear is reason-governed in a human being but not in an animal. On the other hand, in spite of these striking differences between human and animal emotions, Dow argues that the emotions also reveal an important continuity between human beings and other animals: both human and animal emotions are fundamentally capacities to respond with pleasure or pain to situations that are apparently good or harmful to the subject. In this sense, emotion plays a similar role in the lives of humans and in the lives of non-human animals.

Dorothea Frede, in her 'Reasonable and Unreasonable Affections and Human Nature', also focusses on the gap between human beings and the rest of nature. While other natural things develop as they do 'necessarily or for the most part', human beings are distinctive in that their development depends on their own efforts. Human emotions or affections (*pathē*) play an important role in their development. Frede argues that, for Aristotle, human affections have an interesting 'passive-cum-active' character. They differ importantly from actions, in that they do not result from decisions. However, for a human being, experiencing an affection is not simply a matter of being passively affected. Human beings experience affections in response to understanding their situation in a certain way. Because of this, reasoning is in a way involved in the formation of human affections. The process of habituation alters not only how human beings act, but also how they feel. The affective part of the soul, though non-rational, is capable of 'listening' to reason more or less well. Thus, in a human being, affections can be reasonable or unreasonable: a human being who has been well habituated will have reasonable affections, which will cause desires of the right kind; a human being who has not been well habituated will have unreasonable affections, which will cause desires of the wrong kind. Because human affections require habituation, they are not (like animal desires) simply a gift of nature. Thus, the distinctive reason-responsiveness of human affections helps to explain why successful human development cannot simply be attributed to nature.

Part IV: *Action and the Natural World (Aristotle)*

The chapters in Part IV discuss Aristotle's views on the way in which human purposive activity is related to the world of nature. Are there any constraints that are placed on our general account of causation by the need to make sense of the possibility of human intentional action? Does Aristotle hold that moral responsibility is compatible with causal determinism? And how should we understand the analogy Aristotle draws between human intentional (deliberation-based) agency and more general natural purposive agency?

In 'Chains That Do Not Bind: Causation and Necessity in Aristotle', Thomas Tuozzo discusses the relation between causation and moral responsibility. We generally hold adult human beings morally responsible for their actions; yet those actions are also events in the natural world, enmeshed in causal chains that extend backwards in time long before the agent's birth. If the causes in those chains necessitate their effects, it would appear that we must either give up the view that humans are morally responsible for their actions or embrace the paradoxical view that humans are morally responsible for actions necessitated by events over which they have no control. Tuozzo argues that Aristotle's causal theory avoids this dilemma by recognising two distinct types of causal chain or nexus. In one of these, the links between cause and effect are indeed necessary, from beginning to end. But chains of this sort are necessarily finite, with a definite beginning and end. Each of these necessary, finite causal chains is also enmeshed in a different sort of causal nexus, one that does extend indefinitely into the past. But this sort of indefinite causal chain is possible only because it contains links that are not necessitated. This enables Aristotle to account for moral responsibility by locating the necessitating cause of a human action in the agent herself. Nonetheless, Tuozzo concludes, Aristotle's theory does have the paradoxical implication that, although the state of the world at a given time does not necessitate all subsequent events, a complete description of it would, in principle, allow all subsequent events – including human actions – to be predicted.

Ursula Coope's 'Aristotle on Nature, Deliberation, and Purposiveness' discusses Aristotle's puzzling claim that 'craft does not deliberate' (*Physics* II.8). Aristotle makes this claim in response to an imagined objection to the analogy he has drawn between purposiveness in nature and purposiveness in craft. The objection is that craft and nature are not analogous in this way because craft production involves deliberation. Aristotle's response is puzzling in two ways. First, there is the puzzle of what Aristotle means and how the claim that 'craft does not deliberate' can be compatible with the manifest fact that the practitioners of certain crafts (e.g. medicine) do need to deliberate if they are to do their job well. In response to this puzzle, Coope argues (following Sedley) that Aristotle is not denying that particular craftsmen deliberate. His point is rather that the craft itself (which is the primary cause of the production) does not deliberate. However, this leaves us with a second puzzle: how is this claim (that the craft itself does not deliberate) relevant to defending Aristotle's analogy between craft and nature? Surely his opponent can just respond that there is nevertheless an important disanalogy, namely that processes of craft production depend on deliberation in a way that natural processes do not. Coope attempts to solve this puzzle by examining more closely the roles (respectively) of craft in craft production and of nature in natural processes. She argues that Aristotle's point is that it is *the craft* itself that explains the purposiveness of a process of craft production and analogously it is *the relevant nature* that explains the purposiveness of a natural process. Thus, in each case, the source of purposiveness is something that does not deliberate. However, Coope suggests that this solution may in fact raise a new difficulty for Aristotle. Aristotle can perhaps explain the purposiveness of natural processes and of processes of craft production in this way, but it is not at all clear whether he can give any analogous account of the purposiveness of those ordinary human intentional actions that are not cases of craft production. Thus, the purposiveness of ordinary human intentional action turns out to be problematic for Aristotle, in a way that the purposiveness of natural processes (and craft productions) is not.

Part V: *The Naturalness of Goodness*

Many ancient discussions start out from the view that goodness is, in a certain sense, natural. This might mean that all desire (whether human or animal) is naturally oriented to the good, or it might mean that those things that exist by nature are naturally such as to be good. The chapters in Part V take up questions that arise from different ways of developing the idea that goodness is natural. If all desire is naturally oriented to the good, can this fact provide the basis for giving an account of the identity of the good? If things that exist by nature are naturally such as to be good, does this imply that human beings are naturally such as to be good? If so, might this help to explain how human beings are able to achieve a kind of decency (and hence, a kind of approximation of happiness) even when they lack full practical wisdom?

In 'Eudoxus' Hedonism', Joachim Aufderheide uses Aristotle's account in the *Nicomachean Ethics* to reconstruct Eudoxus' argument for the thesis that pleasure is the good. He sets out and explains Eudoxus' argument from universal pursuit: pleasure must be the good because all things seek pleasure. Aufderheide claims that Eudoxus' point is that all animals pursue pleasure in all natural and fitting choices. Pleasure features in every good choice as a good. Eudoxus' naturalism is an important background assumption here. Eudoxus assumes that each animal, by nature, successfully chooses in all situations what is good for itself. This allows him to move from an observation about the universal pursuit of pleasure to the claim that pleasure is a feature of all natural and good choices. Aufderheide argues that the pleasure that features in such choices is overall pleasure. Thus, Eudoxus can allow that animals sometimes naturally choose things that are painful, provided that what they choose contains, overall, more pleasure than pain. Aufderheide ends by suggesting how Eudoxus might defend the claim that pleasure is not merely *a* good, but moreover *the* good. This is not the claim that pleasure is the only thing that is good, but rather that pleasure plays a unique role in relation to choice: it is the only thing that features in all natural and good choices as a good.

Christopher Rowe argues in 'Aristotle and Socrates in the *Eudemian Ethics* on the Naturalness of Goodness' that Aristotle, in the *Eudemian Ethics*, develops a naturalised account of Socrates' divine sign. Aristotle claims that it is possible for humans to act well, and hence achieve a kind of happiness, even in the absence of full practical wisdom. There is something divine in human beings that allows them to do this. But this 'something divine' is not (as it is for Socrates) a private inner voice; it is, rather, a kind of well-naturedness. For Aristotle, goodness is natural: we all, by nature, pursue the good. The goodness of human nature explains how it is possible for those human beings who lack full practical wisdom nevertheless to act well, and to do so reliably. This provides Aristotle with an answer to a puzzle about the relation of good human beings to the natural world. Aristotle holds that human beings are good by nature, but he also seems to hold that fully virtuous human beings are relatively rare. These two claims are hard to reconcile, given Aristotle's usual view that what occurs 'by nature' occurs 'always or for the most part'. By introducing the idea that there is a level of decency that can be achieved, as a result of well-naturedness, even by those who lack full virtue, Aristotle can answer this puzzle. If this decency is achieved by many people, then there is, after all, a kind of good human development that occurs by nature and occurs regularly.

PART I

Humans in Nature: Nature and Law, Humans and Natural Catastrophes

CHAPTER I

Legislating in Accordance with Nature in Plato's Laws

Alex Long

As soon as you look systematically for 'nature' (φύσις) and related words in Plato's *Laws*, you find that they are used not only often but in some surprising contexts.[1] Here are just three examples. Retail trade is said to have a 'natural' function: correcting a lack of commensurability between different goods (918a8–b4). Money itself has a 'natural' reason for existence, which is to serve the needs and interests of the body, the same function that the body fulfils for the soul (εἶναι πέφυκε, 870b5; cf. 743d). The third example concerns the well-known 'preambles' to laws. When the Athenian Visitor complains about the lack of preambles in previous legislation, he says that so far legislators and authors have not brought a legal preamble 'into the light of day', as if preambles 'did not exist by nature' (εἰς τὸ φῶς, ὡς οὐκ ὄντος φύσει).[2] But their preceding discussion has shown that preambles do indeed exist, by which he must mean that they exist *by nature* (722e1–5), despite their absence from all previous legislation.

What follows is not a comprehensive discussion of nature in the *Laws*. I focus on two passages (720e–721a, 858c) where the Athenian speaks of legislating, or examining laws, 'in accordance with nature' (κατὰ φύσιν).[3]

I am delighted to have this opportunity to thank Sarah Broadie for her outstanding generosity as a colleague in St Andrews and to join others in expressing admiration for her enormous contribution to the understanding and appreciation of Greek philosophy. My thanks to Barbara Sattler and Myrthe Bartels for comments on the chapter, and to the other participants at the conference in Milan where an earlier version of it was presented.

[1] I use 'nature' and related words to translate φύσις. I do not have space here to review the Greek word, passages where a translation other than 'nature' should be used, or the relationship between φύσις and νόμος. For a concise overview of φύσις in pre-Aristotelian philosophy, see Section 1.1 of Sattler 2020. Taylor 2007 is a recent treatment of the φύσις-νόμος relationship in Plato and Democritus.

[2] φύσει is not included in Griffith's translation ('as if such a thing did not exist') in Schofield and Griffith 2016. Songs and discourse in general 'naturally' have preambles (723d).

[3] I do not discuss education in mathematics, although the Athenian's proposals in this area too are said by Cleinias to be 'in accordance with nature' (818e3–4). The Athenian is embarrassed by the state of Greek mathematical education (819d–820b) and evidently wants to look beyond what Greek

'Legislating' should be taken to include the reasoned and deliberate creation of norms and customs (another sense of the Greek word νόμος), as
well as the creation of laws, for the Athenian says that he and Cleinias
should aim to provide customs as well as laws for the new city (793a–d).[4]
I try to explain what 'natural' legislation involves and why following nature
is thought to be preferable. But no less important is the following negative
point. When the Athenian explains what it means to legislate 'in accordance with nature', he does not mobilize other parts of the conversation that
venture outside legislation or politics and that, in various ways, concern
nature – namely, his discussions of value, the human soul, and the true
character of the gods and their responsibility for the universe. (As we will
soon see, concerning two of these, value and the gods, his discussion
explicitly refers to 'nature'.) These extra-political or extra-legislative parts
of the *Laws* have attracted particularly close attention in recent scholarship.
The Athenian's silence about all three, when he discusses 'natural' legislation, suggests that they are, to some extent, less foundational for his project
than we might otherwise suppose.[5]

To give more detail: over the course of the *Laws* the Athenian presents
the following three claims or theories. (1) The gods are real, direct the
cosmos and supervise its human inhabitants, and are not swayed or bought
off by human gifts or promises (885b–907b).[6] (2) All humans resemble
marionettes in their susceptibility to being motivated by pleasure, pain,
and their expectation. Nevertheless, it is not naïve to praise some people
and criticize others, and in particular, there is good reason to praise some
people for 'getting the better of themselves' and to criticize others as
'overcome by themselves'. Those terms of praise and censure refer to
whether or not someone follows another internal source of motivation,
reasoning, and uses the law to strengthen its control (644c–645c).[7] (3)

---

educators currently do. The common view that the *Laws* offers a synthesis of Athenian and Doric
customs and laws (see e.g. Gill 2003) helps make sense of the debates in books 1 and 2, but sometimes
the Athenian's ambitions outstrip Greek practice, and so what he offers is not merely such a synthesis.

[4] He refers to what 'ordinary people' call ἄγραφα νόμιμα and πάτριοι νόμοι. All the same, he indicates
that, despite these common ways of speaking, such customs should not in fact be called νόμοι (793a–
b). For further discussion of the scope of 'legislation', see Laks 2000, 263, 265.

[5] The detailed account of gods comes in book 10, after both of the passages I discuss in detail below.
But in the earlier passages the Athenian could have made claims about gods and postponed to book 10
their defence or elucidation. After all, the existence of gods is assumed from the very start of the
discussion, but it is not defended until that book.

[6] For recent commentary, see Mayhew 2008.

[7] See also 732e, 804b3–4 ('puppets for the most part, but to some small extent understanding the
truth'). I follow the interpretation of Schofield 2016. Further discussion is provided in e.g. Frede
2010.

Goods fall into two kinds, 'human' (health, beauty, strength, wealth used with wisdom) and 'divine' (wisdom and the other virtues, 631b–d).[8] The Athenian suggests further nuances as he lists the goods – for example, wisdom is the primary divine good, and human goods in some sense 'depend' on divine goods. (1) and (2) have had a special fascination for recent philosophical readings of the *Laws*, and the first claim, about the gods, is supported with a lot of argumentation, including an elaborate argument for the gods' existence.

All these claims are presented as true independently of laws and conventions. (2) presents facts, psychological and normative, about human souls and their evaluation. According to the Athenian, as he concludes the brief overview of values in (3), the divine goods are ranked before the human goods 'by nature', and the lawgiver should rank them accordingly (631d1–2). He could hardly be more explicit in saying that their higher value does not derive from legislation or convention. And Plato makes a point of emphasizing that the claims about the gods in (1) are not dependent on tradition or legislation. For he stages in book 10 a debate that turns on precisely this point. That gods are the product of laws or conventions is the claim of the atheists against whom the Athenian argues.[9] According to the atheists, things come into being because of nature, chance, or art/craft, and legislation is a form of art.[10] Law and convention falsely assert that the gods are real, and thus – insofar as we can speak of the gods as existing at all – they exist as a result of art and, more specifically, law and convention (889e3–5), not nature. The Athenian then argues against the atheists that no matter what law and convention may or may not say, the natural world and individual heavenly bodies are controlled by rational souls which it is appropriate to call 'gods' (899b). Part of his response takes aim at the atheists' application of the word 'nature'. Whereas for them physical stuffs – fire, water, earth, and air – are natural (889b), the Athenian offers, before he delivers his argument itself, a manifesto about the primacy of soul: if 'nature' refers to what is primary, then soul, not fire or air, should be treated as pre-eminently natural, and the atheists apply the name 'nature' to the wrong items (892b3–c7).[11]

---

[8] See Stalley 1983, 45–58; Frede 2010, 112; Meyer 2011, 402 and 2015, 108–114; Schofield 2013, 16–17, 25. The Athenian discusses value again at 661a–c and 728c–729b.

[9] For discussion, see Sedley 2013.

[10] The atheists thus analyse the familiar dichotomy between *nomos* and *phusis* in terms of what they claim to be a more basic trio – nature, chance, art. Laws and conventions derive from merely one particular form of art or craft, legislation. So, for these atheists, the familiar opposition between *nomos* and *phusis* over-dignifies *nomos*. It is as if one opposed 'nature' to 'cakes' or 'pencils'.

[11] 'Plato recalls and seeks to dissolve the old *nomos/phusis* controversy by claiming that nature itself includes intelligent design at its heart' (Long 2005, 423). Cleinias urges the group to show that law

These claims about the soul, divine and human, and about value are exactly what we would expect Plato to use in order to illustrate what it means to legislate in accordance with nature: legislation should aim to secure what is most in our interests, should be guided by an understanding of human motivation, and should somehow respect and align itself with the divine supervision of the cosmos. But instead Plato gives the Athenian – at least in the parts of the *Laws* we will consider – an account of 'natural' legislation that could be accepted by a reader completely unconvinced by his claims about the gods, the human soul, and value. This has implications for our understanding of the logical structure of the *Laws*, and in particular for debates about whether the discussions of god and psychology underpin the political discussion as a whole.[12]

Natural Legislation and the Doctors: Book 4

The first passage is rather easy to overlook. It is placed within the discussion of preambles, immediately before the Athenian gives an example of introducing the law with a preamble. When the Athenian and Cleinias agree that they should use preambles, the Athenian asks which law they should use for the purpose of illustration:

T1

ΑΘ. φέρε δὴ πρὸς θεῶν, τίν' ἄρα πρῶτον νόμον θεῖτ' ἂν ὁ νομοθέτης; ἆρ' οὐ κατὰ φύσιν τὴν περὶ γενέσεως ἀρχὴν πρώτην πόλεων πέρι κατακοσμήσει ταῖς τάξεσιν;

ΚΛ. τί μήν;

ΑΘ. ἀρχὴ δ' ἐστὶ τῶν γενέσεων πάσαις πόλεσιν ἆρ' οὐχ ἡ τῶν γάμων σύμμειξις καὶ κοινωνία;

ΚΛ. πῶς γὰρ οὔ;

ΑΘ. γαμικοὶ δὴ νόμοι πρῶτοι κινδυνεύουσιν τιθέμενοι καλῶς ἂν τίθεσθαι πρὸς ὀρθότητα πάσῃ πόλει.

ΚΛ. παντάπασι μὲν οὖν.

---

and art exist 'by nature' (890d); later the Athenian claims also that what is 'akin' to the soul, including law and art or craft (892a7–b5), is prior to bodies. He thus implies that law and craft, like soul itself, deserve to be called 'natural' more than bodies do (see 892c).
[12] See, above all, Bobonich 2002 and its account of new political and social proposals flowing from a new moral psychology. But compare Miller's account of the metaphysical foundations of natural justice in Plato: 'Plato's *Laws* represents justice and law as "natural" in the sense of having a divine origin' (1991, 289). One principal contention of my chapter is that we have to look beyond the theology of book 10 in order to understand fully the connections between nature, law, and legislation in the *Laws*. Contrast the judgements on the *Laws* quoted in n. 39 below.

ATHENIAN: Well then, as heaven is your witness, what would be the first law the lawgiver would enact? Will he not follow nature, and in his directives first bring into good order, from a political point of view, the principle of the production of children?[13]

CLEINIAS: No doubt he will.

ATHENIAN: And this principle governing the production of children, isn't it, in all cities, the union and partnership provided by marriage?

CLEINIAS: Of course.

ATHENIAN: So if the laws governing marriage are the first to be enacted, that will probably be the correct thing to do in any city.

CLEINIAS: Absolutely.   (720e10–721a7, trans. Griffith, with modifications)

I expect twenty-first-century readers of the *Laws* often read through this passage comparatively quickly, as many will be *en route* to the subsequent illustration of preambles. The first point to note is that what is 'natural' here is not a law but proceeding in a certain order as one legislates, in such a way as to match the chronological sequence of human generation and life. That is, the passage does not recommend as natural certain *products* of legislation, laws; rather, it recommends performing the work of legislating in a natural manner. This focus on activity, not products, matches the discussion immediately before this passage, to which we will soon turn, where the Athenian says that some doctors, but not all, work and pursue inquiries 'according to nature' (720d3). There, too, he is discussing an activity, practising medicine, not the product, health (which, we might think, is always 'natural', regardless of the expertise or blind luck by which it is acquired). The point needs strong emphasis, as it is easy for us to think that a philosophical connection between legislation and nature must concern a *natural law*, or a *law of nature*, or at least a partial anticipation of one of those concepts, rather than natural *legislating*.[14]

---

[13] Here and in other extended quotations I use the translation in Schofield and Griffith 2016. But at this point I have replaced Griffith's translation ('and use his directives for political purposes, to bring into good order the basic principle governing the production of children?'). πρώτην marks the answer to the question 'what will the lawgiver enact first?', and I suggest that πόλεων πέρι avoids the risk of irreverence in suggesting that procreation needs to be 'put in order'. From a theological and biological point of view, provided in the *Timaeus*, we have been ingeniously motivated and equipped to procreate, but for social and political purposes there is still work for a lawgiver to do. For a certain sequence of thought or discourse as 'natural', compare *Philebus* 50e, *Laws* 853a.

[14] For excellent recent discussion of law and natural law in ancient political philosophy (including Plato's *Laws*), see Annas 2017. For law as 'natural' in the *Laws*, see n. 11 above; 714e–715a; Jaeger 1960, 346; but also the caveats in Stalley 1983, 33–4 and Laks 2005, 158 n. 55. Although I cannot develop the point here, there is a risk of overstating the importance of natural law even in Stoicism. Suppose the ideal Stoic agent rationally and virtuously chooses, in Athens, an action neither required nor forbidden by Athenian law, such as caring for an ill friend. Is there any law that instructs him to perform this action? Yes, Stoics say, the agent's own reason, which itself has the authority of law

But it is quite in keeping with the rest of the *Laws* that the Athenian should get his interlocutors to think about different ways of legislating and their merits. The *Laws* is just as concerned with how to legislate as it is with the result of legislation, laws. Perhaps it is with the aim of putting legislation itself, and the reasoning that should inform it, under scrutiny that Plato has put the discussion some distance away from actual laws. The Athenian is not drafting laws, even though he sometimes speaks as if he were (e.g. 768d–e, 853c, 854a, 854c–d, 874d; but then see 857e = T2 below). Instead he is offering a discussion of law and legislation for Cleinias to consult when, on a later occasion, he and other Cretans engage in a real piece of legislation for a new colony (702c–d).[15] The point has been argued powerfully in a recent book by Myrthe Bartels.[16] But even if the Athenian is not actually legislating, it does not, of course, follow that the work is not profoundly interested in legislation: on the contrary, the preparatory character of the Athenian's project gives him and his interlocutors the time and leisure to reflect on the principles that underpin legislation, and different ways of getting legislation done.

A further passage suggests that there is valuable learning to be gained from examining legislating itself, not only its products (i.e. laws). This is the extraordinary proposal to make the discussion of the *Laws* itself part of children's education (811c–e).[17] The idea that *law* is educational is comparatively well-established, and we find it expressed by Plato's Protagoras (*Prt.* 326d).[18] But of course the *Laws* is not merely a list of laws but a series of reflections on how to legislate, what the legislator should prioritize, and so on. If we take the Athenian at his word, all these reflections, not merely the finished product, laws, are now seen as educational. The city's children must see the reasoning and principles that have gone into the laws by which

---

(Cic. *Leg.* 1.18; compare Diog. Laert. 7.88). We can make sense of this Stoic claim without the notion of *natural* law.

[15] Notice that already in this passage the Athenian is invited to speak as if he were really founding a city (702d1–2). So when the Athenian talks of himself and the others as legislators, we need not suppose that he has not forgotten the actual nature of their task. For fuller references, see Bartels 2017, 140 n. 97.

[16] Bartels 2017. She emphasizes the Athenian's invitation for them to 'test' what they have said in books 1–3 (702a7–b3): 'the lawgiving in *Laws* is presented as an exercise, meant to test the utility of the outcomes of the opening discourse, rather than being the objectively good law code for Magnesia' (2017, 38; see also 2017, 116–23, 129, 134, 142, 151). See also Laks 2000, 261.

[17] It has been suggested that the proposal is to use the 'message or content' of the *Laws* in education, not the dialogue itself (Meyer 2011, 398). But any reproduction of the dialogue's content would have to include reflections on how to legislate, not merely laws. See also Stalley 1994, 174–5.

[18] See also Isocrates 2.2–3; Meletus in *Apology* 24d–e; Socrates (or the 'Laws' themselves) in *Crito* 51c–d. For an overview, see Too 2001.

they must live, and so they must be shown round an active studio, as it were, as well as a motionless gallery.

T1 comes in the context of a comparison between legislators and doctors, and so it is remarkable that following 'nature' does not require anything approaching technical or advanced understanding. Shortly before T1 the Athenian draws a contrast between two types of doctor and argues that his own legislation will resemble the practice of the 'free-born' doctors who employ persuasion rather than bald instructions. One difference between the two types of doctor concerns nature: the doctors whom the Athenian will not emulate 'acquire their skill by observing their masters, and from the master's orders, and by trying things out', but not 'on the basis of nature' (κατὰ φύσιν, 720b2–4). By contrast, a 'free-born doctor', the model he will follow, does learn from nature (implied at 720b4–5), examines illnesses 'from their starting-point and according to nature (ἀπ' ἀρχῆς καὶ κατὰ φύσιν), spends time with the patient himself and his friends, and so both learns something from the patients and, so far as he can, teaches the ill man himself' (720d2–6).

Given that this passage is about doctors, we might assume that working 'from nature' must involve the technical knowledge (of pathology, anatomy, and so on) that a doctor alone possesses, and so that the doctor's political or legislative counterpart will need similarly specialist knowledge (perhaps in human psychology). But in T1 all that the legislator needs to know, in order to follow nature, is that life begins with procreation. This suggests that we should rethink what is being stressed when it is said that the doctors who provide a better model for legislation work and learn from 'nature'. The first contrast, in the discussion of medicine, is between following nature on the one hand and, on the other, being guided by one's own trial and error, following a master's instructions, and observing what the master does (720b2–4).[19] This suggests that following nature involves independence from what is empirically available concerning treatment, including both the doctor's own previous practice and the precedent set by a master. Of course, there will still be empirical input to the doctor's decisions, but it will concern not the success or failure of previous treatment but rather the peculiar symptoms of the patient and so on.

The Athenian does not deny that a doctor who looks to 'nature' will, in some cases, recommend a drug or surgical procedure already used by his predecessors; what makes the doctor a follower of 'nature' is that the

---

[19] As Schofield notes (2016, 163 n. 59), the passage echoes a contrast elaborated at greater length in the *Gorgias* (462a–465d, 500d–501c).

practice of his predecessors has not made up his mind for him. When the Athenian develops the contrast, he adds that the doctor who follows 'nature' will acquire a more thorough knowledge of the illness: he will study illnesses 'from the starting-point and according to nature' (720d3). The contrast is with a hastier doctor who looks only to the current symptoms of the patient, recommends treatment on the basis of previous trial and error, and then rushes off to the next sickbed (720c5–7). The better doctor recommends treatment only when he has brought into view the entire course of the illness, from initial symptoms to the present day, and in order to acquire this larger overview he speaks with friends and family as well as the patient. Here, too, the Athenian does not deny that, after these painstaking conversations, exactly the same drug may be chosen that an in-and-out doctor would have used.

The doctors who follow 'nature' are thus characterized not by the originality of what they prescribe, but by their independence and their thorough overview of the individual illness that they must cure. This matches their counterpart in legislation, for the Athenian's proposal for their city in T1, namely that they begin with marriage and procreation, is not at all original. Xenophon's *Politeia of the Spartans* began with Lycurgus' regulation of marriage and reproduction (1.3–10), as did Critias' work of the same name.[20] Xenophon noted explicitly that he placed the discussion of reproduction first 'in order to start at the beginning' (1.3), and Critias probably intended his readers to notice the appropriateness of his initial subject: 'I begin with the generation of the human being' (B32, Clem. Al. *Strom.* 6.9.2). Not only is it unoriginal to begin with marriage and reproduction, but it is unoriginal even to say that this is where one ought to begin.

What then is advantageous about following 'nature', if it leads, or at least sometimes leads, to the very same outcomes as those recommended by others in the same field? We have already seen that the doctors emulated by the Athenian learn thoroughly how the illness has developed: they are said not merely to study the beginning of the illness, but to study it *from* its beginning (720d3). The doctors must have in view how the illness has progressed from its start to the present day, which suggests that legislators who adopt a similar practice should bring before their mind's eye the entire course through time of their own object of study. According to T1, this – or at least one object of their study – is the sequence of a human life, which is

---

[20] Gray 2007, 43 suggests that the 360s are a 'probable' period of composition for Xenophon's work. Schöpsdau 1994–2011, II, 242 notes the parallel between the *Laws* and Xenophon and Critias.

said there to start with the parents' union, and presumably ends with the person's own death.

In the scholarship it is already recognized that the Athenian's discussion of legislation from book 4 to book 12 in fact follows that order:[21] it begins with parents' marriage in T1, within book 4, and ends with discussion of funerals and tombs (959d–960b) in book 12. There follows the discussion of the council that reviews the entire body of laws, usually called the 'Nocturnal Council'.[22] T1 sets in motion this massive sequence, although, as we will see, there are plenty of interruptions on the way. Given that the passage turns out to have such significance, we should expect to see the rewards of following nature not from T1 alone but from the large-scale architecture of the *Laws*, where each stage of human life is brought in turn before the legislator's scrutiny. The Athenian says nothing in T1 about how and when the order he will follow will cause him to deviate from previous political and social practice, but it would be impossible for him to predict such outcomes before each life stage is actually considered. So Plato's readers must wait for later books before they see where following nature will bear original fruit. One passage where we are shown exactly this is the discussion of education and physical conditioning, and the debate about the age at which they should begin (789a–794a).[23] The Athenian expresses uneasiness about enacting laws in this sphere, but suggests that they can and should look to foster benign customs (790a–c, 793a–d), such as soothing motions to remove fear in infancy (791a–c). He then outlines the educational use of games for children up to the age of six (793e–794a). Cleinias' evident surprise at starting education and physical training at such an early age (789a) shows that the Athenian is proposing something unorthodox, to Cretan ears at least. Although there is no reference back to T1, it is reasonable to connect the Athenian's consideration of infancy and early childhood to the marriage–grave sequence that his legislation as a whole is tracking. It is because he has resolved to bring each stage of life into his field of vision that he, unlike other legislators, sees the potential to begin education and physical training at an earlier age.

---

[21] See e.g. Laks 2000, 265–6; Laks 2005, 29 (the chronology of human life is one of several structuring principles); Bartels 2017, 126–7.

[22] 'Dawn Council' may be more accurate, as it is said at first that they meet early in the morning, not through the night (961b). But later they are said to meet 'by night' (962c, 968a).

[23] Xenophon's discussion of education (*Lac.* 2) draws attention to differences between education in Sparta and elsewhere, but without reflecting on the age at which it starts or should start. Compare the account of Persian education in *Cyropaedia* 1.2.2–16: in Persia there is an effort to stamp out improper desire, not only (as elsewhere) improper action, but Persian education seems to begin at the same age as Greek education (1.2.2–3).

At this point, it must be acknowledged that although the overall trajec-
tory of the Athenian's discussion is from the marriage ceremony to the
grave, it is a simplification to say that the entire legislative project keeps in
step with the sequence of a human life. For example, after he has described
the political officials of the city, the Athenian returns to the topic of
marriage in book 6 (772d–776b), before then moving on in book 7 to his
discussion of education. But he does not turn directly from marriage and
sexual union to the education of the very young: first he considers other
questions concerned with setting up a household, such as property and
slavery (776b–778a). The marriage–grave sequence is hardly underway
before the topic of property is interposed. Although this may reflect
some of the priorities of a recently married couple, it is nonetheless
surprising that the Athenian makes so much of starting at the right place
and then disrupts the sequence. One explanation would be that the
Athenian's discussion illustrates an imperfect approach to legislating,
undertaken without the expertise of a true lawgiver, in a manner similar
to Socrates' discussion of a just city in the *Republic* from a lower epistemic
standpoint than that of its envisaged rulers.[24] But I would be reluctant to
endorse that explanation myself, at least without a convincing account of
why it is problematic to break off from, or interrupt, this particular
sequence. More promising, I think, is to conclude that the point was
never about sticking rigidly to a particular sequence in legislation, but to
ensure that no part of a human life is overlooked by the legislator.[25] That
will be achieved if legislators start with its origin and move to its end, but of
course it is possible to move some way through a human life, address some
other question, and then return later to the human life stage at which the
other question interposed itself. As with the doctor, the objective is
comprehensiveness of vision, not a completely unalterable sequence.

I have argued that the meaning, and the desirability, of following nature
in T1 can be understood only by relating the passage to the previous
discussion of doctors and then to the order of the Athenian's programme
across the *Laws*. If the object under scrutiny develops, independently of

---

[24] Meyer 2011, 395 discusses the Athenian's level of expertise; for the philosophical limitations of the
Laws, see also Schofield 2003 and Frede 2010, 111 and 114. For discussion of Socrates and the
philosopher in the *Republic*, see e.g. Keyt 2006; Morrison 2007; Long 2017.
[25] If the objective were to keep out extraneous subjects, and to stick uncompromisingly to the
marriage–grave sequence, the Athenian would need to give far more justification than he does of
the other subjects that intrude and interrupt the sequence. But viewing the goal as comprehensiveness matches the lack of concern with which additional subjects are brought into the discussion:
there is no reason not to bring in other questions and topics, as long as the legislator returns at some
point to the marriage–grave sequence.

legislation, through stages A, B, C, and D, then the legislator who follows nature will consider each of those stages, even if his predecessors have considered only A, C, and D. (In the case of the doctor, we should draw a contrast with those who look to D alone: that is, doctors who in their haste consider only the symptoms currently exhibited and ignore the previous stages of the illness.) This will be achieved if he starts at stage A and then runs through each of the others, although that does not require the legislator to shut his eyes to other questions that may occur to him along the way. The point is that each of A–D should come to his attention, not that anything other than A, B, C, and D should be disregarded.[26]

Nature and the Masons: Book 9

In book 9, the Athenian returns to his comparison between legislators and doctors. An objection has occurred to him: they should concentrate on making laws and not spend time educating their citizens with meta-legislative reflections and preambles.[27] A similar objection could be made against the 'free-born' doctors whom he has adopted as his model: that these doctors are teaching, not curing, their patients (857c–e).[28] In his answer, the Athenian exploits the fact that he is not actually engaged in legislation, and so he (unlike real legislators, or doctors) need not be troubled by an objection that he is spending time on something else.

T2

ΑΘ. εὐτυχὲς δὲ ἡμῶν τὸ παρὸν γέγονεν.
ΚΛ. τὸ ποῖον δή;

---

[26] An Aristotelian might ask whether the Athenian's discussion needs the notion of what is intelligible *to us* (compare, among other texts, *Ph.* 184a16–21, *Metaph.* 1029b3–12). Comprehensiveness of vision would be achieved equally if life were considered in the opposite direction, from death to parents' marriage, with the legislator's imagination performing a *Statesman*-like reversal. We find it easier to get a full view of a human life if our thinking tracks the actual sequence of a human life, but that may be because of our own cognitive limitations, not (or not only) because of how humans actually develop and age.

[27] I owe the expression 'meta-legislative reflection' to Laks 2005, 30.

[28] These doctors are now said to 'go over the entire nature of bodies' (περὶ φύσεως πάσης ἐπανιόντα τῆς τῶν σωμάτων, 857d3–4) – presumably out loud in discussion with patients, not merely in their own studies, given the complaint that they are almost 'teaching' (857d6–e1). This now adds to what is said about the doctors' study of nature in book 4, where, as we have seen, advanced, technical knowledge in medicine would not match the low-level knowledge of 'nature' required by legislators in T1. If in 857d the Athenian is looking ahead to the lengthy discussion of justice, harm, intention, and punishment (859c–864c), it is now more appropriate than it was in book 4 to represent the analogous medical knowledge as advanced and detailed. What looks like a simple recapitulation of the comparison with doctors thus includes a significant and context-appropriate addition.

Αθ. τὸ μηδεμίαν ἀνάγκην εἶναι νομοθετεῖν, ἀλλ' αὐτοὺς ἐν σκέψει
     γενομένους περὶ πάσης πολιτείας πειρᾶσθαι κατιδεῖν τό τε ἄριστον καὶ τὸ
     ἀναγκαιότατον, τίνα τρόπον ἂν γιγνόμενον γίγνοιτο. καὶ δὴ καὶ τὸ νῦν
     ἔξεστιν ἡμῖν, ὡς ἔοικεν, εἰ μὲν βουλόμεθα, τὸ βέλτιστον σκοπεῖν, εἰ δὲ
     βουλόμεθα, τὸ ἀναγκαιότατον περὶ νόμων· αἱρώμεθα οὖν πότερον δοκεῖ.
Κλ. γελοίαν, ὦ ξένε, προτιθέμεθα τὴν αἵρεσιν, καὶ ἀτεχνῶς ὥσπερ κατεχομένοις
     νομοθέταις ὅμοιοι γιγνοίμεθ' ἂν ὑπὸ μεγάλης τινὸς ἀνάγκης ἤδη
     νομοθετεῖν, ὡς οὐκέτ' ἐξὸν εἰς αὔριον· ἡμῖν δ' – εἰπεῖν σὺν θεῷ – ἔξεστι,
     καθάπερ ἢ λιθολόγοις ἢ καί τινος ἑτέρας ἀρχομένοις συστάσεως,
     παραφορήσασθαι χύδην ἐξ ὧν ἐκλεξόμεθα τὰ πρόσφορα τῇ μελλούσῃ
     γενήσεσθαι συστάσει, καὶ δὴ καὶ κατὰ σχολὴν ἐκλέξασθαι. τιθῶμεν οὖν
     ἡμᾶς νῦν εἶναι μὴ τοὺς ἐξ ἀνάγκης οἰκοδομοῦντας, ἀλλὰ τοὺς ἐπὶ σχολῆς ἔτι
     τὰ μὲν παρατιθεμένους, τὰ δὲ συνιστάντας· ὥστε ὀρθῶς ἔχει τὰ μὲν ἤδη
     τῶν νόμων λέγειν ὡς τιθέμενα, τὰ δ' ὡς παρατιθέμενα.
Αθ. γένοιτο γοῦν ἄν, ὦ Κλεινία, κατὰ φύσιν μᾶλλον ἡμῖν ἡ σύνοψις τῶν νόμων.
     ἴδωμεν γὰρ οὖν, ὦ πρὸς θεῶν, τὸ τοιόνδε περὶ νομοθετῶν.

ATHENIAN: Well, there's a bit of luck for us.
CLEINIAS: Luck? In what way?
ATHENIAN: The fact that there is no absolute requirement to be making laws,
     merely to involve ourselves in an enquiry into social and political systems
     in general, with a view to identifying both the best possible, and also the
     bare necessary minimum (and how it would come into being, if it ever
     did so). There is the added advantage, on the face of it, that it is open to
     us, in our study of laws, to investigate the best possible, if we wish, or, if
     we prefer, just the bare minimum. So let us make a choice which to do.
CLEINIAS: That's an absurd choice to impose on ourselves, my friend – we would
     literally be putting ourselves in the position of lawgivers who, in the face of
     some irresistible necessity, are making our laws today, because tomorrow it
     will be too late. Whereas our position, god willing, is that of stonemasons,
     or people embarking on some other work of construction. We have the
     opportunity to gather together in a pile[29] the materials from which we
     shall select those which are suitable for the proposed construction, and
     what is more, to make that selection at our leisure. Let us take it, therefore,
     that we are not now people building as a matter of necessity, but people
     with all the time in the world who are still partly putting materials on one
     side for future use, and partly engaged in the construction, so that it is

---

[29] Griffith's translation has 'indiscriminately' for χύδην. I have chosen something closer to
Schöpsdau's 'haufenweise' (1994–2011, vol. 3), as Griffith's translation might suggest that there is
no principle of selection at all in the initial phase of collecting building materials, and no mason
would collect, say, twigs, dust, and grass as potential materials and restrict himself to stones only
later. The contrast is with selecting materials with an eye to combining them: at first the builder
selects materials that are, considered on their own, promising, and then considers which of them
work well in combination.

correct to say that some parts of our legislation are in the process of being established, while other parts are still in the future.

ATHENIAN: Certainly, Cleinias, that would be a more natural way for us to carry out our review of laws. To see why – well, my goodness, there's another point in connection with lawgivers which bears examination. (857e8–858c4)

The Athenian says that if he took Cleinias' advice, the review would be conducted in a more 'natural' way. Does T2 contain the full explanation, or do we need to read on? The words at the very end of T2 are translated by Griffith in such a way as to suggest that the explanation is yet to come: 'to see why … '. Against this, Denniston includes the T2 passage among several in late Plato (two of the others are *Laws* 637d1–4 and 926e7–9) where γὰρ οὖν seems to serve as a forward-pointing connective and where, despite the presence of γάρ, it is hard to make out an explanation of what has come before.[30] I will assume for now that T2 gives us what we need to make sense of the comment on 'nature', and that something closer to Saunders' translation for the final words ('well then, may we please notice this point that concerns legislators?') is more accurate.[31] At the end of this section I will consider briefly what would follow for our interpretation if Griffith's translation were correct.

Whereas the Athenian denies that what they are doing is legislation, Cleinias says otherwise: some of the colony's laws are, he says, in the process of being 'established', and so at least some genuine legislation is underway. On this particular question, Cleinias' word counts for more than the Athenian's, for it is Cleinias and his nine colleagues, not the Athenian, who have responsibility for the laws of the new Cretan colony (702b–c). When the Athenian describes what he is offering as merely a 'review' (σύνοψις) of laws, we should not take this as if it were Plato's own description. The Athenian, as Cleinias' adviser or assistant, avoids the immodest assumption that what he proposes will be used by the Cretans as laws,[32] and Cleinias alone has the authority to be more encouraging. So the Athenian's description of their project as a mere 'review' does not show the passage to have no bearing on how legislation itself should be conducted.

What, then, makes their way of legislating, or considering legislation, more 'natural' than others? We cannot simply reapply our interpretation of

---

[30] Denniston 1950, 447–8.

[31] Saunders' translation in Cooper 1997. Compare the translation in Schöpsdau 1994–2011 ('so wollen wir denn, bei den Göttern, folgenden Punkt bezüglich der Gesetzgeber betrachten'). But Saunders' translation hides κατὰ φύσιν in 858c2: 'this will be the more realistic way to conduct our review of legislation'. This illustrates how easy it becomes to miss the many references to nature when reading the *Laws* in English translation.

[32] Later he says – again, I suggest, showing proper deference to Cleinias and the Cretans – that they are not lawgivers yet, although they may become lawgivers (859c).

'natural' legislating in T1 to this passage. For the new comparison between
them and masons, who work with lifeless building materials, shows that
the two men cannot have in mind in T2 an overview of how something (a
human organism, or an illness) develops over time independently of the
human specialist or craftsman. All the same, avoiding narrowness of vision is
a common feature of the two passages. The contrast item in T2 is a specialist
working under the constraint of a pressing deadline. If we put together what
the Athenian says with Cleinias' comparison, the deadline is imagined to be
so urgent – the product is due today, not tomorrow – that the craftsman can
undertake only the tasks that are most essential to getting the work done, or
what is most 'necessary', to use the literal translation of τὸ ἀναγκαιότατον.
In order to meet the deadline, the craftsman must look away from questions
of optimal practice, or optimal materials. By contrast, the 'natural' way
brings into the foreground these further questions and makes time to look
at materials twice, asking first whether each, taken on its own, is suitable for
the task in hand, and then how they work in combination.[33]

Cleinias says nothing about the particular stones that masons will use or
their qualities, except that they are 'suitable', and his silence on that point
suggests that the Athenian's comment on nature ('a more natural way',
858c2, T2 above) does not refer to stones' own nature, or to whatever is
their equivalent in legislation. Instead it must refer to the nature of the
mason's, or legislator's, own craft or expertise: he is not compelled, by some
external constraint, to regard as irrelevant or distracting a question that,
from the point of view of the craft itself, is not at all irrelevant. It is entirely
the business of the mason's craft to consider what the best materials might
be, and how suitable materials would best be combined. Only an external
constraint, which is to say, a constraint external to the craft itself, would
make those questions appear to be distractions, such as a political crisis or
an invasion that compels the legislator to enact laws today rather than
tomorrow.

Cleinias does not say that all legislators work under such constraints,
merely that he and the Athenian will resemble legislators who do so if the
two of them restrict their options for no good reason. But the Athenian's
suggestion that they are lucky *not* to be legislating implies, beyond courtesy
to Cleinias, that often legislation is carried out with what is, from the craft's
own point of view, an arbitrarily – it is tempting to say 'artificially' – tight
deadline. If so, his claim that what they are doing is 'more natural' should
not be taken to imply that it is often found empirically. Remember, after

---

[33] Cleinias notes again later that they are not under any pressure to complete their work quickly (887b).

all, that he has implied, as noted in my opening paragraph, that preambles exist 'by nature' (722e), despite their non-existence in all previous legislation. In T2, their procedure is deemed more natural, despite its rareness in actual political practice, insofar as the craft itself determines which questions deserve an answer.

Let us now suppose, as Griffith's translation implies, that the Athenian's mention of 'nature' is explained or further explained in what immediately follows. The Athenian's next claim concerns what lawgivers should concern themselves with in their writing: it is, he says, thoroughly appropriate for lawgivers' writing to discuss the virtues and virtuous actions, and to provide guidance to other writers as well as to the rest of the citizens (858d–859a). If this is to explain the Athenian's claim about 'nature' in T2, the point must be that the slower and fuller way of proceeding will get them to include subjects which fall squarely within the lawgiver's range of concerns, such as the virtues, and which would be left aside if they were forced to work more hastily. On this interpretation too, then, nature should be connected to what does and does not belong to a craft or activity, and it is 'natural' to practise what is, so to speak, the whole-limbed version of one's craft, and not make it an amputee.

Conclusion: The Atheists and Natural Legislation

Why does Plato not give these reflections on 'natural' legislation more of a metaphysical, theological, or psychological underpinning? Nobody familiar with the *Laws* will be surprised by the absence of Forms from these passages. But it is remarkable that the Athenian does not elucidate what it means for legislation to be natural by means of the theories defended in the *Laws* itself, especially those concerning the gods' existence and character, value, and the soul. In T1 and T2, the speakers speak of the gods when avoiding overconfidence and encouraging each other to answer – 'god willing' and 'as heaven is your witness' – but their comments on nature and legislation do not require the gods' existence, let alone a particular view of their character or role in the cosmos. Neither passage requires, or is informed by, a theory of the soul or human motivation.

When the Athenian speaks of 'natural' legislation, Cleinias and Megillus do not need to be convinced that it is appropriate to speak of legislating in such terms. But the *Laws* mentions other people who would resist this connection between legislation and nature: the atheists of book 10,[34] who

---

[34] Mentioned on p. 17 above.

sharply distinguish between art or craft (τέχνη) on the one hand and nature (φύσις) on the other (888e). On the atheists' account, legislation 'in its entirety' derives from art or craft, not nature, and there is no basis in nature for what legislators say about gods or justice.[35] What is respected as 'just' in a community depends entirely on whatever its legislators happen to have recommended, or formally enacted, most recently, and so 'justice' gets its authority exclusively from craft and convention (or 'laws', νόμοις), not nature (889d8–890a2). Legislators may succeed or fail in their goals but, according to this theory, the point of legislation is not to satisfy 'natural' criteria.[36] The atheists draw a contrast between legislation and other more serious crafts, such as medicine. Whereas legislation is a matter of artificial invention, with no input at all from nature, the doctor's art collaborates with nature: 'those of the arts which really do bring something worthwhile into being, they say, are the ones which combine their own powers with those of nature – medicine, for example, or farming, or physical training' (889d4–6).

We can now appreciate the additional significance, in the broader context of the *Laws*, of what the Athenian says outside book 10 about 'natural' legislation. Whereas the atheists identify legislation as an art or craft in such a way as to detach it completely from nature, the Athenian suggests that it is possible *both* to treat legislators as craftsman, or resembling craftsmen, *and* to recommend certain legislative practices as 'natural'.[37] He illustrates the point by means of one of the activities in which the atheists themselves accept that there is collaboration between craft and nature: medicine. A doctor has to deal with an item, an illness, that changes over time independently of his medical art, and he should turn his attention to the entire course of its development. Similarly, the legislator cares for creatures – human organisms – that develop over time, and exercises his own art 'naturally' if he attends to their development from generation to death. And a legislator, like other craftsmen, works 'naturally' if his own priorities and sense of relevance are aligned with what does and does not belong to his own craft. It is as if the craft itself were naturally oriented towards a certain set of deliberations, and so gives us a standard by

---

[35] I take the antecedent of the relative clause in 889e1 (ἧς οὐκ ἀληθεῖς εἶναι τὰς θέσεις) to be legislation and the clause itself to be non-restrictive (van Emde Boas et al. 2019, 565). The atheists are not saying that merely a subset of legislation – such legislation as lays down falsehoods – derives from art rather than nature. When their theory is elaborated (889e–890a), they do not say that any part of legislation derives from nature.

[36] See Sedley 2013, 343–4.

[37] For legislation as a craft or τέχνη, see also 709b–d, 769b–d; *Gorgias* 464b; *Cratylus* 388e–389a; Laks 2000, 263; Bartels 2017, ch. 2. For the 'political' τέχνη, see 650b, 875a–b.

which to judge as natural or unnatural human attempts to put it into practice.[38]

As we have seen, however, none of these points against the atheists, if they are the target, requires them to renounce their atheism, or for that matter to accept the moral psychology and account of value outlined in my opening section above. Showing how legislating can be judged as 'natural' or 'unnatural' seems to be a project of intrinsic importance for Plato, not merely an extension or corollary of what are now, for modern readers, the dialogue's more familiar claims concerning psychology and theology. Sometimes in the *Laws*, law (or at least legislating) and nature are connected without the gods and divine reason playing a bridging role. The *Laws* thus has something to say about how to judge legislation even to atheists left unconvinced by the theological discussion of book 10. Perhaps, then, it is possible to overstate the importance of the fact that the first word of the *Laws* is 'god'.[39]

---

[38] In *Laws* 875b2, the Athenian speaks of what is the case 'by nature', and he may refer to, among other things, the concerns of the political art (discussed in 875a5–6); if so, he is claiming that these concerns belong to the political art 'by nature'. Arts are 'naturally' honest (921b4–5). Compare the debate between Socrates and Thrasymachus in the *Republic* about the 'natural' function of a craft or art (341d), and the 'natural' aim of the ruler (347d). I discuss 'nature' in the *Republic* in Long (in press). See, in particular, *Timaeus* 17c–d, where Socrates says that the principle of specialization is 'according to nature', and *Republic* 428e–429a, 456b–c.

[39] Contrast the following: 'the second-best state described in the *Laws* is a theocracy from beginning to end . . . . It can hardly be an accident that the first word of this long and appalling work is θεός "God"' (Burnyeat 1997, 9). Schofield 2003, 12 speaks in a much more sympathetic spirit of 'the religious assumptions which underpin [the Athenian Stranger's] whole approach to the question of the best *politeia* and the construction of laws appropriate to it'. For divine or cosmic reason as the bridge between law and nature, see Stalley 1983, 29 and 34 and Taylor 2007, 19–20.

CHAPTER 2

Astronomy and Moral History
in Plato's Timaeus

Barbara M. Sattler

2.1 Introduction

One of the most puzzling features of the structure of Plato's *Timaeus* is that it combines the story of the creation of the universe with a story about ancient Athens, Atlantis, and Egypt without there being an obvious connection between these two topics. The only explicit statement we find in the *Timaeus* for how these two parts are meant to be combined is Critias' quick overview of the programme for the *Timaeus* and *Critias*:[1] Timaeus will start with the coming into being of the world and end with the creation of human beings; Critias will then take these human beings and include them in his story about ancient Athens and Atlantis (27a–b). But this overview is hardly an explanation of any philosophical connection between what we may call cultural and natural history.

The Atlantis story is explicitly meant to fulfil Socrates' request to see the city he has laid out 'on the previous day' in motion and action (19b7–c1), specifically in the action of war, since ancient Athens in its fight against presumptuous Atlantis is meant to embody something that resembles the *kallipolis* from the *Republic*. But why does Critias' programme for the *Timaeus* start with Timaeus' account of the creation of the universe? It is not until close to the end of the *Timaeus* that Plato indicates a systematic connection between the two realms, which may serve as a basis for answering our question:

The first version of this chapter owed a lot to Ulrich Bergmann's inspiration and criticism. I want to thank Sarah Broadie, Ursula Coope, and Verity Harte for their helpful comments on several versions of the text.
[1] The two dialogues are usually seen as forming a compositional unity; see e.g. Johansen 2004, 7 n. 1 (Rashed and Auffret 2017 have, however, argued for the inauthenticity of the *Critias* dialogue).

The motions akin to the divine part in us are the thoughts and revolutions of the universe; these therefore, every man should follow, and correcting those circuits in the head that were deranged at birth,[2] by learning to know the harmonies and revolutions of the world, he should bring the intelligent part, according to its pristine nature, into the likeness of that which intelligence discerns, and thereby win the fulfilment of the best life set by the gods before mankind both for this present time and for the time to come. (90c7–d7; Cornford's translation)

The passage quoted clearly suggests some intimate connection between the human realm and one key aspect of the natural one, the revolutions of the universe.[3] In order to lead the best life, everybody should follow the revolutions of the universe, since they are akin to our divine part. Thus the way in which the natural and the human realms are meant to be connected is by having us human beings adapt to the motions of the heavenly bodies.

However, it is not at all obvious what it could mean that we should follow the motions of the universe, and how literally we are meant to take this passage. Furthermore, the passage quoted sketches a parallel between individual human beings and the cosmos, but what does it tell us about the relation of Timaeus' cosmological account to Critias' story about Athens, Atlantis, and Egypt?

The secondary literature in the twentieth century did not spend much time on explaining the relationship between the two parts,[4] but more recently there have been two accounts of how to understand the connection between the cultural and natural history in the *Timaeus*,[5] by Sarah Broadie and Thomas Johansen, respectively.[6] While Broadie and Johansen ultimately subsume Plato's cosmology under an ethical perspective,[7] some later Platonists seem to have taken the relationship between ethics and cosmology the other way round and subsumed the Atlantis story under cosmology by understanding it as an allegory of

---

[2] Sedley 1997, 334 translates περὶ τὴν γένεσιν as 'concerned with becoming'. I discuss this in a work in progress titled 'Thinking Makes the World Go Round'.

[3] In the following, when I talk about the natural realm, the motions of the heavenly bodies are my main focus.

[4] See Cornford 1997 and Taylor 1928.

[5] In general, there seems to be a new interest in possible connections between natural philosophy and ethics, as can also be seen in Carone 2005 and the current volume.

[6] Broadie 2001; cf. also Broadie 2011; Johansen 2004.

[7] How does the cosmos contribute to making us better people in Johansen's case, how do human beings and the cosmos together contribute to overcome the theodicy problem in Broadie's case. I discuss this in a work in progress currently titled 'Circular Motion in Plato – Systematic Thinking and Historic Development'.

cosmological realities.[8] By contrast, I read the *Timaeus* as answering a problem that has an irreducible ethical and cosmological dimension: how can motion, change, and in general all kinds of processes be made intelligible? This question can be seen as the main problem of natural philosophy after Parmenides and it had already been tackled by Presocratic philosophers such as Empedocles and the atomists. And so we may consider this to be an obvious problem for the cosmology part of the *Timaeus*, but think that it does not apply to the cultural history. However, I will argue that the natural and the human realms confront Plato with a structurally similar problem – how to account for the intelligibility of processes (which include human actions) in the phenomenal world – and that he offers a solution to this problem in which the human and the natural realms are seen as intimately connected.

This explanation will also offer a new lens through which to view and understand the way in which, in the *Timaeus*, Plato conceives of human rationality and the rationality of the natural world as a whole. For Plato, the world we experience is not only (a) itself rationally structured (i.e. it itself possesses structures that are designed on a rational scheme, for example, by employing numerical structures) and (b) intelligible (i.e. it is capable of being understood by rational beings), but also (c) itself a thinking being, whose reasoning is the basis for processes in the natural and human realms.

In the following, we will take the passage quoted above (90c–d) as a first guide. In order to figure out how far the motions of the universe can be a paradigm for human beings and their *poleis* 'set in motion', we will have to investigate first how we should conceive of the motions of the universe, which in turn requires a brief look at the World Soul. Only then can we examine human motions and their imitation of the World Soul on the individual as well as on the collective level.

2.2 The Setup of the Universe – The Structure of the World Soul and the Motions of the Heavenly Bodies

The universe came into being, or so we are told by Timaeus, out of chaotic motions and traces of the elements in the receptacle. The demiurge introduced *metron* and *logos* into this chaos, and formed the elements thus created into the spherical World Body. Spread throughout the

---

[8] See, for example, Amelius according to Taylor 1928, 50.

World Body is the World Soul, which is in constant motion – its motions are the basis for those of the heavenly bodies.

The World Soul is formed from two bands that are mixed out of Being, Difference, and Sameness, each of which is composed of indivisible and divisible components (35a). These two bands define a circle and move in opposite directions. The motion of the outer band is called the 'movement of the Same', that of the inner band the 'movement of the Different', even though both are mixed from Sameness and Difference alike. The circle of the Same moves sideways to the right, which commentators usually understand to mean along the Equator from East to West,[9] while the circle of the Different, which is split up into seven circles, moves diagonally to the left and is understood as motion along the Ecliptic. The stars move in the circle of the Same (40a), whereas the sun, the moon, and the five planets are set into the seven circles of the Different in such a way that each circle of the Different accommodates one of these bodies (38c–d). These seven heavenly bodies move according to both circles, the circle of the Different specific to them and the circle of the Same, which affects them all (38c–39b).

Thus, the motions of the World Soul are the ultimate basis for the motions of the heavenly bodies. The rather odd ingredients out of which the World Soul is made – Being, the Same, and the Different – ensure that it is not only the basis for physical motion, but can itself also perform intellectual motions. Plato's *Sophist* shows that these three Forms are necessary for all possible cognition and thus for rationality.[10] And they have a similar function here in the *Timaeus*. Passage 37a2–c2 explains how the World Soul can acquire true opinions and knowledge: by being made up of divisible and indivisible Being, Difference, and Sameness, the World Soul is of a similar basic structure to what is cognised, which, according to the like-to-like principle, is a necessary condition for cognition[11] – what is cognised *is* (either something divisible, if belonging to Becoming, or something indivisible, if belonging to Being), *is the same as* something, and *is different from* something. Furthermore, cognition consists in affirmations and negations about what is cognised. Sameness in this passage is the basis for affirmations, Difference for negations, since '*x* is F' is understood as 'something is the same as something else', and '*x* is not F' as 'something is different from something else'.[12] What will be important later on is the fact that while the World Soul itself has only knowledge and *true* opinion,

[9] See Proclus, *Commentary on Plato's* Timaeus, III, 237–8; Cornford 1997, 74–86; and Taylor 1928, 147–52.
[10] See, for example, 254d–255e.   [11] Cf. Frede 1996, 38.
[12] I spell out in detail how these motions work in the unpublished piece 'Thinking'.

the construction of cognition sketched in 37a2–c2 leaves open the possibility of falsehood.

The motions of the heavenly bodies in Plato's account are nothing other than the visible manifestations of the cognising motions of the World Soul. Since the motions of the World Soul are regular, the motions of the planets and the fixed stars are also regular,[13] and in this way show on a physical level the rationality of the motions of the World Soul's reasoning. While the Socrates of the *Republic* seems to suggest that the heavenly motions cannot be understood as being regular and intelligible,[14] *Timaeus* 39c explicitly claims that there is a regular pattern for all heavenly motions. For we can use the motions of each individual heavenly body to gain regular units of time, even if it might be difficult for us to actually grasp the path of their revolutions. In 38e–39b Plato gives us a general principle of how to understand seemingly irregular motions, namely by analysing them as the combination of different regular motions. Each planet follows the motion of the circle of the Different specific to it, but is also given a second motion by the circle of the Same (39a). Accordingly, in the *Timaeus* seeming irregularities can be explained as the combination of different regular motions.

We see that one crucial achievement of the *Timaeus* is the establishment of (at least some) natural processes as intelligible. The way Plato guarantees the intelligibility of the motions and changes in the universe is by having them proceed according to the intellectual motions of the World Soul. In the *Republic* and the *Phaedo*, what is intelligible is restricted to that which is and remains always the same, which is without any differences and thus stable.[15] In the *Timaeus*, by contrast, motion in the phenomenal realm too is presented as being both rationally designed and intelligible in so far as it proceeds according to a regular pattern, the path or combination of paths of the circles of the Same and the Different. The terms Plato uses in the *Timaeus* for describing such patterns, which processes follow, are terms for order and harmony (cognates of *taxis, sumphonia,* and *kosmos*).

In the case of static elements, order may be understood as an unchanging arrangement of elements or as a principle underlying such an arrangement. But in the case of processes, order must be a principle that is responsible for a certain arrangement *in spite* of changes and thus must guarantee each

---

[13] See 39b–d and below.

[14] I deal with the possible objection that this is only due to the educational context in the aforementioned work in progress 'Circular Motion in Plato – Systematic Thinking and Historic Development'.

[15] See e.g. *Phaedo* 78c ff., *Republic* 479a; cf. also Parmenides fr. 8.

element its appropriate place in a process. This is what we can call a *rule* – a principle governing or describing conduct (actions, processes, procedures, arrangements), which thus allows processes to be ordered.[16]

The regularity of the heavenly motions demonstrates that there is indeed such a rule in place guaranteeing the rational structure of motions. For it is the regularity which makes it clear that what moves does not simply acquire different places over time, but that there is something that remains the same in these changes: the process will always proceed in the same way, so that, among other things, the *relation* of the different places will remain stable, as will the relation to and between certain times. For example, a certain planet will always be in place y after it has been in x and before it goes on to z, and it will always take the same time to go from x to y and from y to z. This uniformity throughout the change is what makes these motions intelligible and shows their rational design. In contrast to mere invariance, regularity allows for change (for instance, the planets' change of places). Hence, the uniformity guaranteeing intelligibility is not tied to something which remains always the same and is simple. Rather, it is the uniformity something retains by changing in a regular fashion, that is, changing not randomly but according to a rule, which is the basis for regular behaviour.[17]

This regularity can be guaranteed by having the planets and stars proceed in *circular* motions, as circular motions can proceed in uninterrupted uniformity, while a rectilinear motion in a finite universe will necessarily have to come to an end at some point. More exactly, it is combinations of circular motions that Plato employs for his account of the motions of the heavenly bodies. In addition, circular motions can easily be used to measure and thus be compared to other motions. As 39b–c explains, the motions of each planet will give us a unit of time, and can be measured against the motions of the other planets.[18]

---

[16] Plato talks about the order of motions, for example, in 30a when we read that what was given to the demiurge in the beginning was 'in discordant and disorderly motion, and he brought it from disorder to order'; see also 46e. And 47d claims that if the revolutions of our soul are confused, they have to be brought back to order and harmony with themselves.

[17] E.g. the moon revolves at an average distance of 238,875 miles around the centre of the earth in an average of 29 days, 12 hours, 44 minutes, and 3 seconds. So, it moves at the average velocity of $2 \times \pi \times 238{,}875 / 29.5h$, which is the rule for its changes and tells us how to calculate where on its path it is situated at a given time. A Platonic version of this rule may claim that the moon moves along its circle of the Different diagonally to the left for a period of x units of time before it is affected by the motion of the Same and moves straight to the right for a period of y units of time.

[18] This presupposes that the motions of the planets are regular – otherwise, there would not be a quantifiable relation between them.

While in *Republic* 530a–b we are told that there is no ratio (and no *summetria*) between the motions of the heavenly bodies, the *Timaeus* explicitly states in 36d that the seven circles of the Different have a ratio to each other: two of the three circles of the Different move with the same speed, the other four with different speed but in a ratio (*en logō*) to each other. Such a ratio can be understood as a (second-order) rule describing the relation of two motions, each of which itself follows a certain rule. This ratio can be numerically expressed. For example, we can say that the relation of the revolution of Mars around the sun to the revolution of Venus equals 94:31. This ratio gives us the rule which allows us to calculate the position of the two planets with respect to each other.

While the regular motions of the heavens are an expression of rational design, the chaotic motions of the elemental traces 'before' creation and thus 'before' any reason was at work are not imbued with reason and hence not rationally structured. Without a rational structure, however, motion does not follow any pattern or rule, and thus does not show any regularity. It is the *regularity* of the motions of the heavens which shows that, and how, reason is unfolded in nature.[19] That the regular motions of the heavens are rationally structured and intelligible and visibly manifest the cognising motions of the World Soul already indicates why we human beings should follow the revolutions of the universe – for thus we follow the never-erring reasoning of the World Soul.

2.3   Processes in the Human Realm

If we now look at the realm of human beings, we see that our initial question, why Plato combines cultural and natural history in one text, is given a first answer by the fact that he has to solve a structurally similar problem in both realms: how can processes be available for rational understanding? In the *Republic*, processes, human or natural, are not rationally structured, since rationality is a feature of the realm of Being and thus of the purely intelligible world only.[20] In the *Timaeus*, however, an attempt is made to give an account of processes of sensible things, in the natural and the human realms. We will see that in the human realm, too, the way to prove processes to be intelligible is by showing how they can be understood as regular, and hence as proceeding according to a rule. What

---

[19] That regularity indicates a connection to reason is also shown in the idea that these regular motions of the cosmos are what, according to Plato, allow for knowledge and rational understanding (37c).
[20] For a different reading of the *Republic*, see Fine 2003.

guarantees their rational structure and their intelligibility is, in both cases, the intellectual motions of a soul.

In the human realm, we will have to distinguish between the level of the individual human being and the level of the human culture understood as a joint enterprise of human beings. The structural similarity between the individual human being and the universe is to be found within the cosmology of the *Timaeus*, while the actions of cultures as a whole are mainly found in the part preceding the cosmology.

If we regard the history of human culture as a whole in the *Timaeus*, we see that Plato assumes regularity and predictability. While the *Republic* showed that even the *kallipolis* has a natural tendency to decline (book 8, especially 546a ff),[21] with the Egyptians the *Timaeus* presents as paradigm a culture that remains essentially unchanged over millennia. All other cultures follow a regular pattern of development and destruction,[22] the regularity of which becomes clear when the old Egyptian, in his discussion with Solon, refers to the *'usual* period of years' (πάλιν δι' εἰωθότων ἐτῶν, 23a7), after which torrents of rain lead again to the destruction of a culture (23a–b). Thus, on the cultural level, too, there is a regular pattern that resembles to some degree the regularity to be found in nature. In fact, this regularity is caused by natural processes, namely by the regular occurrences of natural catastrophes. Hence, what connects the rational structure in the natural and the cultural realms as a whole is a certain regularity in nature itself, which we see expressed in the regular recurrence of catastrophes. *Prima facie*, it seems as if these catastrophes were only disturbances[23] of the regularity in nature. However, reoccurring at regular intervals (22d1–2), they follow a complex rule that is only detectable over a long interval of time.[24]

The Greeks tell the story of Phaeton's accident with his father's chariot, burning everything (22c); hence, they understand this catastrophe as a one-time irregularity. The Egyptians, by contrast, explain it as a reoccurring event. Thus, it is only seemingly an irregularity; it actually follows a complex rule: 'the truth behind it is a deviation of the bodies that revolve in heaven round the earth and a destruction, occurring at long intervals, of

---

[21] For whatever has come into being must pass away again – a claim that is, however, not unqualifiedly true in the *Timaeus*: the cosmos as a whole, as well as the minor gods, has come into existence, but will not pass away (41b and 38b–c), since the demiurge promises not to dissolve them.

[22] Egypt is an exception due to its special geographic location.

[23] See Timaeus' talk about deviation (*parallaxis*) in 22d1.

[24] Only because the Egyptians keep a record of these events can they capture the regularity in it (cf. also the regularity of the great year in 39d).

things on earth by a great conflagration' (22d1–30).[25] These catastrophes regulate human history on the grand scale, since the pattern of human history as described in the *Timaeus* is ultimately a consequence of effects of and reactions to these natural events. Thus, we get a regular pattern of development and destruction within the history of human culture which is caused by a regular pattern occurring in the natural realm.[26]

If we look at the individual human being, we also find regular motions akin to those in the natural realm, since the individual human being is made up of the same stuff as the universe as a whole: she is an embodied soul; the body is composed of the four elements; her soul is mixed of the same ingredients as the World Soul (41d) and set up with a circle of the Same and another of the Different. Finally, the revolutions of these two circles in the individual share the same structure as those of the World Soul, as becomes obvious in 47b–c:

> the god invented sight and gave it to us so that we might observe the orbits of intelligence in the heavens and apply them to the revolutions of our own thought, which are akin to them.

Since our thinking and the thinking of the World Soul are of the same kind,[27] we human beings can learn more about our own thinking by observing the motions of the heavens. Furthermore, since the circles of our own intelligence are often disturbed, we can also use the heavenly intelligence in order to improve our own thinking. The rational revolutions of the heavens are thus a basis for human science and rational understanding in two ways: (a) they guarantee that the world is available to human beings for rational understanding, as an object of science. However, in order to explain Plato's claim in 90c–d, that everybody should follow the revolutions of the universe, we also need to remember that (b) the rational revolutions of the natural realm are an expression of the *reasoning* of the World Soul itself (37a–c), so that they can be a paradigm for the proper thinking of human beings.

However, it is not clear yet whether and, if so, how this translates into the realm of human *actions*. Besides, the application of the revolutions of the universe to our own understanding is only a possibility. For the human individual can follow the motions of reason she sees in the sky or she can refrain from doing so. The World Soul and we human beings share the

---

[25] Translations in the following by Zeyl, often with alterations.
[26] Cf. also A. A. Long's chapter in this volume.
[27] This can also be seen from the fact that if human beings move their body in accordance with reason, their motions resemble the motions of the heavens, 89a.

same kind of capacity to think in a certain desirable and correct way (47c), which is thus in accord with a certain norm. But the World Soul, in contrast to human souls, necessarily achieves this desirable way of thinking and fulfils this norm. The fact that we are able to perceive the intelligible motions of the universe[28] not only grants us the possibility of striving for a perfect imitation of these motions, but also gives each human being some distance from them. Accordingly, we human beings are not simply forced to follow the motions we perceive in nature; rather we can either neglect these norms or strive to fulfil them.

This difference between the manifestations of reason in the universe and in the individual human being is not unproblematic. If human beings have a rational faculty but do not necessarily use it, does this not undermine the regularity of processes we can reasonably expect within the human realm? Thus the human realm raises an additional problem, which we do not face in the realm of nature. This seems to be one reason for the particular order of the *Timaeus-Critias* sequence presented to us in 27a–b: first Timaeus gives an account of the universe that shows natural motions and changes to be rationally structured; only then do we turn to the real discussion of the human realm with the additional problems it raises.[29]

Thus, an important structural difference between the two realms is that the phenomena in the realm of nature will always proceed in the same way, if there is no external interference,[30] while in the realm of human actions, there is the possibility of irregularity from within; a process need not always take place in the same way. In the human case, there can be a gap between aim and result, expectation and realisation of actions that is based on the very way human beings are set up, as we see in the contrast Plato draws between human beings as they come into being and human beings as they ought to become. This gap in the human case shows that the human and the natural sphere have fairly different structures so that it is not clear how the one could simply adapt to the other. The question is thus whether Plato accounts for this crucial difference or is simply levelling it out. We may think that this difference can be accounted for in a teleological explanation

---

[28] We are given vision for exactly this purpose, 47b–c.

[29] Critias' summary of the story of ancient Athens and Atlantis before Timaeus' account is explicitly introduced as a preview of which all the details still have to be given in order to fulfil Socrates' wish to see the best city in motion (25e–27b). The detailed account is only partial, however, since the *Critias* dialogue breaks off in mid-sentence.

[30] As mentioned above, with 'nature' I focus on the heavenly bodies here; animals are reincarnations of fallen human souls for Plato, and not much discussed in the *Timaeus*. The possibility of external interference is mentioned to capture the talk of deviation (*parallaxis*) over long intervals in 22d, and, counterfactually, a possible intervention of the demiurge.

(and that for Plato both the human and the natural realms follow final causation), since such an explanation can account for normative failure. However, the project here is not simply to claim that Plato works with a teleological world view, but rather to investigate how exactly such a world view can explain this structural dissimilarity between the human and the natural realms. In his introduction of the human realm in the *Timaeus*, Plato clearly accounts for the difference between human actions and the regular processes in nature – otherwise it would be unclear, for example, what it means that the old Athenians through their victory over Atlantis gave back freedom to those enslaved by Atlantis (25c).[31] He accounts for the difference in the way in which rationality is manifested in nature and in individual human beings; and he points out the basis for the irregularities in the human realm in his characterisation of the embodiment of human souls:

> And they [the minor gods] went on to invest this body – into which and out of which things were to flow – with the orbits of the immortal soul. These orbits, now bound with a mighty river, neither mastered this river nor were mastered by it, but tossed it violently and were violently tossed by it. Consequently the living thing as a whole did indeed move, but it would proceed in a disorderly, random, and irrational way that involved all six of the motions . . . . Whenever they [the revolutions of the soul] encounter something outside of them characterisable as same or different, they will speak of it as 'the same as' something, or as 'different from' something else when the truth is just the opposite, so proving themselves to be misled and unintelligent . . . . All these disturbances are no doubt the reason why even today and not only at the beginning, whenever a soul is bound within a mortal body, it at first lacks intelligence. (43a– 44c)

This dramatic imagery shows how we come into being as rational bodily beings by having our soul embodied, a process which causes serious disorientation for our soul and leads to all kinds of falsity. But it is not simply *being embodied* as such that accounts for the disorientation – after all, the World Soul is also embodied. Rather, these disturbances are due to three crucial modifications in human embodiment *vis-à-vis* the embodiment of the World Soul (43b1–2). (1) The ingredients of human souls are less pure than those of the World Soul (41d). (2) The human body has material exchanges with the outside world, for example, through nutrition

---

[31] The freedom talked about in this passage is human freedom as contrasted to slavery; it is not freedom in contrast to the laws of nature. Still, it would not make sense to talk about free human beings, if everyone's actions were fully determined by nature. Thus, Plato does indeed acknowledge this degree of freedom in the human sphere.

and perception (42a and 43b–c), which can disturb the circles of the soul. By contrast, the body of the universe encompasses everything so there is nothing outside it (33c6–7). (3) Finally, the World Soul is stretched out throughout the World Body, while the rational part of the human soul is situated only in the head.[32]

Let us now consider the structural differences between the natural realm and the cultural realm where this means human beings acting together. We saw above that Timaeus assumes a regular pattern in human history caused by natural processes. However, this does not mean that Plato takes human culture as a whole to be designed in just the way that nature is. Nature only determines certain limits within which human beings can act independently of nature.

Within these limits, there is no given structure that human history has to follow. Within each circle that is delimited by the natural pattern, human beings can act either in an orderly or in a disorderly fashion. This is made obvious by the Egyptians' introduction of a normative framework: they record those events that are good and noble (τι καλὸν ἢ μέγα γέγονεν ἢ καί τινα διαφορὰν ἄλλην ἔχον, 23a3). To call events good and noble in the human realm seems reasonable only if they could have taken place otherwise, if there is some freedom to choose; normative ideals and normative judgements (of goodness or nobility) only make sense within a context that allows for the possibility of normative failure and improvement.

These normative judgements may seem to apply only to the behaviour of individual human beings.[33] However, in the first part of the dialogue, the good and noble actions referred to are the actions of a *polis*. While we do not get the parallel between individual soul and the whole *polis* stated here as explicitly as in the *Republic*, we see nevertheless that the same kind of normative judgement applies to both. The normative judgements about a society as a whole that are central in the *Timaeus* concern Plato's characterisation of the war between the valiant Athenians and the wanton people of Atlantis (25b–c). The Athenian people represent normative success, the people of Atlantis normative failure.

The difference between the cultural and the natural realms is seen not only with this normative characterisation. Rather, it is already clear from the description of the battle between Atlantis and Athens, which

---

[32] These differences explain human imperfection, but in such a way that they do not challenge the claim of an intelligent cosmos.

[33] As we find it, for instance, in 42c–d.

is a single event – according to the *Timaeus*, it is the biggest war in human history, and as such not a regular occurrence. It is the singularity of the occurrence itself that indicates a basic difference between human processes in the cultural realm and the natural ones of the heavenly bodies.

While we saw that Plato does indeed accommodate the structural difference between the natural and human realms, we have yet to answer the question of whether human imperfection undermines the regularity we have seen him attribute to human motions and actions.

2.4 Structural Similarities in the Human and the Natural Realms

The *Timaeus* tries to show that the structure specific to the human realm does not lead to total chaos, which would indeed undermine the possibility of regular motions. Chaos and arbitrariness can be remedied on the individual level by employing a norm, a standard of decency for human actions, and on the collective level by coordinating the actions that are performed according to such norms, for instance, with the help of laws, as Timaeus describes it in the case of ancient Athens and Egypt. The fact that human actions can be *regulated* by such rules, norms, and laws is what allows Plato to see room for a substantive *parallel* between human reasoning and actions, on the one hand, and the rational structure of the heavens, on the other, in spite of the differences between the two realms. These differences include the fact that rules in the human realm are instructions for how people ought to behave, while with the motions of the heavenly bodies, rules describe how they do in fact 'behave'. But the human 'ought' should adapt to the heavenly bodies' 'is'.

On the individual level, a decrease in external disturbances after a certain time gives human beings the possibility of escaping from the chaotic motions brought about by embodiment:

> But when the stream that brings growth and nourishment diminishes and the soul's orbits regain their composure, resume their proper course, and establish themselves more and more with the passage of time, their revolutions are set straight, to conform to the configuration each of the circles takes in its natural course. They then correctly identify what is the same and what is different, and render intelligent the person who possesses them. And to be sure, if some right nurture lends help towards education, he'll turn out perfectly whole and healthy, and will have escaped the most grievous of illnesses. But if he neglects this, he'll limp his way through life and return to Hades uninitiated and unintelligent. (44b–c)

After the initial shock of growth and nutrition, time brings about a comparatively restful period in which the external interferences diminish, so that the soul can follow the natural tendency of its own circles again. However, education is needed to lead the motions of the soul back to its proper harmonies and to regulate the interplay between body and soul. Then the circles of the soul can correctly state what is the same as something else and what is different from something else. In this way, education leads the human soul to knowledge and true opinion, though the soul retains the possibility of error. Plato explicitly leaves room for failure by pointing out that without education, human beings will die ἀτελὴς καὶ ἀνόητος (44c3).

Following the circles of the Same and the Different and controlling the body again by reason (*logos*) is, according to Plato, what brings a human being back to its 'former and best state' (42d). Only a soul whose circles of the Same and the Different are *moving regularly* again can acquire knowledge. As Plato points out in 87a–b, knowledge can prevent us from acting badly, it is proscribing; and it is prescribing in giving us some positive rules or norms for our actions (which are based on understanding what are the right things to do; in this sense they are rationally structured norms). This becomes obvious in the case of the Egyptian habit of 'keeping the good and noble deeds'. If this evaluation was not made against a certain norm or standard of what should be done, then these deeds presumably could not be called good and noble. Norms prescribe in general which actions we should pursue and which we should refrain from. A morally good person will follow these norms and, accordingly, her actions will become more regular and less chaotic as they will be in accord with what the norms make us expect. In this way, norms lead to more regularity within the realm of human actions. Thus, on the individual level, chaos and arbitrariness are remedied to a certain degree by norms for our actions, certain rules.

Such norms ensuring learning are also in place on the collective level, when the Egyptians secure learning for the whole of society by their laws (24b–c). By contrast, the Greeks of Solon's and Critias' time do not seem to learn from what has gone before. A lack of education is thus responsible for disorder in the individual soul (44b–c) as well as in a *polis* as a whole. This becomes obvious also from the account of the decline of city states in the *Laws*: while the decline of all *poleis* seems to be unavoidable in the *Republic*, in the *Laws* a *polis* declines due to lack of knowledge and moderation (695e). Sparta protects itself from this danger by the right education and is preserved as a well-ordered *polis*. The 'contemporary' Athenians of the *Timaeus* do not use the regular circles of destruction and reconstruction well, as they do not build on the developments of the preceding circles. They start anew with each circle and so they are, as an Egyptian priest expresses it, 'in constant infancy' (22b). This may seem like the unavoidable outcome of bad luck, since the Athenians live in a region undergoing natural catastrophes in regular cycles, in contrast to the Egyptians, who are not affected by these catastrophes. However, Plato makes it clear that the actual reason is not bad luck, but the Greek attitude towards their history: they see their history as a mere succession of individual events that they tell like a 'nursery tale', rather than as a reservoir of possibilities from which to learn (22a–23c).

   We have seen that the regularity on the natural level imposes a certain structure on the cultural level, but within these limits, within a cycle, a human culture can either learn and thus behave regularly, or not. Furthermore, regularity on the individual level does not automatically ensure regularity on the cultural level. For even if all individuals acted rationally for themselves, the combination of all their actions could lead to irregular outcomes, if they are not coordinated. This becomes obvious in the case of a battle – the situation in which Socrates wants to see the best city: even if all individuals in an army acted most rationally in a battle, they might still act badly if their actions are not harmonized and, for example, obstruct each other. On the cultural level, regularity is only possible if there is rational coordination of the different actions and agents in place. In the Platonic picture, we do find such regularity within a culture, in old Athens as well as in Egypt. So there must be some coordination going on, presumably with the help of laws – at least part of what we hear about the laws in ancient Athens is a coordination and ordering of who is doing what: it is laid down by law that there is a strict division between the classes of priests, warriors, and craftsmen, and the warriors are meant to do nothing but take care of war (24a–b). These laws, we are told, formed a crucial reason for why ancient Athens was so outstanding – 'Athens excelled itself by the excellence of its laws' (εὐνομωτάτη, 23c6).[34] Since it is due to their laws that the Athenians stood out amongst other peoples as most excellent, these laws seem to have been the basis for their overarching *aretē*. This is also in accord with what we are told is the purpose of the laws in Plato's *Laws*: virtue in its entirety (630e–631a).[35]

---

[34] Cf. also 23e and 24d.

[35] Cf. also 628c. It is surely not a coincidence that Timaeus is introduced in the dialogue as coming from a most supremely governed state (εὐνομωτάτης πόλεως, 20a).

Furthermore, the *Laws* makes explicit what, given the outcome, can be found also in the *Timaeus*, namely that laws do not simply encapsulate human traditions and conventions, but have an intimate connection to reason: 'For of all studies, that of legal regulations (*nomoi*), provided they are correctly framed, will prove the most efficacious in making the learner a better man; for were it not so, it would be in vain that our divine and admirable law bears a name akin to reason (*nous*)' (957c–d). In the *Timaeus*, the laws allow for establishing the sciences in society and for the cultivation of *phronēsis* (24b–c), and thus ensure learning on the collective level. It is the very same legislation that we find in Egypt, which thus presumably owes its successful avoidance of moral decline to these laws.[36] Even Atlantis was virtuous, as long as its citizens obeyed the laws (*Critias* 120e), which they did as long as the divine nature in them was strong enough.

Thus, it is such laws that are responsible for regularity on the collective level. We can understand these laws as a body of binding and enforceable rules governing human conduct that will coordinate human actions by regulating the societal order, the relations and interactions between human beings, and thus their common life as a culture. They determine which kinds of actions should occur and are thus likely to be performed in a good state,[37] and which are not permitted to occur in a state, to which degree, and under which circumstances.

Synchronically, laws governing the actions of all individuals within a culture can lead to regularity and allow for the best possible culture. Diachronically, regularity is possible if one culture learns from what has happened before – from failure, as in the case of Atlantis, and from success, as in the case of ancient Athens – either in their own or in another culture.[38] Both on the level of culture and on the level of individual human beings, there is space for learning and improvement through developing rational structures, as well as for failure and decline of rationality.

---

[36] In the *Laws*, Plato plays with the fact that *nomos* can mean 'law' as well as a musical mode or strain, which also fits his usage of cognates of *sumphonia* in the *Timaeus* for describing regular patterns and the order in the natural world. Cf. also his usage of *plēmmelēs*, 'being out of tune', in order to describe the unregulated, chaotic motions before creation in 30a.

[37] Regarding laws also positively as norms of what should be done with respect to virtue is the prevalent understanding of laws that we find in Plato's *Laws*; see 628c and 630e.

[38] In *Laws* 692c we hear from the Athenian that once there has been a *paradeigma* in history, like the Spartan constitution, it is not difficult to learn from it. On the other hand, in 695d–e it is pointed out that the Persian king Darius does not appear to have learned anything for the education of his successor from history.

That education with the help of norms and laws is needed in the human realm in order to avoid chaotic motions not only stresses the difference between the natural and human realms. It also makes clear why bringing these different realms together in the *Timaeus* is nevertheless instructive, as indicated by the quotation stating that everybody should follow the revolutions of the universe. For we have seen that the embodiment of the human soul initially leads to total confusion. And a culture can be thrown back to cultural infancy through natural catastrophes. Accordingly, the right way to proceed is not immediately obvious to the embodied human soul or to a culture in infancy. Rather, souls have to learn how to return to their cycles of reason, cultures how to orientate themselves by rational norms. This process of learning is supported by watching the heavens and their motions, since with the divine planets and stars, human beings can see how other souls deal with being embodied in a rational way.

Not only is the cosmos rationally structured and hence cognisable for us, its motion also visibly manifests the World Soul's own reasoning, so that looking at it we can learn more about our own cognition in general. Again the like-to-like principle is crucial: it is the basis to explain not only why we can understand the motions of the heavens (because the same circles of the Same and the Different underlie the motions of the heavenly bodies and our thinking), but it also tells us why we should follow the motions of the universe (because these revolutions visibly manifest paradigmatic cognitions, and we, cognising them, learn what knowledge and true opinion really are). Examining the motions of the universe can thus be a basis not only for establishing science and rational understanding, but also for self-reflection. While the regular processes of a culture are not based on its own societal circles of the Same and the Different, the individual soul's ordered intellectual motions along the circles of the Same and the Different are necessary conditions for it.

Summing up, I have argued that the reason why Plato connects cultural and natural history in the *Timaeus* rests on the fact that he has to solve the same problem in both realms: how can processes in the natural as well as the human realm be understood as intelligible? The way he solves this problem is by binding intelligibility no longer to complete uniformity but to a rule. This rule is expressed in the regularity of human and natural processes, even if we are dealing with different kinds of rules in these two realms – norms and laws for actions in the one case, ratios and descriptive rules for the motions of the heavenly bodies in the other. While regularity is achieved in different ways in the two realms, we see in both that without reason motions proceed in all directions, without any rule or order that is expressed in regular motions.[39] And in both realms motions are, or should ultimately be, related to the motions of the World Soul, which ensures the knowability of the world of change: the regularity of the motions of the heavenly bodies is grounded in the reasoning motions of the World Soul, while our human reasoning should adjust itself to the heavenly revolutions.

Observing the revolutions of the heavens as well as their harmonies will make our thinking follow the heavenly revolutions, and thus the revolutions of the World Soul (90d4). We are promised that following these revolutions will win us 'the fulfilment of the best life set by the gods before mankind' (90d).[40] And if we do well in this life, controlling our sensations and feelings, and acting rationally, we will be able to return home after our earthly life to the star we belong to (42b); thus we will not only assimilate ourselves to the motions of the heavenly bodies, but finally also join them.

---

[39] In the case of nature, we have seen this with the pre-cosmic chaos, while in the human case we have seen it at the birth of an embodied soul.

[40] For different interpretations of this claim, see Sedley 1997, 332 ff.

CHAPTER 3

Natural Catastrophe in Greek and Roman Philosophy

A. A. Long

As we proceed into the third decade of the twenty-first century, there is an unprecedented recognition that we are on the brink of natural catastrophe on a global scale. To call climate change catastrophic is not just to say that it is hugely threatening. Catastrophe is the most appropriate word because, borrowing from the ancient Greek word *katastrophe*, the English term originally signified a *dramatic* event that *changes* or *ends* the order of things.[1]

Human beings have always experienced catastrophe, whether it be the outcome of purely natural conditions or of human actions like war and genocide. Greek philosophers from the beginnings of their inquiries into nature offered explanations of such devastating phenomena as earthquakes.[2] How did they accommodate catastrophe within their understanding of causality and theology? Our own climatic dangers and fears could have no ancient anticipations but, given the basic invariance and

---

For Sarah Broadie – with great admiration and affection.

[1] The ancient Greek *katastrophe* does not signify *natural* disaster, but rather an enforced change, such as a military subjugation (Herodotus 1.92), or simply an end; hence the word on its own frequently signifies death, though not necessarily a violent or emotionally charged demise. Our word 'cataclysm' also comes directly from ancient Greek. There it literally means a 'deluge'. In English, 'cataclysm' has become virtually synonymous with 'catastrophe' on the widest scale. Latin has a rich language for specifying violent events of great magnitude. Without attempting to be exhaustive, I instance *clades* (calamity, military disaster), *ruina* (downfall), *exitium* (destruction, ending), and *calamitas* (calamity). My impression is that *ruina* and *calamitas* may be used to signify what we call catastrophes, but our derivatives 'ruin' and 'calamity' lack the connotations of violence, suddenness, and finality for which we use the word 'catastrophe'. *Exitium* is more or less equivalent to the Greek noun most commonly found in contexts describing natural catastrophes, which is *phthora*. Derived from *phtheirō*, meaning 'decline', 'fade', or 'die', connotations of ending (as in English 'catastrophe') are present in *phthora* as well as, obviously, in *exitium*. These Greek and Latin expressions (even *kataklusmos* in its metaphorical usage) pertain to both natural and to humanly caused disasters. In this chapter, I will focus on natural catastrophe, with the proviso that 'natural' may include divinely caused events, as in the expression 'acts of God', which British insurance companies use to exclude their liability for unpredictable and uncontrollable contingencies. The American insurance company ALLSTATE provides a Catastrophe Readiness Clearing House.

[2] See n. 7 below.

consistency of human psychology, we may reasonably expect that the leading ancient philosophers would have had interesting thoughts about natural catastrophe. Plato and Aristotle, especially Plato, will feature importantly in this study, but we shall find the philosophers most relevant to contemporary anxieties to be the Epicurean Lucretius and the Stoic Seneca.

*****

Early modern science generated a debate in geology that had already been pertinent in Greco-Roman thought – the question of whether the earth, viewed over long time spans, stays more or less uniform, its major changes being cyclical and repeatable, or whether, on the other hand, the earth began and will end in a set of linear and more or less uniform events. Thus the early nineteenth-century Cambridge scientist William Whewell coined the term 'catastrophism' to distinguish the theory that extraordinary and unrepeatable events (for instance, uniquely convulsive volcanic eruptions) have shaped the world's geological structure, as distinct from the theory he called 'uniformitarianism', which proposed ongoing and repeatable processes, with the same principles at work now as have operated in the past.[3] Catastrophism in its original context was deeply influenced by a literal reading of the biblical Genesis, but its influence persists in our secular understanding today. No one expects the terrestrial conditions that favoured the flourishing of the dinosaurs to repeat themselves; and if the dinosaurs were destroyed as a result of a gigantic asteroid's impact on the earth, as current theory supposes, we do not expect that a similar impact will recur during humanity's foreseeable existence, even if it is a statistical possibility.

To the extent that we can find *theories* of natural catastrophe in Greek and Roman literature (as distinct from myths such as Hesiod's story of Typhoeus, seemingly inspired by eruptions of Mt Etna), they presuppose the repetition of devastating events rather than their singularity. Stoic *ekpurōsis* – the theory that the entire universe will eventually end in a mighty 'conflagration' – might seem to be an obvious counter instance. But actually, in spite of its catastrophic connotations, the *ekpurōsis* was presumed to be an eternally repeated ending to the one and only world that is eternally and identically re-created. The Epicurean Lucretius, too, though he posited the eventual and absolute ending of our world, was

---

[3] For a convenient outline of these notions, see Wilson 1973.

a uniformitarian in the sense that he regarded nothing in his infinite universe to be unique or unrepeatable (5.97–109, 2.1067–89).

A further point that differentiates ancient and modern conceptions of natural catastrophe concerns the practical and emotional responses to such events. Widespread suffering, loss of life, and terror will always accompany catastrophe, but our linear and progressivist thinking generates such responses as 'never again if we can help it', or 'we must do better next time', or 'this could have been prevented if only . . .'. Modern engineering has made those of us who live in developed countries far more secure from the perils of natural catastrophe than were the inhabitants of ancient Greece and Rome. Such technological security, however, is entirely relative. When a partly preventable disaster such as Hurricane Katrina's devastation of New Orleans does occur, progressivist ideologies and political expectations hinder our fully coming to terms with the *natural* causality of the event in terms of meteorology and geography. Seneca sagely (*Natural Questions* 6.1.12) counsels his readers against complacently thinking that any part of the world might be immune from earthquakes. It would be absurd to suppose that ancient peoples were less traumatically affected by natural catastrophes than we ourselves are, but because they lacked naive confidence that all would or could be well, they were better prepared than we are to face nature's wrath. Contrast our indignation when officialdom fails to perform as we think it should.

For the historians of classical antiquity, earthquakes, floods, fires, volcanic eruptions, plagues, and famines were the most frequently mentioned examples of natural catastrophes.[4] They did not envision long-term damage to the earth's ecosystem. Nuclear fallout such as occurred at Chernobyl or the chemical pollution by Union Carbide at Bhopal furnish types of catastrophe unimaginable to the ancients, but I set aside such examples of humanly generated disasters.

We start then with an intriguing incongruity when comparing ancient and modern thinking about natural catastrophe. In Greece, with its seismic instability, many people experienced earthquakes and many more must have feared their occurrence.[5] Their mythological and religious tradition emphasised the unpredictability of territorial security and other life-supporting conditions. Our everyday lives, broadly speaking, are much

---

[4] Details and discussion are amply assembled in Olshausen 1998. The effect of earthquakes on the conduct of Greek politics, policy, and military strategy is excellently treated by Mosley 1998. On ancient pandemics, see Harper 2017.

[5] It was not for nothing that Poseidon was given the epithet of 'earth-shaker' in Homer (*enosichthōn, ennosigaios*).

more secure. Yet, the kinds of catastrophes that may give us nightmares are still more terrifying than those that our classical forebears could have imagined.

*****

In ancient Near Eastern and Mediterranean cultures, people pictured natural catastrophe most vividly as a deluge that wiped out virtually everyone. The flood is already an important feature of the Gilgamesh epic, where the gods set out to destroy humanity because of the noise people are making as a result of population expansion. We may suppose that an actual event – a tsunami perhaps, generated by a gigantic volcanic eruption – prompted imagination of this global cataclysm. In the Bible the flood is a divine punishment for human wickedness. Sin and community are causally related in this story with its theological pessimism, tempered at the end, thanks to Noah's righteousness, by God's covenant that he will never again destroy his special creation (Genesis 9:8–17). In essentially the same tradition, when Zeus was minded to destroy all human beings by a deluge, Deucalion with his wife Pyrrha, on the advice of philanthropic Prometheus, survived by means of an ark, and began the repopulation of the earth (Apollodorus 1.47). For Greek myth, like the Judaic belief system, catastrophe on the scale of a global deluge was a unique and unrepeatable event. In its singularity, the great flood served as a benchmark against which historical time or something like it could be presumed to start. No Greeks traced their ancestry back beyond Deucalion and Pyrrha. Similarly, the Bible includes elaborate genealogies for Noah's three sons and their descendants, but only the first-born sons of the long-lived descendants of Adam are recorded.

When Plato and Aristotle give rationalising accounts of natural catastrophe, they continue to mention the flood associated with Deucalion as a quasi-historical event (*Timaeus* 22a–c; *Meteorologica* 1.14, 352a32). Yet, rather than viewing it as a singular and unrepeatable occurrence, they seem to treat it as no more than an especially memorable instance of the cataclysms that are constantly repeated on a long view of history, a theory that Seneca too will endorse, as we shall see.

Already with the Presocratic thinkers, attention had shifted from myth and folktale to extraordinarily naturalistic explanations of earthquakes and similarly disturbing events. Our intellectual tradition has viewed the Presocratics as innovative philosophers rather than pioneering scientists. In fact they were both. As late as Seneca (see his *Natural Questions*), they were remembered especially for their theories of numerous natural phenomena, whether regular meteorological events and seasonal happenings like snow and hail and shooting stars, or occasional and especially striking occurrences such as earthquakes and tidal waves. Removing such phenomena from the divine and mythological domain was a momentous shift in human consciousness. By bringing these events within the scope of empirical intelligibility, the Presocratics sought to control them not only intellectually but also – something rarely remarked on – emotionally.[6]

These thinkers differed in their opinions concerning the world's duration. The majority of them seem to have held that, in as much as our world itself had an origin, so too it will eventually end. However, that thesis could be combined with a belief in the world's everlasting oscillation between complete unification and complete separation of its constituents (as with Empedocles), or with a theory that innumerable worlds are always being created and destroyed (so Democritus), as Epicurus too would later propose. Most strikingly, Heraclitus (though anachronistically credited with the Stoic theory of *ekpurōsis*) anticipated Aristotle in denying a beginning or end to the present world, giving it the status of dynamic equilibrium (DK22 B30, 31, 94, 114).

*****

Seismology was a staple of Presocratic investigations and of all Greek scientific speculation thereafter.[7] It was given terrifying immediacy one winter night in 373 BC. In a mere few hours, an earthquake followed by a tsunami completely overwhelmed and inundated Helikē, a prosperous city state situated on the north-west coast of the Peloponnese. This event, which left no survivors or intact

---

[6] If this observation seems unduly speculative, consider the way Heraclitus cajoles his hearers to wake up, heed experience, and expect the unexpected as they investigate natural events (DK22 B1, 17, 18, 35). Such injunctions were among his most important lessons for the Stoic philosophers, who followed his lead in their goal of living an unimpassioned life in agreement with nature. See Long 1996b.

[7] Anaximander is reported to have advised the Spartans to leave their homes because of an impending earthquake affecting Mt Taygetus (DK12 A5a). Some hundred years later, Anaxagoras, on the basis of secret Egyptian records, is said to have predicted earthquakes by stones falling from the sky and by handling mud from a well (DK59 A10), a theory which, in its presumed signs of pre-seismic instability, anticipates the most current seismology at Berkeley. The significance of these reports is not their accuracy but the fact that Presocratic thinkers were regarded as figures with the kind of know-how that could be of enormous practical benefit. Thales, who set the scene for this applied science with his nautical observation and mathematics, cannily likened an earthquake to a ship's motion in waves (DK11 A15). The younger Milesian scientist Anaximenes (DK13 A7) held that seismic phenomena are due to extreme changes of the earth in consequence of heating and chilling. Archelaus (DK60 A16a) and Democritus (DK68 A98) also offered intriguing accounts of when and why earthquakes occur.

buildings, was the greatest natural catastrophe of classical Greece. It is mentioned in all the obvious sources.[8]

A few years later, according to the standard chronology of Plato's dialogues, Plato himself was writing works that display a virtual obsession with natural disasters and their effects on human history and culture. This theme occurs in the *Timaeus* and its truncated sequel the *Critias*, in the *Statesman*, and most fully in the *Laws*. What prompted Plato to dwell so strongly on such catastrophes? At the time he began writing about them, the instant destruction of Helikē was still recent, but there is more than circumstantial reason to think that this event may have remained vividly in his mind. Plato's description of the violent end of Atlantis bears a strong resemblance to the recorded fate of Helikē, including the city's instant inundation and sea-girt location.[9]

Socrates begins the *Timaeus* by giving a reprise of Plato's *Republic* (supposedly the topic of the previous day's discussions). He then expresses the desire for someone else to describe that ideal community's competition with other societies, especially in its conduct of war. This request is answered by Plato's great-grandfather, Critias, who reports that a still older Critias heard the tale of how Athens, some 9,000 years previously, defeated the great invading power of Atlantis. The older Critias had learned of this 'history' from the illustrious Athenian lawgiver Solon, who had heard it in his turn from an ancient Egyptian priest.

Solon had begun his conversation with this personage by tracing the proximate origin of the Greeks back to Deucalion and Pyrrha (*Timaeus* 22b). He then attempts to compute the time between them and their descendants down to the present. Solon's narrative provokes the ancient Egyptian to criticise his childish naiveté. The Greeks, he says, have no true grasp of their own antiquity because they lack the requisite historical records. How so? 'There have been, and there will continue to be, numerous disasters (*pthorai*) that have destroyed human life in many ways. The most serious of these involve fire and water, while the lesser ones have numerous other causes' (22c).[10]

---

[8] See Lafond 1998. Sources include Aristotle, *Meteorologica* 343b, 368b6; Strabo 8.7.2; Diodorus Siculus 15.48.1; Pausanias 7.24.13; Seneca, *Natural Questions* 6.25.4. The three historians, but not Aristotle, attribute the catastrophe to divine anger, and specifically the wrath of Poseidon to punish the Heliconians for killing suppliants in the god's sanctuary. Diodorus, however, observes that *phusikoi* attribute the disaster to natural conditions. Poseidon, by grim irony, was Helikē's patron divinity.

[9] See Giovannini 1985, who makes the comparison and notes that Strabo's main source for his account of Helikē's catastrophe was Plato's student Heraclides of Pontus.

[10] I take translations of the *Timaeus* from Zeyl 2000. At *Critias* 111a, Plato refers more vaguely to the occurrence of many great 'cataclysms' in the 9,000 years separating the Athens that fought Atlantis from the contemporary state.

The Egyptian now mentions the Phaethon myth, interpreting it as a story about a global conflagration, and continues:

> This tale is told as a myth, but the truth behind it is that there is a deviation (*parallaxis*) in the heavenly bodies that travel around the earth, which causes huge fires that destroy what is on the earth across vast stretches of time. When this happens, all those people who live in mountains or in places that are high and dry are much more likely to perish than the ones who live next to rivers or by the sea [such as the Egyptian Nile dwellers]. On the other hand, whenever the gods send floods of water upon the earth to purge it (*kathairontes katakluzōsin*), the herdsmen and shepherds in the mountains preserve their lives, while those who live in cities, in your region, are swept by the rivers into the sea.

Egypt, the priest proceeds, thanks to its climate and its geographical location, is not subject to such catastrophes to the same extent, and the survival of its people assures their continuing literacy and historical records. In Greece, by contrast,

> No sooner have you achieved literacy and all the other resources that cities require, than there again, after the usual number of years, comes the heavenly flood. It sweeps upon you like a plague, and leaves only your illiterate and uncultured people behind. You become infants all over again, as it were, completely unfamiliar with anything there was in ancient times, whether here or in your own region. (*Timaeus* 23a)[11]

Solon is told that the Athenians recall only one flood, rather than the great many that there have actually been, and that they have no recollection of their finest hour 9,000 years ago, when they combated the aggressive empire of Atlantis, an event that occurred 'before the greatest of these devastating floods'.

We need not follow up the narrative of the war between Atlantis and ancient Athens save for its conclusion (25c):

> Athens prevented the enslavement of those not yet enslaved and generously freed all the rest of us who lived within the boundaries of Heracles. Sometime later, excessively violent earthquakes and floods occurred, and after the onset of an unbearable day and a night, your entire warrior force

---

[11] *Critias* 109d–110b repeats the claim that only illiterate mountain people survive the repeated catastrophes, but expands on the *Timaeus* account in the following ways: the names of the 'good autochthonous' early citizens, such as Cecrops and Erechtheus, are remembered, but not their 'works'; and the survivors were too concerned with the sheer necessities of life to pay any attention to history, which requires leisure. An analogous point was made by Aristotle if Iamblichus reports views that he advanced in his *Protrepticus* (fr. 8 Ross).

sank below the earth all at once, and the Isle of Atlantis likewise sank below the sea and disappeared.

When the younger Critias returns to the story of Atlantis, he states that the city's land (like the historical Helikē) is now buried by earthquakes (*Critias* 108e).

There are four principal motifs in this account of natural catastrophe: (1) long-term periodicity; (2) conflagrations or floods as the typical manifestation of such disasters; (3) enormously destructive effects on human habitations; and (4) devastating effects on culture and memory. All these motifs recur in at least one of Plato's other treatments of catastrophe, though the *Timaeus* version is exceptional in the contrast it draws between Athens and Egypt. It is also distinctive in attributing the floods to a divinely caused 'purgation' of the earth (22d, 23a).[12] These details may be a sign that Plato was dependent on Near Eastern traditions for the essence of his narrative; for it blends astronomy with religion in ways that point to a likely Babylonian origin.

The central point of this prelude to the *Timaeus* is the bearing of natural catastrophe on human history and the development of culture. That theme emerges with much greater clarity and depth in the remarkable discourse assigned to the Athenian spokesman in the opening of *Laws* book III. I summarise as follows.[13]

How are we to suppose that society (*politeia*) originated? The best way to find out is to study changes over a very long period. Even if we cannot calculate how long human beings have lived in communities, we should assume that tens of thousands of states have come into existence and equally many have been destroyed. We must also assume that all states have been subject to growth and decline, and to improvement and deterioration (676a–c), a thought that Plato likely owes to Herodotus.

Why have these changes occurred? Let's accept the long-standing tradition that numerous catastrophes have repeatedly wiped out human beings 'by floods, plagues, and many other means', leaving only a remnant of survivors (677a). Now, let us take one such instance – a flood from which almost the only survivors were shepherds living on mountain tops. It is necessary to suppose that such persons were technological innocents and

---

[12] See Harvey 2020, who argues, on the basis of *Laws* book X, that 'the occurrence of periodic disasters fits the gods' aim in caring for human affairs, namely the victory of virtue over vice on the whole (904b1–6)'.

[13] For an excellent account of how Plato's treatment of cultural vicissitudes fits his overall project in this dialogue, see Nightingale 1999.

unfamiliar with the dirty tricks city dwellers play on one another. As for low-lying settlements, these will have been completely destroyed along with their implements, technology, and political know-how. Hence we should suppose that for *millions* of years our remote ancestors lived in ignorance of such things (677d). Then, 'only yesterday as it were', such figures as Daedalus, Orpheus, and Palamedes made their civilising discoveries.

How, to continue, should we describe the state of humanity after these catastrophes? A good deal of fertile land was still available. Most livestock had perished, but some cattle and probably goats survived, enough to provide for the few remaining herdsmen. What had completely gone, we must presume, was any trace or memory of organised society (678a). From this condition of primitive subsistence, modern culture and community life gradually developed as the hill dwellers fearfully descended to level ground, encountered one another, and slowly rediscovered such techniques as mining and the ability to make tools and forms of transportation.

The Athenian spokesman proposes that, in the absence of social organisation, the few original survivors were neither completely virtuous nor completely vicious (678b). Their successors, however, thanks to their isolation, the smallness of their populations, and the availability of food and other basic resources, were not motivated to quarrel or fight one another; and in the absence of precious metals, they remained poor, free of crime, and, in a word, naively 'good' (679c). Waxing eloquent over the 'manliness' and other excellences of these early people (679e), the Athenian reminds his audience of the purpose of his account, namely, to show when human beings first came to feel the need for law.

This need was not registered by the 'excellent' people just described. Having no written records and hence no codified laws, they lived on the basis of custom (*ethos*) and 'so-called ancestral norms' (680a). This was the first type of social system developed after the great catastrophe. Its name is 'autocracy' (*dunasteia*) because the eldest son inherits authority from his parents, and the others follow his lead (680b). The Athenian claims that this social system is still prevalent in parts of the contemporary world, both Greek and non-Greek. Setting further details aside, let us ask about Plato's reasons for connecting a theory of *periodic* catastrophe with anthropology and the history of culture. We may start from comments by Solmsen.

Supposing, probably rightly, that periodic catastrophes were not part of the Presocratic scientific tradition, Solmsen writes:

Floods may have provided the most convincing explanation for the short span of recorded human history. The three late dialogues of Plato which embody the doctrine of catastrophes use it primarily for that purpose. Here the advantages of the flood theory come to light when Plato himself points out that civilization makes greater strides in the river valleys than in the lonely mountains. Therefore, when inundations occur and the settlers in the valleys suffer, much greater damage is done than when the illiterate mountain dwellers become the victims of a conflagration.[14]

Such a train of thought was surely subordinate to Plato's main reasons for emphasising periodic catastrophes. In the *Timaeus* and *Critias* and in the *Laws* his ethical focus is clearly to the fore. The superiority of ancient Athens to Atlantis is supposed to offer evidentiary and patriotic support for the real possibility of a state like Socrates' ideal *Republic*. That point is made in both the *Timaeus* (24b) and the *Critias* (110c–d), where we are told that, in the Athens that fought Atlantis, the soldiers, like those in the *Republic*, were distinguished as a special class from the populace engaged in agriculture and economic production. There is no reason for attributing to Plato an intrinsic interest in the 'short span of recorded human history'. The point of mentioning Egypt's antiquity in the *Timaeus* is to give the verisimilitude of ancient tradition to the Egyptian priest's tale of Atlantis. In the main body of the *Timaeus*, where Plato's focus is specifically cosmological, the topics of cultural history and catastrophe are not resumed.

In the case of the *Laws*, the Athenian proposes a hyperbolic account of primitive humanity's longevity (millions of years) and cultural change (tens of thousands of communities waxing and waning). I have no idea why he gives such exaggerated numbers to his story but, in contrast with the *Timaeus*, he does not base his thesis of periodic catastrophes simply on 'tradition'. In effect, he argues in favour of uniformitarianism with the intriguing hypothesis that periodic catastrophes wipe out all the implements and technology of the previous civilisation (677c): 'If these things had survived throughout at the same level of development as they have attained today, how could anything new be being discovered?' That is to say: given the proposed longevity of humanity's existence, if culture had continued uninterruptedly, everything would have been invented by now, contrary to our actual experience.

The extraordinary myth of the *Statesman* gives further support for taking Plato's interest in natural catastrophe to be primarily motivated

[14] Solmsen 1960, 432–3.

by his ethical and political concerns. The *Statesman* resembles the *Timaeus* in attributing what it calls 'the greatest and most complete change' (270b) to a huge shift (actually in this case, a 'reversal') in celestial motions. A result of this catastrophe, which includes a great earthquake (273a), is the large-scale destruction of life, as in the other two accounts I have discussed. Peculiar to the *Statesman*, however, are the bizarre effects of cosmic reversal: as God withdraws from the world, the surviving human beings grow progressively younger until they wither away to nothing. A new generation of 'earth-born' humans succeeds them (271a). This was the fabled era of Cronus, when human beings lived easy lives and had no need of political organisation. In course of time, however, the world underwent a further reversal, again without overall divine supervision. Finally, we have the present genus of human beings who have to struggle for survival.

The moral of this tale is that human society, in the absence of divine governance, requires leaders who will draft appropriate laws. Here, then, we see again how Plato's treatment of catastrophe feeds into his overriding political concerns. In all these stories a mythical past is envisioned, to throw light on the condition and needs of present-day society. The ideal Athens that defeated Atlantis was irrevocably blotted out by catastrophe. This state had the finest social system on record (*Timaeus* 23d). It thus serves not only as a reminder of Athens' most glorious past but also as a model for its future. In the *Laws* and the *Statesman*, the human beings who survive catastrophe or who come into being soon after lack the vices of urban life and political corruption.

Plato's catastrophic events are sketched with a broad brush. Though described as thoroughly devastating and periodically repeated, they are too impersonal and paradigmatic to evoke any emotion, let alone anxiety, in the reader. We may compare and contrast the enormous pathos Homer achieves with his narrative of the plague in the opening lines of the *Iliad*. Is Plato's use of catastrophe in his political contexts pessimistic or optimistic, teleological or purely objective? Such questions are probably too precise to be answered categorically, but I incline to the optimistic and teleological response. Even if, as Plato's theory maintains, our present civilisation will eventually be destroyed, human society will reconstitute itself. As it evolves, perhaps with the help of reading Plato (should his works survive), it may avoid some of the errors of the past, or at any rate recognise the value of studying cultural history.

*****

Aristotle followed Plato in supposing that civilisation is endlessly cyclical with arts and institutions being lost and reinvented (*Politics* 7.1329b25). He also conjectured the long-term occurrence of 'a great winter' (an ice age?) and periodic deluges (*Meteorologica* 1.14), citing the 'so-called flood in the time of Deucalion' as a Greek instance of the latter. In contrast to Plato, however, Aristotle offered few thoughts about how such catastrophic events affect the life and culture of the people involved.

His main thesis in the *Meteorologica* is the regularity and gradualness of large-scale changes affecting the earth (1.14, 351a21–6):

> Mainland and sea change places and one area does not remain earth, another sea, for all time, but sea replaces what was once dry land, and where there is now sea there is at another time dry land. This process must, however, be supposed to take place in an orderly cycle. (trans. Lee)

The orderliness of such geological events is due to the reciprocal alternation of heat and cold under the influence of the sun's cyclical motion.

When it comes to earthquakes, what interests Aristotle is not only refuting earlier theories and offering his own superior explanations, but also telling his readers when and where earthquakes are most prevalent and severe, for instance (*Meteor.* 2.8):

> Earthquakes occur most often in spring and autumn and during rains and droughts ... . When an earthquake is severe the shocks do not cease immediately or at once, but frequently go on for forty days or so in the first instance, and symptoms appear subsequently for one or two years in the same district .... Earthquakes are rarer in islands that are far out to sea than in those close to the mainland.

I do not imagine that Aristotle took himself to be offering practical advice in such passages. Still, we had better suppose that he thought he knew what he was talking about, and that in an environment as prone to seismic catastrophe as Greece, he intended his ideas to be useful, as well as theoretically sound.

In terms of uniformitarianism and catastrophism, Aristotle firmly aligned himself with the former theory. Though he was well aware of the prevalence of earthquakes, he viewed geological time as exponentially different from human time, as we observe in the following passage:

> Such [changes as silting and gradual inundation] escape our observation because the whole natural process of the earth's growth takes place by slow degrees and over periods of time which are vast compared to the length of our life, and whole peoples are destroyed and perish before they can record the process from beginning to end. Of such destructions (*phthorai*) the most extensive and most rapid are caused by war, others by disease, and others by famine. (*Meteorologica* 1.14, 351b8)

Unlike Plato, Aristotle does not invoke floods, or conflagrations, or even earthquakes, in accounting for the shortness and defectiveness of human records. We can only admire his prescience in citing war, disease, and famine, all three of which, within the last hundred years, have exacted a far greater human toll than natural catastrophes. In this respect, his account of catastrophe has an empirical plausibility that contrasts with Plato's mythical instances of nature's destructive effects on civilisation.

*****

In November 1755, Lisbon was devastated by a powerful earthquake and the Algarve coast by a related tsunami. No single event has done more to shatter naive beliefs in divine providence. This catastrophe prompted Voltaire to abandon his Leibnizian optimism and compose the satirical refutation of it in his novel *Candide*. Such dramatic influence of natural disaster on theological thought prompts reflection on the dispassionate tone in which Plato and Aristotle report their ideas concerning periodic catastrophes by floods and so forth. We might expect that belief in recurrent disasters would have prompted Plato to engage in extensive theodicy and Aristotle to qualify his universal teleology. It appears instead that both philosophers took the world's rational structure and divine causality to be too well entrenched to be threatened by natural catastrophes, even though Plato supposed that these events wipe out whole civilisations. His advice on how to dispose oneself in the face of severe misfortune is terse, not to say bleak.[15]

Plato's detachment is particularly striking if, as I surmise, he had the catastrophic end of Helikē in mind while composing his fiction of Atlantis. Surprising as it may seem, we need to turn to a Stoic philosopher for a thoroughly sympathetic treatment of the human impact of such a disaster. In two contexts addressing his friend Lucilius, Seneca gives graphic and highly moving accounts of catastrophe (*Moral Letters* 91, *Natural Questions* 6.1). In one of these, he describes the complete destruction by fire of the city of Lyons, 'the jewel of Gaul'. In the other he recounts details of an earthquake that devastated Pompeii and neighbouring towns in 62 or 63 BC.[16] Seneca leaves his readers in no doubt that these were appalling events.

In the case of Lyons, he describes its conflagration as uniquely destructive and shocking:

---

[15] See *Resp.* 10, 604c.
[16] Tacitus, *Annals* 15.22, describes the Pompeii catastrophe with no trace of emotion.

Such a range of splendid structures, any one of them capable of embellishing an entire city all by itself – and a single night has levelled them all! During such an extensive period of peace, we have suffered a greater loss than anything we might have feared from war .... In the past, people afflicted by a general disaster have at least had the opportunity to fear such an eventuality before the fact; nothing of great importance has been wrecked in a mere instant. But here, a single night marked the difference between a mighty city and none at all. Its end took less time than I have spent in telling you of it .... It would be some relief to our frailty and our concerns if everything came to an end as slowly as it comes into existence. The reality is that it takes time for things to grow but little or no time for them to be lost .... We should set before our eyes the entire range of human fortunes, and calibrate our thoughts about the future not by the usual scale of events but by the magnitude of what could happen. (trans. Graver and Long)

Concerning Pompeii and the other affected areas of the Bay of Naples, he comments first on the consternation the earthquake caused, and then concludes that of all disasters, earthquakes are the most lethal owing to the vast area they damage and human helplessness before them. In addition to the ruin of buildings at Pompeii, he reports, hundreds of sheep were killed, statues were cracked, and people wandered around out of their minds. In both literary contexts the challenge Seneca set himself is twofold – how to console the victims of such catastrophes and how to help people come to terms with their fears.

As a Stoic, Seneca should believe that this is the best of all possible worlds with the conditions of life divinely organised for human benefit. He does believe these things, but for a Stoic the world's excellence and human benefit are not measured in terms of fair weather, conventional fortune, and success. What happens by nature, which is equivalent to what divinity determines should happen, could not be otherwise. In order to reconcile such determinism with divine benevolence, the Stoics had to engage in the kind of intellectual gymnastics that every theodicy requires.[17] Their position includes the fact that everything natural is ultimately subject to dissolution and that 'the law of mortality' is no respecter of persons.[18]

---

[17] Chrysippus, to his credit, acknowledged the difficulty of reconciling undeserved suffering with providence. I have discussed his position in Long 1968. There are no *natural* evils according to Stoics, only humanly caused harms by bad agents.

[18] See Inwood 2005, 237. At *Natural Questions* 6.3.1 Seneca exempts earthquakes from divine causality, saying that they have their own causes, which are 'defects' such as affect our bodies; but in the earlier work *On providence* he cites the fact that they have 'their own causes' as congruent with universal providence. For discussion of the inter-entailment of determinism and providence in Stoic theology, see Long 1996c.

The recommended Stoic response to natural catastrophe was to incorporate it within a rational understanding of causality. Thus Seneca says (*Epistle* 101.5): 'Each person ought to promise himself nothing about the future'.[19] Chrysippus had characterised the virtuous goal of life as 'living according to experience of the natural course of events' (*kat' empeirian tōn phusei sumbainontōn*).[20] This formula glosses the standard Stoic phrase 'living according to nature' by including *experience* of natural happenings. We are reminded, as Chrysippus no doubt intended, of Aristotle's celebrated focus on human beings' universal desire for the knowledge that generates experience (*Metaphysics* A 1). Stoic sources (*Stoicorum veterum fragmenta* II, 28.18) repeat Aristotle's account of experience as a product of multiple memories, but the experience that Chrysippus envisioned must also include a kind of worldly wisdom – a mentality and understanding that went well beyond individual memories and could incorporate history, anecdote, and imaginative storytelling.[21]

Seneca draws on this admonitory appeal to experience as an antidote to suffering and natural catastrophe. It is central to his use of Stoicism in his *Moral Letters* and *Natural Questions*, as when he writes: 'A mind that is upright and sound corrects fortune's wrongs, softens its hardness and roughness with the knowledge of how to endure, receives prosperity with gratitude and moderation, and shows firmness and fortitude in face of adversity' (*Moral Letters* 98.3). He likes to make use of what we may call a worst-case scenario, using his rhetoric and hyperbole to say, as it were: 'You think you know the worst; try this then'. A good example of the strategy is his imagined description of the great flood that will prelude the earth's final destruction (*Natural Questions* 3.27–9).[22] In this virtuoso passage, Seneca includes horror, pathos, moralising, and an optimistic coda concerning eventual renewal. The passage is too long to be reproduced in full, so I summarise it and quote some purple passages.

When the fated day of the flood arrives, entire cities built over many generations will be destroyed in an hour. 'Nothing is difficult for nature when she hastens to destroy herself'. It takes great care and effort to raise a child, but no effort at all for the child to be destroyed. Seneca pictures

[19] See Inwood 2005, 235–41 on Seneca's theme of rational adaptation to natural inevitabilities.
[20] Diogenes Laertius 7.87. For full context and discussion, see Long and Sedley 1987, vol. 1 text 63C.
[21] Schopenhauer 1966, 147 aptly explains Chrysippean 'experience of natural events' as the knowledge that results from maintaining due 'proportion' between 'what we demand and expect and what comes to us'.
[22] Seneca draws on Ovid's account of the great flood in *Metamorphoses* book 1. He also describes global apocalypse in *To Marcia* 26.6 and with rhetorical panache in *Thyestes* 789 ff. See Williams 2012, 124–32.

incessant rain and cloud, constant fog, waterlogged and collapsing buildings, forests swept away by torrents from melted snow, farms and livestock
washed away, people taking refuge on mountain tops: 'In their extremity,
their only source of comfort was that fear had turned to bewilderment …
a single day will bury the human race; all that the long indulgence of
fortune has cultivated, all that it has elevated to pre-eminence'. But there is
light at the end of this global catastrophe, not for its imagined participants,
but for humanity in the long run. The world will be reconstituted afresh
and innocent, so life may begin anew.[23]

We will not be as ready as Seneca to invoke fatality and fantasy as
antidote to natural catastrophe. That is because, as I said earlier, our
technology and expectations of government make his *blanket* recourse to
the inevitable acts of 'fate' and 'nature' unpalatable. Nor will we agree with
his claims that the causes and timing of death should make no difference to
the emotional attitude one brings to its occurrence (*Natural Questions* 6.32,
2–5, 12). Still, it is hard to see how anyone at Seneca's time could have done
better both in acknowledging the horrors of natural catastrophes and in
suggesting how best to come to terms with them emotionally and
intelligently.

Because providential theology in Stoicism was tantamount to thoroughly determining causality or universal determinism, Seneca would
not have found the Lisbon earthquake a major intellectual challenge to
his theology. For a reader of the cosmology of Plato's *Timaeus*, however,
especially one who takes the divine demiurge of the dialogue literally, that
creator's providence and the supreme excellence of the world he manufac-
tures (30b, 92c) does not chime well with the work's earlier account of
recurrent catastrophes that destroy civilisations. As I mentioned, Plato
makes no reference to these phenomena in the cosmological parts of the
Timaeus. A charitable interpreter could say that Plato covers himself by his
theory of the world's having a necessarily unstable aspect, as shown, for
instance, by our bodies' liability to diseases. Just so in the *Statesman* (270d),
Plato makes his spokesman withhold immutability from the world because
of its bodily nature. An uncharitable reader, on the other hand, could set
the two parts of the *Timaeus* against one another and use the recurrent
catastrophes of the first part to cast doubt on the optimistic doctrines of
the second. That is precisely what Lucretius did.

---

[23] Williams 2012, 128 writes aptly of Seneca's 'portrait of nature as an all-powerful guileless and
beneficent agent of physical/moral change that collides with' a portrait of human nature as 'self-
interested and partial'.

The theme of the first part of *On the Nature of Things* book v is the world's origin and mortality and the absurdity of supposing it to be the product of divine creation. Lucretius does not name Plato as his specific opponent, but it soon becomes clear that the cosmology of the *Timaeus* is his principal target. Plato's spokesman had taken the world to be impervious to destruction (32c–33d), but Lucretius insists that anything made of bodily parts is liable to death as well as birth (235–323). Next he addresses Platonic ideas that we have encountered earlier in this study, and turns them against the notion that the world could be everlasting.

According to the cultural theory found in the *Timaeus* and *Laws*, arts and crafts are constantly being rediscovered in the aftermath of recurrent catastrophes. Lucretius proposes instead a single linear model of cultural development on the grounds that there is no evidence for the hypothesised efflorescence of former civilisations subsequently destroyed by natural catastrophes (324–38). Still, he proceeds:

> If you believe that all these things have been the same before, but that the generations of men have perished in scorching heat, or that their cities have been cast down by some great upheaval of the world, or that after incessant rains rivers have issued out to sweep over the earth and overwhelm their towns, so much the more you must own yourself worsted, and agree that destruction will come to earth and sky. For when things were assailed by so great afflictions and so great dangers, if then a more serious cause had come upon them, there would have been widespread destruction and a mighty fall. (338–47; trans. Smith)

Here Lucretius cites 'the same three causes and types of catastrophe that figure in Plato's scheme: conflagration, flood, and earthquake'.[24] Rather than supposing, with Plato, that natural catastrophes can devastate civilisations but leave the world itself (apparently) intact, Lucretius argues that if such natural catastrophes have occurred, there is no good reason to think that the world as a whole can be immune from destruction (5.95–106):

> The mighty and complex system of the world, upheld through many years, shall crash into ruins. Yet I do not forget how novel and strange it strikes the mind that destruction awaits the heavens and the earth, and how difficult it is for me to prove this by argument .... Nevertheless I will speak out. My words will perhaps win credit by plain facts, and within some short time you will see violent earthquakes arise and all things convulsed with shocks.

---

[24] See Solmsen 1951, 11–12. At 5.396–415, Lucretius gives a rationalising interpretation of the Phaethon myth and also mentions the tradition of a great flood.

As a good Epicurean, Lucretius is adamant that 'death is nothing to us'. Yet, every reader of his monumental work notices that it is not only permeated by references to death but also constantly alludes to death in thoroughly graphic and disturbing ways.[25] For example:

> Thus the door of death is not closed to the heavens, nor for sun and earth and the deep water of the sea, but stands open and awaits them with vast and hideous maw. (5.373–5)

If we find Lucretius incongruous in this respect, we shall have to apply the same judgement to Seneca; for he, too, as a Stoic, wants his readers to regard death as nothing or at least nothing bad or fearful. Yet, in his philosophical writings (not to mention the baroque deaths recounted in his tragedies) Seneca was as ready as Lucretius to give vivid and scary accounts of the mortality that his personages experience.

I have mentioned Seneca's admonitions concerning the mutability of fortune, and we find a similar precautionary stance in Lucretius. One of his central notions, straddling physics and ethics, is *finis*, 'limit':

> A limit has been fixed for the growth of things after their kind and for their tenure of life . . . and it stands decreed what each can do by the ordinances of nature (foedera naturai). (1.584–6)

The Epicurean prescription for a happy life is to live within the natural limits set by physiology, psychology, and ecology. Both philosophers had known humanly caused catastrophe, whether that of civil war in the case of Lucretius or Seneca's experience of the horrors perpetrated by the emperor Nero. They ask their readers to face the risk of disaster and the eventual certainty of death head on. At the same time, in order to be positive if not comforting, they indict us (human culture, I mean) as responsible for many of our fragilities and vulnerabilities: if only people refrained from thoughtlessly encroaching on nature's domain, settling instead for a simpler life, they could greatly mitigate the risks to their bodies and well-being.[26]

*****

Natural catastrophe signifies sudden and likely irreparable damage – to the environment, to living beings, and to property. People of Greco-Roman antiquity were ill-equipped to anticipate such disasters and to manage them. Yet their religion, with its many gods in charge of sky, sea, and land, relieved them of the illusion that what we call nature can be easily

---

[25] See Segal 1990.
[26] See Lucretius, 2.1–36, 5.1105–35, 6.1–35; Seneca, *Moral Letters* 89.20–2, 90.7–43, 119.

controlled or be manipulated with impunity. Ancient philosophers accommodated natural catastrophe within their cosmologies: to them it was both intelligible and in principle predictable, given the fact that the world is constructed from materials that are liable to undergo extremes of heat, cold, flood, and drought. That outlook helps to explain the emotional detachment we find in Plato and Aristotle when they comment on the periodic destruction of civilisations. It also explains why Stoics and Epicureans make *our* infringement of 'nature's laws', and not natural events as such, the principal cause of environmental and personal catastrophe.[27] At our time of extreme ecological peril and much self-harming behaviour, these Hellenistic philosophies have lost none of their practical relevance.

[27] Lucretius' term is *foedera naturae* (a metaphor drawn from the notion of a treaty or compact). Seneca writes literally of *leges*, and also of nature's rights (*iura*) and decrees (*decreta*); see Inwood 2005, ch. 8.

PART II

Humans as Godlike, Gods as Humanlike: Presocratics and Platonists

Anthropomorphism and Epistemic Anthropo-philautia: The Early Critiques by Xenophanes and Heraclitus

Alexander P. D. Mourelatos

The phrase 'critique of anthropomorphism' may be taken in two ways. Sometimes we criticize a doctrine or pattern of thought for *indulging* in anthropomorphism, and sometimes we investigate and assay the way in which a thinker *diagnoses and criticizes* anthropomorphism that may be detected in one or another context of human endeavor or in the thought of others. There will be moments of both 'critiques of' in this essay. But it is primarily in the latter sense that I undertake to approach the critiques of anthropomorphism in two sixth- to fifth-century BCE Presocratics: Xenophanes of Colophon and Heraclitus of Ephesus. As is usual in the study of early Greek philosophy, I shall be drawing on evidence that is either explicitly attested, or persuasively implied, in the sources (either fragmentary quotations from writings of the Presocratic figure, or testimony from later authors, and in either case as retrieved from the latter). My aim will be to identify different moments, scopes, and grades of anthropomorphizing and of opposition to it. But I shall also introduce a special type of anthropomorphism, for which I have coined the name 'epistemic anthropo-*philautia*': not *philautia* narrowly understood as one individual's 'self-love' or 'self-promotion' or 'vanity', but rather the *species-philautia* we as humans may indulge in, as we project upon the cosmos (or upon parts or aspects of it) structures and forms that have intuitive appeal for us, ones that seem familiar, congenial, and even comforting. It will emerge that neither Xenophanes nor Heraclitus, fierce critics of anthropomorphism though they were, had escaped the pull toward epistemic anthropo-*philautia*. Examining the thought of these two pioneers in the history of philosophy through the prism of

I dedicate this study to Sarah Broadie in friendship, with affection, with admiration, and with keen personal thanks for all she has contributed to the study and the teaching of ancient Greek philosophy, both at my own university and across continents.

anthropomorphism brings out important conceptual affinities and contrasts, both within early and classical Greek philosophy, but potentially also within the history of ideas and even within philosophy proper.[1]

Anthropomorphism Generally, and Its Most Pronounced Form in Ancient Greek Thought

An obvious first step is to review 'anthropomorphism' as it is commonly understood, viz., as the tendency or practice of attributing human characteristics to divinity, or to animals, or to some or all living things; or to natural phenomena, or indeed to any entity which, outside of an anthropomorphizing or anthropomorphist scheme, would regularly be considered inanimate or even abstract. As this rather long list of disjuncts suggests, anthropomorphism arises in many contexts, and it comes in many special types. Moreover, we can envisage an 'extreme' or 'pronounced' form of anthropomorphism, and correspondingly different attacks on, or critiques of, anthropomorphism at various grades of strength.

In the ancient Greek context, Hesiod's *Theogony* provides the obvious and historically germane paradigm. The entire universe is a society of living beings: most of them are humanlike in their behavior, if not exactly in their figure; some have the behavioral characteristics and the approximate appearance of animals known to humans; and yet others are liminal or hybrid beings or monsters. Cosmogony is theogony, as all generations subsequent to the primordial quartet of Earth, Underworld, Chaos, and Eros arise through biological reproduction – albeit not always through sexual pairing – and thus gradually fill in the various other regions of the cosmos, or add to its components and to its forces. Strife among the cosmic

[1] An earlier and shorter version of the section on Xenophanes, which I prepared in my native modern Greek, was delivered at a ceremonial occasion at the University of Crete, Rethimno, in October 2017. The Greek text has subsequently appeared in *Ariadne*, the periodic publication of the School of Philosophy of the University of Crete, issues 23–4 (2016–17 & 2017–18), 217–30. In addition to the presentation at the University of Crete, working drafts of this study have also been presented to academic audiences at the following venues: the Conference of the History of Philosophy Society, at Texas A&M University; Queen's University, Ontario, at the Gregory Vlastos Memorial Lecture; Texas Christian University, at the Ronald E. Moore Humanities Symposium; the Scuola Normale Superiore in Pisa; and the special 'Ex Ionia Scientia' conference that was hosted by the National and Kapodistrean University of Athens. To the organizers of these events and to the sponsoring institutions, respectively, I offer my sincere and deep appreciation. I also thank the audience members whose questions, on each of these six occasions, sharpened and enhanced my argument. For critical comments on intermediate or penultimate written drafts, I am grateful to Chloe Balla, Barbara Sattler, Greg Scott, Johanna Seibt, Thomas Seung, to the anonymous reviewer of Cambridge University Press, and (as always) to Olive Forbes.

gods develops almost immediately – already by the third generation – and warring between older and younger gods becomes a prominent and pervasive theme in the narrative. Saliently absent is any action of demiurgy (i.e. of world-making or world-fashioning by a god). The last of the generations of gods is that of the Olympian gods, who, under the enlightened despotism of Zeus, establish the world order that is familiar to human beings – in effect, a world-society of partly cooperating and partly antagonistic divine agents.

Epistemic Anthropo-*philautia*: the Paradigms

If we were to search the ancient Greek philosophical tradition for a corresponding case of an extreme of the special type of anthropomorphism for which I have coined the term 'epistemic anthropo-*philautia*', the obvious candidate would be Protagoras of Abdera, author of the famous *homo-mensura* doctrine:

> Of all things the measure is man, of those that are, that they are; and of those that are not, that they are not. (DK80 B1)[2]

But much more apposite to the present analysis is an example I shall draw from early modern philosophy, because of the amplitude of detail it offers, as well as its clarity and precision in formulation: the idealism of George Berkeley.

It will be recalled that in Berkeley's ontology the only 'beings', the only 'substances', are minds or spirits. One such spirit alone, God, has the infinite power to imprint upon the consciousness of finite spirits (i.e. human beings) empirical perceptions: all the various visual, auditory, tactile, olfactory, or gustatory impressions experienced by human beings at any one moment or in the course of their lives. But in addition to this *passive* ability finite spirits have to receive the empirical perceptions that God imparts on their distinct consciousnesses, there is also an *active* ability that even such finite spirits have: to recall memories and mental images of

---

[2] References to Presocratic texts are in accordance with the long-established standard of Hermann Diels and Walther Kranz, *Die Fragmente der Vorsokratiker*, in the abbreviation 'DK' (many editions). Texts considered to be actual quotations from writings by the philosopher at issue are marked by the letter 'B', followed by the fragment number in DK. Testimonia (reports of doctrine) drawn from ancient authors are marked by the letter 'A'. In the cases of Xenophanes and Heraclitus, the chapter numbers in DK (21 and 22, respectively) will be omitted in my references. For other authors, the chapter number in DK will be shown immediately after the 'DK' – English translations (above and throughout) are drawn from Graham 2010, with occasional modifications.

what has previously been experienced, and to compound these and uncompound them at will, so as to create new thoughts.[3]

This active ability of 'mental causation', so intuitively familiar as it is to every human being, provides Berkeley with the analogical basis for making sense of the demiurgic power of God. We humans have the second-order ability to *create* in thought and imagination, drawing on those first-order 'ideas' God has imparted to us as sensations. But the infinite spirit that is God also has the exceptional power to bring about the occurrence of sensory experiences in the minds of finite spirits. It emerges thus that the whole universe, the whole of God's creation, is something intimately familiar to human beings: nothing other than a totality of sensory experiences.[4] It is in this respect and in this connection that Berkeley's idealism furnishes a clear and arresting paradigm of epistemic anthropo-*philautia*.

The Earliest Foe of Anthropomorphism: Xenophanes of Colophon

In many and notable ways, the thinkers who are traditionally considered the first of the Greek philosophers break away from the Hesiodic paradigm. I have in mind the three sixth-century Milesians: Thales,

---

[3] To forestall the possible objection that allusion to Berkeley introduces anachronism, it is appropriate to recall that the ability possessed by the human mind to conjure up images and memories is something that had already been celebrated in Homer, at *Il.* 15.80–3. In that passage, the speed with which gods (specifically Hera) can move physically from one location to another is said to be similar to the swiftness with which human thought can transport itself to favorite places previously visited:

ὡς δ᾽ ὅτ᾽ ἂν ἀΐξῃ νόος ἀνέρος, ὅς τ᾽ ἐπὶ πολλὴν
γαῖαν ἐληλουθὼς φρεσὶ πευκαλίμῃσι νοήσῃ
ἔνθ᾽ εἴην ἢ ἔνθα, μενοινήῃσί τε πολλά,
ὡς κραιπνῶς μεμαυῖα διέπτατο πότνια Ἥρη.

As when a man's mind might dart, a man who, having traveled over much earth, should bring to his mind, 'I wish I were there, or there!', and should entertain many such full-of-longing reveries, that is how swiftly, with ardent eagerness did august Hera dash out.

Two types of mental speed are envisaged in the simile. The adverbs *entha . . . entha* point to the speed with which the mind in reverie can transport itself from one site previously visited to another. But the sequence of (perfective-aspect) aorists, *aixēi, noēsēi, menoinēēisi* (linguists would refer to these as 'achievement predications') correspondingly points to the instantaneous fulfillment through vivid memory of the longed-for return to one's favorite places.

[4] And when it comes to the physicists and cosmologists who claimed high standing in his day, in particular Isaac Newton, Berkeley views the latter's theories (and similar theories of others) as marvelously sophisticated algorithms that make it possible for humans to grasp the natural laws in accordance with which God projects sensory experiences onto the distinct minds of finite spirits. And knowledge of these laws allows humans to make *predictions* about sequences of future sensory experiences, or to understand the conditions under which certain events known to have been experienced in the past can be *explained*.

Anaximander, and Anaximenes. And yet it is also clear that Hesiodic anthropomorphism still has some grip on their speculative schemes. For we have reports of animistic doctrine in Thales (DK11 A22 and A23); Anaximander spoke of cosmic powers – such as Hot, Cold, Dry, and Wet – as 'committing injustice' by overstaying their seasonal term, and thus having to render 'compensation to one another' (DK12 B1); and the single cosmic Air of Anaximenes, which by contraction or relaxation produces the immense variety of substances in the world, 'encompasses (*periechei*) the cosmos' in the way in which 'our own soul, which is air, holds us together (*sunkrateei*)' (DK13 B2).[5]

Against this background of Hesiodic theogony-cosmogony and the survival of elements of the latter in Milesian cosmologies, it is utterly astonishing that the first attack on anthropomorphism came early and with little foreshadowing or anticipation. The attack is direct and determined, and it is arguably among the strongest.[6] It was launched in the second half of the sixth century BCE by one of the brightest stars of the Greek Enlightenment: the poet, social critic, and natural philosopher Xenophanes of Colophon.[7] General histories of philosophy, or even ones specifically of Presocratic thought, discuss mainly Xenophanes' attack on features and aspects of anthropomorphism that are found in traditional religion. But I shall be arguing that his denial of anthropomorphism has much broader compass. Still, it would be right to review first the familiar theme of Xenophanes' critique of anthropomorphism in religion.

Critique of Traditional Religion and Positive Theology in Xenophanes

According to Xenophanes, human beings generally, and Greeks in particular, conceive of their gods as having been born and as having minds and bodies that are humanlike (B14, B23). Gods are likewise thought to wear

---

[5] Even though terms such as *sunkratei*, *periechei*, and *pneuma* (all included in the Diels 'fragment') may come from later characterizations of the causal role of 'soul', there is no reason to set aside the core testimony by Aëtius (the source for the text at issue) that Anaximenes viewed the air-to-world relation as similar to that of soul-to-body (or soul-to-human person). Cf. Laks and Most 2016, 11, 363. While noting that DK13 B2 is a 'paraphrase', Laks and Most nonetheless include the Aëtius text in the 'D' section (Doctrine) of the Anaximenes chapter as well as in the same chapter's 'R' section (Reception).

[6] More modest estimates, which emphasize points and aspects of continuity between Xenophanes, on the one side, and his predecessors in the tradition of poetry on the other, have been offered in Eisenstadt 1974 and Granger 2013. For a more balanced account, see Sassi 2013.

[7] By name he is associated with the Ionian city of Colophon (southwestern coast of Asia Minor), but this is somewhat misleading for, though born and raised in Ionia, Xenophanes emigrated as a young adult to the Greek West of Sicily and Southern Italy, and it is there that he achieved his fame.

clothing and to use language (B14), and they are assumed – which in Xenophanes' judgment is preposterous – to practice on one another what even humans recognize as acts of immorality: stealing, adultery, lying, and deception (B11, B12), as well as engaging in strife and in acts of violence (B1.22–3).

Not limiting himself to this fierce critique of traditional religion, Xenophanes famously also offers a positive conception of divinity. This is articulated in a series of poetry fragments, which I cite here as though they formed a continuous text:[8]

> One god, greatest among gods and men,
> not at all like to mortals in body nor in thought. (B23)
> All of him sees, all thinks, all hears. (B24)
> He remains ever in the same place, moving not at all,
> nor is it fitting that he should travel
> at one or another time to one or another place. (B26)
> Rather, without any toil he makes all things shake and quiver
> (*kradainei*) by the thought of his mind (*noou phreni*). (B25)

A modern interpreter might argue that by conceiving of God not as a cosmic force but as an entity that has attributes of personhood, including mind and perceptual faculties, Xenophanes has *ipso facto* made a huge concession to anthropomorphism. The exact sense in which this is right is an issue I shall postpone taking up. For the question is best dealt with after we have also reviewed the essentials of Xenophanes' natural philosophy, which will reveal that wider compass of anti-anthropomorphism to which I alluded earlier.[9]

Anti-Anthropomorphism in Xenophanes' Natural Philosophy

From the time of Hesiod, and no doubt even earlier, the ancient Greeks had bestowed divinity not only on the familiar figures of the Hellenic pantheon but also on celestial phenomena and objects, including what we today class as meteorological phenomena. Accordingly, the sun, Helios, first of the offspring of the Titan Hyperion, inherits from his father the ability of 'traveling above' (*huper* + *iōn*), and does so in a diurnal journey

---

[8] Translations as in Graham 2010, I, III, with slight modifications for B26 and B25.
[9] Natural philosophy is a part of Xenophanes' thought that is often neglected in modern accounts. The interpretation presented here is based on my three separately published studies: Mourelatos 2002, 2008b, and 2016.

that serves to provide light and heat to earth's creatures. The moon, Selene, was the divine agent who played a role in fertility by regulating the menstrual cycle. The goddess Iris, who showed herself to mortals in the form of the rainbow or halo, was the dispatcher of omens in her role as special messenger of Zeus. The atmospheric phenomenon we call St. Elmo's fire was an epiphany of the twin sons of Zeus, the Dioscuri, who often benevolently intervene to provide rescue or reassurance to sailors in a perilous storm at sea.

Xenophanes offered a naturalistic explanation specifically of each of these, and indeed globally of all the *meteōra* (i.e. all the 'things suspended in the skies') – sun, moon, stars, shooting stars, comets, rainbow, halo, as well as of the rest of what *we* consider atmospheric effects of luminescence. All are different types of cloud formation. The immense variety in the visible forms of ordinary clouds provided good support for the grander generalization. And as for the effect of luminescence, it had long been noticed that ordinary clouds become briefly but brightly luminous when they are suddenly torn by a gust of wind (what we call 'lightning').[10] The steady luminescence of *non*-ordinary celestial clouds (sun, moon, stars, etc.) must be due, Xenophanes reasoned, to some continuous internal agitation. And the ultimate source and cause of that agitation would not be hard to seek: it is that 'shaking' and 'quivering', the one which Xenophanes' one God imparts on all things, and specifically on the essentially aqueous objects that are the sun, moon, and stars.

Not only the domain of *meteōra* but the earth, too, in its horizontal expanse and in its depths was, for the ancient Greeks, rife with the presence of the numinous. The 'limits of the earth' were marked by the presence and the guarding sway of dread primordial deities. Traditional myth had pictured the earth's horizontal 'limits' as located rather vaguely somewhere in the remote west, or as set by the encircling cosmic river, itself a deity, Oceanus. For the limits of what lies 'below', Hesiod had described an abysmal chasm that terminated at the uttermost depth or floor of Tartaros, the underworld.

By contrast, Xenophanes serenely and sagely points out that there is just one cosmic limit, none other than the one with which we are intimately and unavoidably acquainted: the surface, with a small part of which our

---

[10] This intuitive explanation of lightning had already been advanced by Xenophanes' Milesian predecessors. Anaximenes, in particular, had put forward the following analogy. When the oars of ships forcefully cut the dark blue of the sea, a patch of luminous white foam is produced (*parastilbei*). In like fashion, when a gust of wind cuts through the mass of vapor in the sky, a streak of white light is produced (DK13 A17).

feet come to be in contact, whether we firmly touch the ground or happen softly to touch the shallow bottom of the sea, or of a lake, or river. Geographically and cosmographically speaking, this limit is a vast corrugated plane that separates the realm 'above' from the realm 'below'. I refer to this plane as 'corrugated' because it tracks the contours of earth mass, which in some regions thrusts upward to form mountains or hills and in others drops below the waters of rivers, lakes, seas, and oceans. The domain above this single corrugated plane is constituted mostly by vapor (both near the earth and in the skies) and by water (some in the skies, and some where the waters have pooled over areas of the earth). Of course, within the particular region of the 'above' that is proximate to us, there are dispersed amounts of earth, such as dust; and there can also be temporarily suspended clumps of earth, such as pebbles, stone, or other projectiles. Moreover, at the interface of the cosmic masses, there exist formed compounds of earth and water: notably, plants, trees, terrestrial animals, birds, insects, and aquatic creatures. The domain of 'below' is mostly earth, with many pockets of water (aquifers, wells, springs), and rather more sparsely of fire (volcanoes).

Xenophanes conveys the geometric irregularity of the plane that separates the two cosmic masses of earth and water by using the verb *prosplazō*, which in Homer describes the breaking of waves against the land that produces the irregular contours of the coastline:

γαίης μὲν τόδε πεῖρας· ἄνω παρὰ ποσσὶν ὁρᾶται
ἠέρι προσπλάζον. τὸ κάτω δ' ἐς ἄπειρον ἱκνεῖται.

The limit of the earth is this: (here) above, it is seen [or 'can be seen'] at our feet as it thrusts up against the air. As for below, it [the earth, or the limit] keeps stretching [or 'extends'] without limit [or 'unendingly' or 'indefinitely']. (B28)[11]

This thrusting and counter-thrusting involves epochal movements of land masses into what previously were seas or other bodies of water, and contrariwise the inundation of large areas of land. The more enduring of these changes take place over long stretches of time. Xenophanes intelligently infers that in the past there have been land upthrusts that succeeded periods of inundation. The evidence is in the findings of fossils of marine creatures in earth strata that are conspicuously or even at great heights

---

[11] Often overlooked in translations of this fragment is the emphatically ostensive *tode* in the first half of the first line. For an analysis of the text that supports the punctuation and translation above, see Mourelatos 2002, 334 and Mourelatos 2016, 30–1.

above sea level. So, the proverbial battles of the elements that humans witness at the time of storms are, for Xenophanes, brief moments of epochal dynamic processes and cycles. And just as the occurrence of storms is traceable to their 'generator' (*genetōr*), the 'Great Deep' (*megas pontos*), which is the sea (B30), the agitation of the latter manifestly reflects and recalls that 'shaking and quivering' (B25, see above) that is imparted to aqueous substances and to the cosmic waters by the one God.

The 'One God' of Xenophanes

As we have seen, Xenophanes' God does have a mind and a body; but neither of these, he cautions, is in the least like (*ou ti . . . homoiios*, B12) the mind and body of humans. The perceptual faculties of Xenophanes' God are holistic – unlike those of humans, which involve distinct organs and faculties. It is God as a whole that sees, and God as a whole that hears.[12]

The *noos*, *noēma*, and *phrēn* of Xenophanes' God are his 'mind', 'awareness', 'intelligence', and 'thought' or 'thinking'. All these, too, are holistic in the way in which God's 'hearing' and 'seeing' are so. And given that seeing and hearing involve awareness, the omnidirectional seeing and hearing of God must imply that God has some sort of awareness of the world and its contents; this is confirmed by the one-line fragment that speaks of God's 'shaking things' not by any toilsome process but through the sheer 'thought of his mind' (*noou phreni*, B25).

Conspicuously absent, however, both in the fragments of Xenophanes' poetry and in reports about his doctrine and teachings, is any reference to divine providence. Yes, the phrase *promētheiēn theōn*, which in other uses and in later authors does have the sense 'care (of living things) exercised by the gods', occurs in the final line of Xenophanes fragment B1; but the whole passage there makes it clear that the genitive *theōn* is syntactically a genitive of the object, not of the subject: in other words, the 'care' at issue

---

[12] Does holistic perception also entail that God sees and hears everything? A direct and explicit statement to this effect is not found in the preserved fragments. And yet the implication is hard to resist. Let me first observe that I tend to discount the interpretative option that is favored in some late ancient sources, viz., that Xenophanes is a pantheist or panentheist. In other words, I discount the possibility that Xenophanes' world is somehow identical with God in either of two ways: by virtue of God's permeating or suffusing the world, or because the world is a part of God, contained within God. Given that Xenophanes' God has a body, then, on either alternative, God's total immobility is compromised. For inasmuch as all bodily things are 'shaken' by God, then either God as a whole or an inherent part of God (his body) would be constantly undergoing motion. Even so, a God who is distinct from the world but has holistic perception must nonetheless have the capacity to see and hear in every direction, which strongly suggests – albeit without logically entailing – that no part of the world can escape God's seeing and hearing.

is that which humans have 'of the gods', viz., the 'reverence' and 'esteem' they ought to show toward them. And whereas we have no evidence of a doctrine of divine providence in Xenophanes, we do have a report that Xenophanes 'completely rejected divination' (*divinationem funditus sustulit*, A52, from Cicero's *On Divination*). This makes perfect sense: if there is no divine plan for the world, or not even episodic divine plans for certain periods or circumstances, the practice of divination is totally undercut as pointless.

Xenophanes does countenance the possibility of prayer; but unlike the standard prayer which beseeches a god or gods for blessing on specific undertakings or for succor in circumstances of adversity, the prayer Xenophanes prescribes is austerely abstract, self-hortatory, and indeed god-deflective:

> (pray)... that we should be able (*dunasthai*)
> to do what is right (*ta dikaia*) – for that surely is what is more in hand
> (*procheiroteron*). (B1.15–16)

Anthropomorphism and Ordinary-Sense *Philautia* (Vanity)

There is good evidence that the driving motive in Xenophanes' anti-anthropomorphism is contempt for *philautia*, in the regular sense of 'vanity', 'vainglory', or 'narcissism'. In addition to the four passages cited earlier apropos Xenophanes' critique of traditional religion, two other fragments are regularly cited in this connection. I shall again put them together as though they formed a continuous statement:

> Africans <have their gods> be snub-nosed and black;
> Thracians have them blue-eyed and with a ruddy complexion (*purrhous*). (B16)
> But if cattle, <horses>, or lions had hands,
> or if they had <the capacity> to paint with their hands
>   or execute such acts of <sculpting> as men <have the capacity for>,
> then horses would draw the figures of gods to be just like those of horses,
>   and cattle just like those of cattle,
> and they would draw the figures of gods and sculpt their bodies
> <to be> just like the <sorts> of body humans variously (*hekastoi*) possess.
> (B15)[13]

---

[13] My translation, for both fragments. For the second line of B16, I have adopted the translation of *purrhous* in Sassi 2013, 291 n. 20.

Apart from the contribution these two fragments make to Xenophanes' critique of traditional religion, the one I cited first (B16) is also assayed by modern commentators as the earliest attestation of the doctrine of cultural relativism. But the counterfactual thought experiment that mentions horses and cattle in B15 has a distinctly more caustic import. Xenophanes is not just recording – as an anthropologist would do, or as Herodotus does a century later – the marvelous and intriguing facts of diversity in human culture, nor is he discrediting traditional religious belief by deploying a version of the skeptical trope of *isostheneia* (i.e. the argument that there is no more reason to believe in gods of type *A* than there is for gods of type *B*, *C*, and so on). Rather, he puts forward with biting sarcasm his judgment that at the root of the traditional religious beliefs and practices among both Greeks and non-Greeks is a motive of *philautia*, of self-love and self-flattery. By projecting upon divinity the image of their own body, humans vainly arrogate to themselves something of the exalted status of divinity. The sheer vainglory and even absurdity of this projection is brought out by the counterfactual thought experiment: if only beasts had hands to draw and to sculpt, they would make their gods theriomorphic.

Xenophanes' antipathy for conduct that has qualities of vanity or self-promotion is instanced in two other contexts in the fragments. In B3 he diagnoses self-indulgence as the vice that allowed the decline and ultimately the demise by conquest of his home city of Colophon in Asia Minor:

> Having learned useless luxuries from the Lydians, . . .
> they would come to the city assembly clothed in purple mantles,
> . . . boastfully exulting in resplendent long hair,
> and exuding the fragrance of expensive perfumes. (B3.1, 3.3, 3.5)

In another fragment, B2, he launches a most un-Hellenic attack on what is preeminently the most Hellenic of institutions, the Panhellenic athletic games. Athletes who win in these games are showered with gifts, honors, and privileges by their home city and by their fellow citizens (B2.1–9). But these feats by champion athletes, Xenophanes protests, make no contribution either to the *eunomiē*, 'good governance', of the city-state or to its 'treasury' (B2.19 and 2.20). The 'trivial gratification' (*smikron charma*, B2.19) that is experienced by the city and its citizens (*polei*, B2.19) from the successes of home athletes involves the same self-indulgent projection that is at the root of anthropomorphic religion. The collective entity, the city, arrogates to itself the success of select individuals; and the individual fellow citizens of the champion athlete illegitimately claim back for themselves a measure of the merit the athlete himself has earned. And in a very telling concessive clause that is reminiscent of the theriomorphy thought experiment of B15, Xenophanes observes, in the same spirit of biting satire, that in many cases the athlete arrogates to himself merit that is not properly his. For in the cases of horse riding or racing chariots, the merit is primarily and properly earned by the horses the athlete happens to be riding or driving: *eite kai hippoisin*, 'even if by virtue of the horses' (B2.10).

Xenophanes' Crucial Concession to Anthropomorphism

Let me now return to the issue that I bracketed earlier. It would be wrong to argue that Xenophanes slips into anthropomorphism when he uses the masculine gender in speaking of the one God. Greek, famously or notoriously, is one of the many languages in which grammatical gender is morphologically compulsory, and it is also a language in which masculine is the unmarked, or default, grammatical gender. Indeed, as has often been pointed out, *theos*, whether with the definite masculine article or without it, very often carries the sense of 'the numinous' or 'divinity' or 'godhead'.

One might also urge, perhaps, that in light of the cautioning rider, 'in no way similar in mind or in body to humans', we should not rush to the ruling that Xenophanes anthropomorphizes in his conception of God when in B24 he attributes to him seeing and hearing, or when in B23 and B25 speaks of him as possessing a *noos*, 'mind'.[14] In this case, however, Xenophanes' 'in no way' is undercut by his own epistemology. For there is good evidence that what passes as Xenophanes' 'skepticism' is better understood as a position of 'epistemic comparativism', viz., that for any subject X and any characterizing property F, we should never say that X is absolutely or without qualification F – rather we ought to say that X is more F (or less F) than some other Y is.[15] Indeed, B23, the very fragment which introduces the 'in no way' rider, also proclaims God as *megistos*, 'greatest'. It is made immediately clear that the superlative applies to God not absolutely but comparatively: *en te theoisi kai anthrōpoisi*, 'among gods and human beings'; which presumably means, 'compared to any of the gods worshipped either by Greeks or by non-Greeks – let alone compared to human beings themselves'. So, there must be enough real affinity between God and human beings to make the comparison possible.

But there is yet another concession, one that is conceptually more hidden and philosophically more profound, and indeed crucial. It involves

[14] The *noei* of B24 could be translated either as 'thinks' or as 'perceives/has awareness'.
[15] I develop the diagnosis of Xenophanes as an epistemic comparativist in Mourelatos 2016.

Xenophanes' speaking of God as 'making all things quiver by the thought of his mind' (*noou phreni*, B25). The first half of the line provides the relevant contrast: 'without toilsome action' (*apaneuthe ponoio*). God's action is purely psychokinetic: soul or mind directly, without any intervening physical processes, causes a change in a physical object. Here it is relevant to recall that the most compelling insight we humans have into causality is in the exercise of our ability to bring up or conjure up thoughts at will – as in, 'I shall now think of a blue square' (and the thought presents itself). More than two millennia after Xenophanes' time, Berkeley exploited, as was shown earlier, the analogy with mental causation so as to make intelligible the causation involved in cosmogony or world creation. I have already referred to this conceptual move by Berkeley as an instance of *epistemic anthropo-philautia*. In Xenophanes we don't have direct imprinting on other minds; rather we have direct imparting to the world of that quivering motion which causes and sustains all cosmic processes across times and epochs. What makes *noou phreni* conceptually attractive is the intuitive support it draws from that intimate awareness humans have of acts of mental causation. Ironically, the first castigator not only of anthropomorphism but also of ordinary-sense *philautia*, makes a move very similar to Berkeley's.

Heraclitus as Critic of Anthropomorphism

Heraclitus was obviously aware of Xenophanes and of Xenophanes' philosophical message, for he refers to him by name and rather scornfully as a 'polymath' (B40). And yet, for all that scorn, Heraclitus was obviously influenced by Xenophanes. A clear instance is in Heraclitus' doctrine that 'the sun is new every day' (B6), which recalls Xenophanes' doctrine concerning the nature of the sun and the moon, viz., that these are not enduring single objects but diurnal type-identical (as distinct from token-identical) successions of solar cloud formations and lunar cloud formations that are sustained by watery emanations from seas, lakes, and rivers.[16]

---

[16] According to Xenophanes, the constitutions (or properly 'reconstitutions') of these two ephemeral luminaries occur after a total eclipse, and the corresponding processes of dissolution are manifest over the first half of a total eclipse (A41, A41a). In our use of the term 'eclipse', total lunar eclipses occur, of course, episodically, and only at the time of full moon. But, as Xenophanes understands the term (= extinguishment), total lunar eclipses also occur regularly, every month, over the two-to-three days of dark moon; and partial lunar eclipses occur at all other times, except for the time of full moon.

Moreover, Heraclitus shares Xenophanes' critical stance *vis-à-vis* traditional religion. But the critique by Heraclitus is more strident than that by Xenophanes. Blood sacrifices as rites of purification, Heraclitus remarks, are acts of madness (*mainesthai*). The madness is like that of taking a mud bath in order to cleanse oneself of mud after one has slipped into a muddy puddle. Praying to statues is likewise mad: as mad as an act of talking to the walls of a house (B5, mentioning both examples of alleged madness). If a crowd of men were to sing an ode to a human phallus, it might well be considered flagrantly vulgar and offensive; so, why should it not be considered so when this is done as a hymn in a rite worshipping Dionysus? (B15).[17] The Greeks practice elaborate religiously sanctioned rites when bodies of the dead are prepared for burial; but dead human bodies need faster disposal (*ekblētoteroi*) than human excrement (B96).[18]

Heraclitus is famously the author of one of the most striking statements on the subject of cosmogony in all of Greek philosophy:

> This cosmos, this world order (*kosmon tode*), the same for all, was created neither by one of the gods nor by one of men. Rather, it has always existed, exists (*ēn aei kai estin*), and will continue existing (*kai estai*): an ever-living fire, kindling itself in measures and being quenched in measures. (B30)

The reference to possible creation 'by one of men' is of course deliberately paradoxical, conveying the sense '*let alone* (*per impossibile*) by one of men'. But the mere reference to divine creation has an element of paradox and sarcasm in it. For with the exception of hints of partial world creation by a god in the fragments of the mythographer Pherecydes of Syros, we have no evidence of divine world creation in the sources for Heraclitus' antecedents, whether poets or philosophical cosmologists. The rhetorical zeugma in the phrase 'created neither by one of the gods nor by one of men' works persuasively in the way the analogues of 'madness' in Heraclitus' B5 and B15 do. And it correspondingly has the same rhetorical force as Xenophanes' counterfactual thought experiment in which beasts are imagined fashioning images of gods; for it is as absurd and 'mad' for humans to worship anthropomorphic gods as it would be to imagine animals worshipping gods that are zoomorphic. To suggest that the

---

[17] Also worth notice here is the parallelism with the Xenophanean counterfactual thought experiment 'if cattle and horses had hands ...'.

[18] Graham 2010, I, 170, text 116 – and many other translators – rather squeamishly translates *kopriōn* as 'dung'. But cattle dung, as manure, has good human uses. Clearly, Heraclitus intends something of no use whatsoever.

whole cosmic order was fashioned by a god is as mad as it would be to suggest that it was created by a human being – that is the message of B30.

World-making by a god is, of course, among the strongest forms of anthropomorphism – and, for that matter, of epistemic anthropo-*philautia*. So, even though this particular conception is only marginally attested for the early stages of Greek cosmological speculation, Heraclitus' curt dismissal of *the mere conception* of it is highly significant. If we take this dismissal together with Heraclitus' strident critique of traditional forms of worship, it would seem right to regard Heraclitus as at least as much a foe and critic of anthropomorphism as Xenophanes was.

Evidence to the Contrary and Qualifications

And yet, the measure just given of Heraclitus as a critic of anthropomorphism appears to be contradicted, undermined, or at least weakened when evidence from other Heraclitean fragments is taken into account. A biographical report has Heraclitus commenting that gods are also present in the vicinity of the house oven (A9, from Aristotle's *Parts of Animals*), which is reminiscent of the animism of the Milesians. In two fragments, we find references to a cosmic *Dikē*, 'Justice', who enforces moral law (B28b, cf. B23); and in another, *Dikē* is said to control the size of the sun, and thus also its emission of light and heat, with the help of the infernal deities of vengeance, the *Erinyes*, 'the Furies' (B94).[19] Moreover, we have language of 'universal governance' of world processes (γνώμην ... ὁτέη ἐκυβέρνησε πάντα διὰ πάντων, B94), a remark that even processes of opposition or strife unfold 'in accordance with what is right' (*kata chreōn*, B80), and another that human laws are 'nurtured' or 'under the tutelage' (*trephontai*) of divine law (B114).[20]

But could it not be the case that the language of action by divine subjects that have attributes of personhood, and notably the action of world governance, is essentially metaphorical? Very instructive in this respect is B64: 'And thunderbolt steers all things (*panta oiakizei*)'. If 'thunderbolt' is taken as a metonymy for Zeus, then the line loses philosophical import: it merely states the Zeus-thunderbolt association familiar from traditional myth. If, however, 'thunderbolt' is instead a metonymy for cosmic fire, then the entire statement becomes figurative and symbolic. The violence

---

[19] Before the discovery and editing of the fragments of the Derveni papyrus, it was generally thought that the 'measures of the sun' that will not be 'transgressed' were those of the sun's seasonal trajectories in the heavens. See Mourelatos 1993, xxvi–xxvii.

[20] On details of translation of B114, see Mourelatos 1965; cf. Schofield 2015, 53.

and jagged course of the thunderbolt are transparently a metaphor for the violence and the to-and-fro complexity that is ever-present in world processes.

Heraclitus' Rife-with-Paradox Conception of Divinity

Outside the context of disparagement of traditional conceptions of divinity, the distinctly Heraclitean statements of the nature of god are famously couched in language that is contradictory and paradoxical:

> God is day night, winter summer, war peace, satiety hunger. (B67)

> To god all things are beautiful, and good, and just (*kala … agatha … dikaia*). It is human beings who assume (or 'have taken' or 'have perceived', *hupeilēphasin*) some things to be unjust but others just. (B102)

> (The) one thing (*hen*) which alone (*mounon*) is the wise (*to sophon*) is unwilling (*ouk ethelei*) and is willing (*ethelei*) to be called (*legesthai*) by the name of Zeus (*Zēnos*). (B32)

> The wise (*sophon*) is something quite separate (*kechōrismenon*) from everything. (B108)

The last of these sayings may perhaps be taken more broadly, as referring to wisdom of all kinds and at its best. On this reading, the 'thing that is quite apart from everything' is deep knowledge. But the similarity in the use of 'the wise' in B32 and B108 makes it likely that god or the world principle is the thematic focus in B108 – even if the entire statement in this fragment is given the broadest possible scope.

The second fragment quoted above, B102, provides, I think, the key to interpreting all four. Unavoidably, incorrigibly, judgments as to what is just, or beautiful, or good, reflect specifically human sensitivities, preferences, and predilections. Indeed, in most cases they reflect the attitudes, the laws, and the mores of the nation or city-state in which the judging subject has been brought up. God's standard as to what is 'just' is so singular, so totally 'apart' or 'separate' (cf. *kechōrismenon*) that it abolishes and transcends the epistemologically parochial 'just'/'unjust' distinction humans draw – and, of course, *mutatis mutandis* for 'beautiful' and 'good'.

What is said and implied about god's standard of the 'just' can be generalized as a statement of god's nature. The latter is so very much 'apart' that the distinctions humans draw in language have no purchase on divine nature.

Epistemic Anthropo-*philautia* in Heraclitus

True as all this may be about Heraclitus' conception of God, none-theless, in a broader perspective, Heraclitus too slides into anthropo-morphism in one important way. As in the case of Xenophanes, it involves what I have been referring to as epistemic anthropo-*philautia*.

There is no doubt that the central and most important concept in Heraclitus' philosophy is that of *logos*, the 'account' he offers of the whole universe. This *logos* is not just his own 'discourse', or 'speech', or 'book' – let alone that of others (B50). It is something at the widest scale public (cf. *xunou*, B2), 'always existing' (*eontos aei*, B1), intensely and ineluctably present (*toude*, B1; cf. *to mē dunon*, 'that which never sets', B16), albeit widely missed or misunderstood by human beings in general (B1). The *logos* is memorialized in the monistic principle, 'all things are one' (B50); and, as the very name *logos* conveys, this principle is intimately related to something uniquely human, viz., *language*. For it is markedly exemplified in those linguistic forms and structures whereby polar opposites are 'one' inasmuch as they have something in common: high-low/height; deep-shallow/depth; humid-dry/humidity; day-night/day (i.e. diurnal period), etc.[21] Moreover, understanding the nature of the universe is strongly linked to under-standing special devices of language such as deliberately ambiguous or cryptic utterances and oracles (B92 and B93).[22] Accordingly, 'Eyes and ears are poor witnesses for human beings if they have souls that do not understand their language [that of eyes and ears]' (B107).[23] Indeed, as I have myself argued on an earlier occasion, Heraclitus views the universe as being textured by the structures and forms of human discourse;[24] or, as one more recent interpreter has suggested, Heraclitus is the first to have introduced and exploited the metaphor of the *liber naturae*, of the universe as a script that has to be properly parsed and read.[25]

---

[21] See Laks and Most 2016, III, 160–7, texts D47–62.
[22] Cf. Hölscher 1993, 233: the language of Heraclitus 'must be one of paradox, simile, and riddle, precisely because it seeks to proclaim the essence of what-is'.
[23] My translation of κακοὶ μάρτυρες ἀνθρώποισιν ὀφθαλμοὶ καὶ ὦτα βαρβάρους ψυχὰς ἐχόντων. Laks and Most 2016 translate, 'who possess barbarian souls'. The switch from the dative *anthrōpoisin* to the participle in the genitive, *echontōn*, indicates that the latter has hypothetical force. Moreover, as has often been pointed out, 'barbarian' here means '[persons] who do not understand the language' (as though eyes and ears spoke in 'intelligible' Greek, but the 'souls' are 'foreigners', who cannot understand what was spoken).
[24] Mourelatos 2008a, 317–24.   [25] Lebedev 2017, 231–67.

Friends and Foes of Anthropomorphism in Later Thought

Let me close by reconnecting with the general remarks at the start of this chapter. Xenophanes and Heraclitus are not unique in making concessions to anthropomorphism and epistemic anthropo-*philautia*. This is rather the pattern in most of subsequent philosophy. By contrast, extremes in opposition to anthropomorphism are rather a modernist development, and otherwise quite rare. For a case in point, one could turn to the most advanced 'high-level' (in explanatory scope) scientific theories of our time in physics and in cosmology.[26] These theories introduce theoretical constructs so totally defying ordinary human intuitions that they can only be captured abstractly: in mathematical terms and through equations.

For an example from the ancient Greek context of extreme opposition to anthropomorphism, we might turn to Parmenides. For I believe a good argument can be made for the thesis that Parmenides generalized Xenophanes' critique in the following way: it's not just that God must not be conceived in anthropomorphizing terms; what counts as 'being' should be free of the sort of traits that are imported by epistemic anthropo-*philautia*.[27] It ought to be conceived as altogether different from the comfortingly familiar entities of the observable physical world. The *eon*, 'being', or 'what-is' – to quote the main deductions in the main fragment (DK28 B8) of Parmenides' poem – must conform to these four requirements: (i) not liable to birth or death (*agenēton, anōlethron*); (ii) simple and indivisible (*adiaireton*), totally cohesive (*homou pan hen, suneches*);

---

[26] Provided proponents of these theories have a 'realist' and not a Berkeley-like 'conventionalist' interpretation of the concepts and algorithms at issue.

[27] Parmenides' poem is certainly replete with images of divine agents who behave in anthropomorphic ways. In the narrative proem of B1 we have, for instance: divinities who abduct a mortal on a very physical chariot, the wheels of which 'squeal' from acceleration (B1.6–8); and we have a stern infernal deity who can be 'swayed to action' by *malakoi logoi*, 'soft, gentle words' (B1.15–17). In the 'Doxa', for instance, we have an 'all-governing' divinity who drives women to have sexual inter-course with men, or men to have either heterosexual or homosexual (*arsen thēluterōi*) intercourse (B12.5–6). And even in 'Truth', the main part of the poem that expounds Parmenides' own ontological doctrine, we have personified deities that see to it that *genesis* and *olethros* ('coming into being' and 'perishing') should be 'driven far away' (cf. *tēle mal' eplachthēsan*, B8.27). One of these personages, *Ananke*, 'Constraint', places 'fetters' on 'what-is' so as to 'hold it fast' (passim) and to 'constrict it all around' (*amphis eergei*, B8.31). This quite strong and colorful imagery in 'Truth' makes it absolutely clear that, especially in this all-important context, the anthropomorphist language may *only* be taken metaphorically. For there is no significant component or detail or aspect in these images that can pass all the austere criteria of reality that Parmenides explicitly deduces. By the same token, it is clear that the anthropomorphism of B1 is blatantly allegorical. And where in the 'Doxa' the anthropomorphism might not come across as transparently metaphorical, it is still subject to all the riders and cautions Parmenides attaches to that natural-philosophical part of his poem.

(iii) unchanging and not moving (*akinēton*); and (iv) *tetelesmenon*, 'totally complete', 'perfect', 'fully actualized' (i.e. not admitting of 'iffy' properties, such as potencies or powers). That nothing ever experienced in the world by human beings satisfies all these requirements would not have fazed Parmenides. No doubt, he viewed his deductions as a program or prophecy for any logically legitimate understanding of the ultimate or fundamental nature of reality.[28]

It is nonetheless relevant and intriguing that, at least in classical Greek philosophy, there is one entity that succeeds in meeting – with no need of qualification – all of Parmenides' requirements, viz., Aristotle's God, as the Unmoved Mover. Unlike Xenophanes' unmoving God, the Aristotelian Unmoved Mover does not act psychokinetically, and therefore no analogy with mental causation is appealed to in its conception. And yet there is epistemic anthropo-*philautia* in this otherwise most austere and abstract conception of divinity. For it is *noēsis*, 'thought', that is the essence of the Unmoved Mover; and *other* things 'are moved' by him (or 'it') in the way in which 'lovers' are drawn to the person or to the object of their love.

Plato's attitude *vis-à-vis* anthropomorphism and epistemic anthropo-*philautia* also merits attention – and in this connection, we are in the happy position of giving the last word to Sarah Broadie. Early in her *Nature and Divinity in Plato's* Timaeus, she makes this observation, rather in the spirit of Xenophanes and Heraclitus: 'If our own views on the nature of the finest world are shaped by standards peculiar to us, our attempts at hermeneutic cosmology are useless'.[29] But the argument she diagnoses in Plato, and which she brilliantly explicates and reinforces in her book, is that there are compelling conceptual requirements 'for infusing cosmology with the most refined *human* values of formal beauty and intellectual fitness', and that accordingly we are 'not to hold back in envisaging a cosmos framed to satisfy our own *a priori* criteria of fitness and perfection'.[30] So, if there is epistemic *anthropo-philautia* in Plato, it does not come about as a result of a thematic concession or slide; nor does it have the aggressive ideological tenor of the *homo-mensura*. Rather, Plato offers us a determined and yet exquisitely developed argument in support of his conviction that 'it is a central, indeed fundamental, fact about *the one and only cosmos* that it has in it beings like us'.

---

[28] For an account of the 'prophetic' character of Parmenides' overall argument, see Mourelatos 2013, esp. 107–12.

[29] Broadie 2011, 37–8.   [30] Broadie 2011, 279.

CHAPTER 5

Nature and Divinity in the Notion of Godlikeness
Li Fan

I

But it is not possible, Theodorus, that evil should be destroyed – for there must always be something opposed to the good; nor is it possible that it should have its seat in heaven. But it must inevitably haunt human life, and prowl about this earth. That is why a man should make all haste to escape from earth to heaven; and escape means becoming as like God as possible (ὁμοίωσις θεῷ κατὰ τὸ δυνατόν); and a man becomes like God when he becomes just and pious, with understanding.

(*Theaetetus* 176a5–b2)[1]

This frank remark on the human condition lies at the heart of the *Theaetetus*;[2] yet it is relatively neglected in contemporary scholarship on the text. That is hardly surprising, given that the remark comes within a digression from the dialogue's central epistemological arguments. (It is said *parerga*, as Socrates himself puts it at 177b8, referring to 172c–177b.) On the other hand, this digression, with its notion of becoming like god (ὁμοίωσις θεῷ), is as prominent in the ancient Platonic tradition as it is marginal in contemporary Plato scholarship.[3] For instance, in chapter 28 of Alcinous' *Handbook of Platonism* (*Didaskalikos*), we are told that in Plato's ethics, the

---

Ursula Coope read the draft of this chapter, and generously gave detailed comments and suggestions helping me to improve it in many ways, from argumentation to language. I gratefully acknowledge her kind assistance.

[1] All translations of Plato are from Cooper's edition, modified when necessary.

[2] The *Theaetetus* extends from Stephanus page 142 to 210, of which page 176 stands precisely at the centre.

[3] Sedley 1999, 309; Annas 1999, 52. Note, though, that in very early Platonism (i.e. in the Sceptical Academy), godlikeness is not named as the *telos*. As a matter of fact, even the first doctrinal Platonist (Antiochus of Ascalon) agrees with the Stoics in describing the *telos* as 'living according to nature'. Godlikeness first comes to be regarded as the *telos* in the Alexandrian Platonists (Eudorus and Philo), probably under the influence of Pythagoreanism, and this remains the view of later Platonists; see Dillon 1993, 171–2.

90

telos of a human being is precisely 'becoming like god as far as possible (εἰς ὅσον δυνατὸν ἄνθρωπον ὁμοιοῦσθαι θεῷ)' (181.19–20), or alternatively, 'following god' (ἕπεσθαι θεῷ, 181.37).[4] To account for this notion, Alcinous refers above all to the *Theaetetus* digression.[5] Similarly, Plotinus in his treatise on virtue alludes to the same passage to present godlikeness as the human *telos* (1.2.1–5).

One might say that it is hard for us modern readers of Plato to make sense of the idea of becoming like god, and that this is partly because we are more attuned to alternative notions of the *telos* – those of Aristotle, Stoicism, and Epicureanism. We are more inclined to think that the *telos* is 'living according to nature', which implies that our final end lies in fulfilling our human nature, rather than in approaching divinity.[6] However, it is one thing to say that the notion of godlikeness and that of fulfilling human nature are rivals in the history of ideas, it is another to say that they are philosophically incompatible. Actually, they are compatible, provided that the fulfilled human nature is conceived of as divine or quasi-divine (as it is on the view that the best part of us is some sort of deity). To take a well-known example, in the first book of Aristotle's *Nicomachean Ethics*, the ultimate human good or happiness is defined, in the light of Aristotle's conception of human nature, as activity in accordance with virtue (1.7); towards the end of the *Ethics*, in the tenth book, Aristotle asserts, picking up that thread of thought, that happiness is activity in accordance with the virtue of our best part; given that our best part is something divine, happiness is the activity of that divine part of us, that is, the activity that consists in living a divine life (x.7). Therefore, according to Aristotle, the life that fulfils human nature is a divine life (1177b30–1). By the same token, it is hardly surprising that some of the Platonists also identify the human *telos* with the fulfilling of human nature, for instance, Speusippus' definition of happiness is precisely 'a state of perfection in respect of things according to nature'; and Antiochus of Ascalon, presuming ultimate agreement between Plato and Aristotle, asserts that the human *telos* is nothing but 'living according to nature', that is, living according to human nature.[7] In other words, there is no difficulty in maintaining both

---

[4] Translations of the *Handbook* are Dillon's.

[5] In addition, Alcinous alludes to *Republic* x 613a, *Phaedo* 82a–b, *Laws* iv 715e, and *Phaedrus* 248a. Another passage in question, *Timaeus* 90b–d, is not cited by Alcinous, but by Arius Didymus; see Annas 1999, 57 n. 16.

[6] Annas 1999, 52–3.

[7] Dillon 1996, 72–3. Speusippus' definition is found in Clement of Alexandria, *Stromata* 2.133; Antiochus' view is found in Cicero, *De finibus* 2.34, 5.26–7.

the idea of the *telos* being assimilation to god and the idea of the *telos* being the fulfilment of human nature.

A striking fact concerning the ancient notion of godlikeness is that becoming like god is said to be a sort of flight (*phugē*) from the world, that is, a flight from here, where good and evil are mixed together, towards somewhere beyond, where good alone exists. The *Theaetetus* digression most powerfully explicates the idea of flight by embodying it in the figure of the philosopher in the digression (173c9–174a2). The figure is depicted as lacking concern for his surroundings, namely the world of the city and of the customary, yet concentrating upon something remote and of a higher order. An example of such a figure is Thales, who fell into a well while gazing aloft (174a–b). The things aloft, the objects of the philosopher's gaze, are said to be the things that (in reality) are (*ta onta*, 174a1), for instance, 'what it is to be human, what actions and passions belong to human nature (*phusei*)' (174b4–5), justice or injustice itself (*autē*, 175c2), etc. Moreover, the philosopher is said to speculate about things from the perspective of the whole universe, so that those things that seem to be grand from the human perspective turn out, on his view, to be trivial and petty (174d–175b).

This idea of flight, so vividly presented in the *Theaetetus* passage, is anything but an exception in the Platonic dialogues. In addition to the *Theaetetus*, Alcinous' *Handbook* also alludes to the *Republic*, *Phaedo*, *Phaedrus*, and *Laws*. In the *Phaedo*, godlikeness is achieved through philosophy, with philosophy being construed as a practice of dying and being dead, and as catharsis. This is clearly in tune with the *Theaetetus* passage in advocating the idea of flight.[8] In the *Phaedrus*, godlikeness is identified as the ultimate aspiration of the soul, and there the idea of flight is no less evident: the originally winged soul, gazing aloft, eager to rise up, and paying no attention to this world, is buried in the body, unable to ascend (249d).

The idea of flight, however, is not easy to understand. In Plato's dialogues, 'becoming like god' is interpreted as improving oneself in regard

---

[8] It should be pointed out that the *Handbook* misinterprets *Phaedo* 82a–b: 'So then, said he, the happiest and (truly) blessed, and those who go to the best place, are those who have practised the popular and political virtues, which they call self-control and justice' (181.32–6). The *Handbook* clearly assumes that godlikeness in the *Phaedo* is achieved through practising popular (*dēmotikē*) and political (*politikē*) virtues. That, however, is incorrect. '[T]he happiest' (*eudaimonestatoi*) is qualified in the original text by a partitive genitive 'of those men' (*toutōn*, 82a11), referring to those who have not managed to purify themselves from the pollution of the body, and who will soon sink into this world by reincarnation (cf. 81b ff.). The happiest of those men possess virtues generated from 'habits and training' rather than 'philosophy and intelligence' (82b1–2). Those souls will depart to be reincarnated in the social animals such as bees or wasps or ants, rather than departing to the divine realm, for '[n]o one may join the company of the gods who has not practised philosophy and is not completely pure when he departs from life, no one but the lover of learning' (82b10–c1).

to virtue. In the *Theaetetus* passage mentioned above (176a5–b2), 'becoming like god' is glossed as 'becoming just and pious with understanding'; at *Phaedo* 82a–b, it is glossed as becoming moderate and just; at *Republic* x 613a, it is glossed simply as becoming just. Various virtues are named to gloss the notion of godlikeness. For Plato, becoming like god is nothing but becoming virtuous in general. If so, becoming virtuous must also be a flight from the world (cf. Plotinus 1.2.1.5).

This conception of virtue is peculiar. Virtue is usually held to be a good disposition that is manifested in a person's dealings with his surroundings (e.g. in treating other people justly, in sacrificing to the gods properly). To be more specific, virtue is usually held to be a disposition of coping with evils that exist in the human condition but are absent in divine life. If becoming like god is becoming virtuous, the virtue in question must not be conceived of in this way. The question therefore arises as to how to make sense of becoming virtuous as a flight from the world. In the second section, I shall present a popular mode of understanding the idea of flight, on which fleeing from the world is understood as engaging in *theōria* as opposed to *praxis*, and I shall trace this understanding back to the ancient tradition. In the third section, I shall challenge the *theōria-praxis* mode of interpreting the idea of flight. In its place, I shall offer a new interpretation of this idea and of the notion of godlikeness. I shall argue that flight is compatible with practical action in the natural world. Although our souls are temporarily associated with human bodies and rooted in the natural world, their nature as souls is to have a divine part that transcends this world. In advocating flight, Plato is not claiming that we should cease engaging in practical activity, but is instead making a claim about the *manner* in which we should act. His claim is that the standards that guide our (practical or theoretical) activity should be drawn from the divine transcendent realm and not from the natural realm in which we, as human beings, are temporarily located.

II

In contemporary studies of the notion of godlikeness, fleeing from the world is taken to be equivalent to fleeing from practical engagement in human affairs,[9] and, more often than not, to be equivalent to engaging in theoretical activity.[10]

---

[9] See Rue 1993; Annas 1999; Sedley 1999; Armstrong 2004; Mahoney 2004; Lännström 2011.

[10] This is clear in Sedley 1999 and Armstrong 2004, and also in Annas' treatment of the *Phaedo*, where she suggests that the significance of the idea of flight lies in its novel conception of virtue as

This mode of understanding is based on the Aristotelian antithesis between *theōria* and *praxis*. Speaking of the best kind of life, or happiness, Aristotle refers to the life of god. In a famous passage, he rejects the idea that divine life consists in any sort of practical activity (*Eth. Nic.* 1178b10–18):

> [W]hat sorts of actions should we attribute to them [the gods]? Just actions? But will they not obviously be ridiculous if they make contracts, return deposits, and so on? Courageous acts, then, enduring what is fearful and facing dangers because it is noble to do so? Or generous acts? To whom will they give? And it will be absurd if they have money or anything like it. And what would their temperate acts consist in? Is such praise not cheap, since they have no bad appetites? If we were to run through them all, anything to do with actions (τὰ περὶ τὰς πράξεις) would appear petty and unworthy of the gods.[11]

In short, the gods engage not in practical activities but in theoretical activity alone. Since a typical human life here on earth consists mainly, if not wholly, in engaging with practical matters, engaging in *theōria* (namely philosophical contemplation in Aristotle's sense) could be reasonably said to constitute a flight from the human condition. Along that line of thought, Aristotle distinguishes between the virtue of *theōria*, namely *nous*, on the one hand, and the virtue of practical activity, either the moral virtues or prudence, on the other (x.8). According to Aristotle, the former is divine while the latter merely human. Therefore, the practice of theoretical virtue, so to speak, constitutes a sort of flight from humanity to divinity.

Much indebted to the Aristotelian philosophy, the middle-Platonist *Handbook* maintains the superiority of the theoretical life to the practical life, and identifies the former with becoming godlike (ch. 2).[12] But in the chapter on the notion of godlikeness (ch. 28), the antithesis between *theōria* and *praxis* is not applied directly. Rather, becoming godlike seems to be conceived both practically and theoretically (182.3–8):

---

philosophical understanding, in comparison to the ordinary view that virtue is conceived as practical knowledge (1999, 61), and in her treatment of Plotinus, whose intellectual virtue she believes to constitute a flight from the world (68–9). Lännström 2011 focuses on the choice of the philosopher in the *Republic*, where the alternatives are fleeing to theoretical study on the one hand, and taking part in ruling on the other.

[11] Cf. Annas 1999, 59–60. Plotinus has a similar account, which he probably wrote with Aristotle's words in mind; see *Enneads* 1.2.1.10–21. Translations of Aristotle are from Barnes' edition.

[12] For the meaning of *theoretikos bios* vs *praktikos bios*, see Sedley 2012.

We can attain likeness to god, first of all, if we are endowed with a suitable nature, then if we develop proper habits, ways of life, and good practice according to law, and most importantly, if we use reason, and education, and the correct philosophical tradition, in such a way as to distance ourselves from the great majority of human concerns (τὰ πολλὰ τῶν ἀνθρωπίνων πραγμάτων), and always to be in close contact with intelligible reality.

It seems that being 'in contact with intelligible reality' means nothing but contemplating the intelligible. One becomes more godlike in doing so than in developing 'proper habits, ways of life, and good practice'. There is an implicit distinction lurking here between different levels or grades of godlikeness, and the higher level of godlikeness consists in fleeing into theoretical activity.

What is implicit in the *Handbook* is made explicit in Plotinus. Plotinus distinguishes two levels of virtue: political virtue and cathartic virtue. The term 'political virtue' (*politikē aretē*) is picked up from Plato, but acquires a different denotation. When Plotinus employs the term, he does not mean to refer to the virtue of the city (cf. Pl. *Resp.* 430b9–d2); nor does he mean to ground the virtue in habits rather than in intelligence (cf. Pl. *Phd.* 82a11–b2, *Resp.* 619c–d). This term, in Plotinus, is used to denote the sort of virtue that limits and gives measures to the appetite (*epithumia*), or the affective states (*pathē*) of the soul. This sort of virtue brings an intelligible pattern into psychic matter (*hulē*), creating in the latter some sort of order (1.2.2.10–18). Plotinus believes that political virtue makes the soul resemble to some extent the intelligible world and the One, because political virtue is itself a sort of measure; yet, it is limited because it is the measure in matter (1.2.2.18–20). Therefore, political virtue is able to assimilate the soul to god in a limited way, namely, in the way in which the unmeasured matter participates in the measures of intelligible reality (1.2.2.20–6, 1.2.1.21–6). In god, however, there is no matter to which political virtue gives measure, that is, in god there are no affective states, which are acquired only in incarnation (iv.8.2.42–50). Therefore, through political virtue one cannot achieve godlikeness without qualification; that is only achieved through cathartic virtue, that is, through virtue as purification (1.2.3). Plotinus, alluding to the *Phaedo* (69c1, 82a11), conceives of purification as freeing the soul from the pollution of the body. According to him, virtue in this sense can no longer be conceived of, like political virtue, as what gives measure to the affections, because the soul, when freed from the body, is free of affections (*apathēs*, 1.2.3.19–21). In this case the virtues must be redefined.

Plotinus defines the cathartic virtues in both negative and positive ways, so to speak. Negatively speaking, wisdom is the soul's no longer believing what the body believes; moderation is the soul's no longer being affected by that by which the body is affected; courage is the soul's no longer fearing separation from the body; justice is the soul's following reason without appetites fighting against it (1.2.3.14–19). The positive definitions are more informative. The soul freed from the body engages in the pure activity of intellect, namely, contemplation (*theōria*) of intelligible objects. Wisdom consists precisely in this contemplation (1.2.6.12–13), moderation in turning inwards to intellect, courage in a lack of affection that is a consequence of being assimilated to the unaffected object of contemplation; even justice, usually believed to presume a multiplicity, is redefined as this contemplative activity, for that activity is 'doing of one's own job' in the highest sense (1.2.6.19–27).[13] It is clear that all cathartic virtues are defined in terms of contemplation. According to Plotinus, political virtue and cathartic virtue are concerned respectively with two types of life: in exercising political virtue, one leads the life of a good man, whereas in exercising cathartic virtue, one leads the life of god. The superior virtue makes us step beyond the realm of man (1.2.7.21–30).

In this way, Plotinus qualifies as 'political' the virtue that is necessary for a good man's life (this conception of virtue is more familiar to us), and places it beneath the cathartic virtue that exalts us beyond this world. What is more important is that Plotinus construes the cathartic virtues as those acquired and developed in philosophical contemplation; the political virtues, on the other hand, are construed as those displayed mostly in practical life. Plato already distinguishes between two levels of virtue: philosophic virtue, as purification, coming about from intelligence, especially from studying philosophy, and popular/political virtue, coming about from customs and habits (*Phd.* 82a11–b2, *Resp.* 619c–d).[14] However, Plato does not construe political virtue as the virtue of practical activity and cathartic virtue as the virtue of theoretical activity. Plotinus, however, effectively interprets the flight as the idea of engaging in theoretical activity, and the virtue in question as theoretical virtue.

---

[13] Some scholars assert that Plotinus in fact mentions three types of virtue: the political, the cathartic (the purifying), and the intellectual; see e.g. Cooper 2013, 342–3. But, in fact, Plotinus' treatise on virtue (1.2) provides no evidence that he distinguished between cathartic virtue and intellectual virtue. To establish this distinction, Cooper appeals to a tentative question in Plotinus: whether the (true) virtue is identical to purification or follows purification (1.2.4.1–4). Plotinus, however, never distinguishes two types of virtue on the basis of that question. In any case, it is beyond doubt that purification points to contemplative/intellectual activity.

[14] Cf. O'Meara 1993, 101; Dillon 1996, 331; Emilsson 2017, 298.

III

In this section, I shall call into question the *theōria-praxis* mode of inter-preting the idea of flight. More specifically, I shall disentangle the idea of flight from the theoretical conception of godlikeness. Fleeing from the world, I shall argue, should not be understood as engaging in theoretical activity. Rather, the flight in question involves practical engagement in human affairs as much as theoretical contemplation. Moreover, I shall inquire into this question: in what sense can a life involving wide-ranging practical engagement in human affairs be seen as a flight from the human condition? I shall consider, in turn, the digression in the *Theaetetus*, the description of the philosopher in the *Republic* and the description of the soul's flight in the *Phaedrus*.

Let us first look at the dialogue that introduces the idea of flight, namely, the *Theaetetus*. Given Socrates' vivid description of the philosopher's withdrawal from the world, one must ask about the kind of activity in which the philosopher engages. Does the philosopher in flight engage only in theoretical activity? Not exactly. Admittedly, theorising the truth of the universe and of intelligible reality is said to constitute a crucial, if not central, part of the philosopher's life (173e–174a), and abstract discussion is said to be his trade (174a–b, 175b–d). However, the philosopher is pre-sented as engaging in non-theoretical activities as well: he may come into contact with his fellows; he may have to speak in a law court; he may be expected to comment on personal scandals or to make compliments in conversations (174b–175b). On all those occasions, the philosopher turns out to be an object of ridicule. The philosopher's flight from the world seems to be compatible with his engaging in these non-theoretical activities as well as in the activity of theorising.

Moreover, in the passage where Socrates introduces the idea of flight (176a5–b2), he lists justice, piety, and wisdom as the representatives of virtue (176b1–2). Among them, justice seems most central, and is said to be the primary characteristic of the gods: 'In God there is no sort of injustice whatsoever; he is supremely just, and the thing most like him is the man who has become as just as it lies in human nature to be' (176b8–9). According to some scholars, justice is the virtue concerned with treating other people appropriately; if becoming like god is becoming just above all, godlikeness seems to consist in treating other people in a proper manner, rather than engaging in theorising. Therefore, either Plato in the same passage fails to realise the connection between the idea of flight and the virtue of justice, or in the *Theaetetus* passage the idea of flight should not be conceived of in theoretical terms alone.[15]

Plato's most complex and thorough treatment of the virtue of justice is in the *Republic*. Usually it is not considered to contain the idea of flight, because, unlike in the *Theaetetus* digression, the best life presented in the *Republic* is not said to be one of withdrawing from practical engagement in worldly affairs. As in the *Theaetetus*, becoming godlike in the *Republic* is also said to be achieved by practising the virtue of justice (613a). In the core books of the *Republic*, the philosopher turns out to be the just person *par excellence*. According to Socrates in book vi, the justice of the philosopher implies disengagement from love of money, and from slavishness, boastfulness, and cowardice (486b6–8); he is disengaged from love of money, because he has no interest in what money can buy (i.e. bodily pleasures); he is disengaged from slavishness and boastfulness, because he cares about the whole rather than the trivial; he is disengaged from cowardice, because he takes interest in the true beings, thus considering the life of a man insignificant and death not dreadful (485d–486b). In other words, the philosopher's justice, or rather his refraining from injustice towards other people, is due to his lack of interest in the things that interest other people. Soon it is made clear that the philosopher is just because of his passionate concern for what is beyond the world (500b8–d9):

> No one whose thoughts are truly directed towards the things that are, Adeimantus, has the leisure to look down at human affairs (κάτω βλέπειν εἰς ἀνθρώπων πραγματείας) or to be filled with envy and hatred by competing with people. Instead, as he looks at and studies things that are organized and always the same, that neither do injustice to one another nor suffer it, being all in a rational order, he imitates them and tries to become as like them as he can. Or do you think that someone can consort with things he admires without imitating them?
>
> I do not. It's impossible.
>
> Then the philosopher, by consorting with what is ordered and divine . . ., himself becomes as ordered and divine as a human being can (κόσμιός τε καὶ θεῖος εἰς τὸ δυνατὸν ἀνθρώπῳ γίγνεται).
>
> That's absolutely true.
>
> And if he should come to be compelled to put what he sees there into people's characters, whether into a single person or into a populace, instead of shaping himself (ἑαυτὸν πλάττειν) alone, do you think that he will be a poor craftsman of moderation, justice, and the whole of popular virtue?
>
> He least of all.

---

[15] Mahoney 2004, 324 refers to the tension between the demand of justice and the idea of flight as 'the key problem the passage raises'; also cf. Rue 1993, 90; Lännström 2011, 114.

Though the philosopher takes part in worldly affairs, such as shaping the minds of his fellow citizens, he does so in an unworldly spirit, so to speak, with his thoughts directed towards transcendent reality. In this sense, he is also fleeing from the world (cf. also 518b–d, 529b).[16] The philosopher's lack of concern for this world and his passion for what is beyond it stand in tension with the fact that only the philosopher is competent in ruling the city, the greatest worldly achievement. This tension, I believe, is critical to understanding the figure of the philosopher in the *Republic*.[17]

Between contemplating the Forms and transforming the city, there is another kind of activity mentioned: self-transformation, or, in Socrates' own words, 'imitating' (*mimēsthai*) intelligible reality, thereby 'shaping himself' (*heauton plattein*). Here Socrates speaks of this imitation as an inevitable consequence of 'consorting with', that is contemplating, intelligible reality. But such a contemplator of truth hardly arises as a matter of course. Socrates has to engage in a long discussion of the making of such a figure, especially of his education. This education turns out to consist not in putting knowledge into an ignorant soul, but in turning the soul's intellect around towards the right direction (518c4–d1):

> [O]ur present discussion, on the other hand, shows that the power to learn is present in everyone's soul and that the instrument with which each learns is like an eye that cannot be turned around from darkness to light without turning the whole body. This instrument cannot be turned around from that which is coming into being without turning the whole soul until it is able to endure looking at that which is and the brightest thing that is, namely, the thing we call the good.

---

[16] Cooper, on the basis of his interpretation of philosophic education as aiming at the management of the city rather than as having an otherworldly orientation, asserts that the philosopher in the *Republic* is a person who cares for the good life *in this world* (2013, 313–14). We cannot agree with this interpretation. First, though it is true that, for the purpose of the city's legislators, philosophic education is employed to instruct the city's competent ruler, it is not right to say, in the context of the *Republic* (and other Platonic dialogues besides), that the purpose of philosophic education itself is political. Philosophic education aims primarily at turning the soul from here to there, to what really is (518b–d, cf. 529b), rather than preparing the soul for political rule. Second, it is one thing to say, as Cooper does, that the philosopher necessarily lives 'here' on earth, leading a virtuous life in this world, but it is another to say that the philosopher is attentive to this world and to the life, virtuous as it may be, in this world.

[17] This tension is evident in the notorious problem of the philosopher's being compelled to rule, for it is precisely because of the philosopher's passion for the intelligible world that he is said to take part in ruling only through compulsion. There has been much debate over how one should interpret Socrates' assertion that the philosopher is compelled to rule. Scholars are anxious to argue that the philosopher is after all willing to rule, despite his being compelled, as Socrates says (typically in Kraut 1973, Irwin 1995, Caluori 2011, among others). This anxiety actually suggests that the idea of flight is stubbornly rooted in the figure of the philosopher in the *Republic*.

The intellect, as the eyes of the soul, can only be turned around together with the whole soul. What is the point of this? The reader must remember that the biggest obstacle in the process of ascending out of the cave consists in the temporary pain and dimness caused by the light of reality (515c–d, 518a–b); that pain and dimness arises not because the prisoner is unable to see, but because he has become too used to the darkness of the shadows to endure looking at things in true light. That is to say, our soul fails to grasp intelligible reality not because its cognitive ability is deficient, but because it is still accustomed to the world it dwells in, not yet adapted for the world beyond. Therefore, what we need to do is not to employ our intellect solely for contemplating intelligible reality, which is not possible before our soul as a whole is turned around, but to transform ourselves so that our soul may become accustomed to intelligible reality.

Socrates in the *Symposium* illustrates such transformation as a productive activity, namely the act of giving birth; the transformation of the soul gives birth to true virtue (212a). This transformation is at the same time a sort of practice, that is, a rearranging of one's own life. In the *Republic* we learn that the philosopher, having transformed his life, loses interest in the things that attract the other prisoners (516c–d); now his entire life, everything he does in public or private, aims at a single goal (519c2–4). Although his soul must return from the light of reality to the cave, 'sitting at his same seat', taking his own part in the shadow games as he used to (516e), his life has been reformed in light of the truth, the truth outside the cave. Once he is used to the darkness, he will be much better at seeing shadows than those who stayed inside, for he will look at the shadows knowing they are just shadows, and knowing of what each of them is a shadow (520c). Clearly, the turning of the soul has formed new foundations for human life. Here what matters is not whether you engage in *theōria* or in *praxis*, but whether you live your life in light of the transcendent truth.

For the rest of this chapter, I shall turn to Plato's *Phaedrus*. I shall argue that this dialogue sheds further light on the nature of the soul and on the ideals of godlikeness and of flight from the world. The *Phaedrus* explicitly expresses the notion of godlikeness, and chapter 28 of Alcinous' *Handbook* makes allusion to it, but in contemporary scholarship on the notion of godlikeness the dialogue is rarely discussed, and if discussed, plays no significant part.[18]

Alcinous' *Handbook* alludes to *Phaedrus* 248a: 'the soul that follows and likens itself to god'. One must understand the context of this remark.

---

[18] A few remarks can be found in Annas 1999, 63; Sedley 1999, 315.

There is the physical universe, and there is a region beyond the universe, a region which contains the things that really are, invisible to eyes yet visible to intellect. All souls once lived in the heavens, the imperfect souls as well as the perfect, divine souls (i.e. the gods); and each imperfect soul by its own choice follows one of the eleven gods. The gods rise up to the top of the universe and, stationed on the outer edge, they gaze at the reality beyond the heavens. The imperfect souls can catch a glimpse of reality insofar as they succeed in following, and assimilating themselves to, the gods. The soul that 'follows a god most closely, making itself most like that god' enjoys a better, albeit limited, view of reality than the others (246e–248b). Clearly, being like god in such a way consists in emulating the divine contemplation of reality.

That, however, is not the only place in the *Phaedrus* where the notion of godlikeness is mentioned. Actually, becoming like god is pursued not only by the souls patrolling the heavens; it is also pursued by human souls on earth. But godlikeness is not for all human souls. The soul that aims at godlikeness must be uncorrupted on the one hand and inspired by a beautiful boy on the other. Such a soul is able to recollect its origin in the heavens, particularly the god it used to follow back then (252e7–253a5):

> They are well equipped to track down their god's true nature with their own resources because of their driving need to gaze at the god, and as they are in touch with the god by memory they are inspired by him and adopt his customs and practices, so far as a human being can share a god's life (καθ' ὅσον δυνατὸν θεοῦ ἀνθρώπῳ μετασχεῖν).

The 'customs and practices' (τὰ ἔθη καὶ τὰ ἐπιτηδεύματα) of a certain god refers first to the way in which the lover treats his beloved: for example, the lover of Jovian nature treats his beloved with dignity, whereas the lover of Martian nature is vindictive in his relationships (252c3–7). Moreover, the phrase refers to the way in which the lover treats everyone else (252d3–5); in general, the phrase refers to the overall pattern and way of life which the lover and his beloved strive to resemble *in every way* (253a–c). Here godlikeness is achieved in every aspect of living, without particular connection to theoretical activity, but with emphasis on how the lover and his beloved treat each other, when engaged in activities that are clearly of a non-theoretical nature.

But in such a life, with its many non-theoretical components, there is nonetheless a striking inclination towards being uprooted from one's surrounding world: not only does the lover neglect everything he used to take for granted, such as family and friends, and despise the things he used

to value, among which are wealth and decency (252a–b), but similarly also
the beloved, when captured by the lover's passion, regards his lover as
immeasurably superior to his close relations and friends (255a–b). The
couple see in each other something divine, which cannot be found in this
world, but only 'up there' – this is what is called 'divine madness'
(249d5–e1):

> [W]hen he sees the beauty we have down here and is reminded of true
> beauty; then he takes wing and flutters in his eagerness to rise up, but is
> unable to do so; and he gazes aloft (βλέπων ἄνω), like a bird, paying no
> attention to what is down below (τῶν κάτω δὲ ἀμελῶν) – and that is what
> brings on him the charge that he has gone mad.

'The beauty down here' refers to the physical beauty of the beloved; 'true
beauty', on the other hand, refers to the beauty up there among the realities
of the super-heavenly region. The madness of love furnishes the soul with
wings, stirring it to depart from the body and to fly back to its divine origin
after its incarnate life (256b3–7). There, according to Socrates, the soul is
showered in pure light, untouched by the evils of this world (250b5–c6).
Clearly, its life on earth has turned into a preparation for the journey
beyond. This account clearly agrees both in language and in idea with the
Theaetetus digression. It is without doubt another expression of the idea of
flight.

In the *Phaedrus*, once again, we do not find the identification that is
presumed in contemporary scholarship, namely that of fleeing from the
world with withdrawing from practical affairs and engaging in theoretical
activity. It turns out that the life recommended in the *Phaedrus*, broadly in
line with the flight of the *Theaetetus*, involves a great deal of non-theoretical activity. As in the *Republic*, fleeing from the world consists in self-
transformation, or the rationalisation of one's life (256a7–b3; cf. 253e5–
255a1). Here in the *Phaedrus*, such transformation is inspired by love – to be
specific, by the memory of one's own god revealed in love. One's own god
in memory is one's paradigmatic self, which embodies all sorts of paradigmatic 'customs and practices'. The lover and beloved transform themselves
in accordance with that paradigm. Therefore, the transformation in question consists not in developing one's cognitive ability, but in adapting
every aspect of one's personality to a divine paradigm.

Each divine paradigm has its own distinctive character, but every one of
them is a model of virtue, for the divinity of a god derives from its
association with the transcendent Forms (249c6), and the Forms mentioned in the *Phaedrus* are the Forms of the virtues: Justice (*dikaiosunē*),

Moderation (*sōphrosunē*), and Knowledge (*epistēmē*) or Wisdom (*phronēsis*) (247d5–7, 250d4),[19] not the Form of Big or the Form of Equal, and not even the Form of Good.[20] That is to say, the divinity of a god consists in its being perfectly just, perfectly moderate, and perfectly intelligent – in a word, in being perfectly virtuous. Actually, the Forms of the virtues are prescribed not only for the gods (i.e. the divine souls), but for all souls in general. The Forms of the virtues are, as Socrates puts it, the true nourishment of the soul, both divine and non-divine (247a8, 247d1–5, 248b5–c2; cf. 248b4–5).

Given that becoming godlike concerns every aspect of one's life, rather than theoretical activity alone, the following question arises: in what sense can such a way of life be seen as a flight from the human condition, given that it involves wide-ranging engagement in human affairs? In order to answer this question, one must understand Plato's view of the human condition.

Here in the *Phaedrus*, what is most striking and also most important is that no soul is a human soul by nature. There are souls by nature perfect and hence divine, and there are souls by nature imperfect and non-divine (cf. 246e4–247a7, 248a1–b1). Of the non-divine souls, some remain in heaven; some fall down to earth and enter human bodies, and thus come to be human souls (248c2–e5). The very same souls could also be reincarnated in animal bodies after their human lives (249b1–5) or, if they pass their human life rightly, they could hope to strip off their human shape and be restored to their original place in the divine chorus (one single thing that is said to be in the human soul's nature is that such souls all used to be in the divine chorus gazing at the reality; see 248c8–d2, 249e4–250a1). In other words, a human soul is identified as human not by its own nature, but by the human body in which it happens to reside. Its ultimate aspiration, however, is to depart from its human body, that is, to flee from the human condition. Therefore, the human condition is constituted by the implications of the fact that we are in a human body.

The first implication of having a (human) body is the simple fact that we, as humans, all have parents. That is taken for granted; and our life is built on that simple fact above all: because we all have parents, we are born and raised up in a family, where we learn our first, arguably most decisive, lessons. Family is thus the first and the natural institution in human life. But that would not be the case if each of us were just identical with his soul.

---

[19] It is noteworthy that Beauty (*kallos*) does not enter this list until the speech turns to an account of recollection (249d5).

[20] Cf. Burnyeat 2012, 254. It should be noted that in his second speech in the *Phaedrus*, Socrates never calls the virtues by the name *idea* or *eidos*.

A soul by itself is not born from other souls; a soul only transits from one body to another. Second, we, as humans, live with friends, or those dear to us. Our family is dear to us, of course; and there are others dear to us, too, in different ways and to various degrees. For the Greeks, the highest form of community built on the basis of friendship is the *polis*, and the political life is widely regarded as the highest form of human life. If we were identified with our soul, however, we would resign all that, for our physical existence is one of the basic parameters of almost every sort of friendship known to the Greeks. Admittedly, the inspired lover and his beloved are best friends. Eager to depart this world ultimately, they remain in their human body as long as they are alive. Their friendship is built in the light of their heavenly, non-physical experience: they are friends because they, as two souls, used to belong to the same divine chorus back in the heavens, following the same god (252d5–e1). They do not belong to the family, and they do not belong to the city; they only belong to each other and never to any sort of human community. Therefore, the third implication of our physical existence is that we live with the standards and principles of the communities of which we are a part, the standards and principles by which honour and disgrace are distributed. In a word, our way of life is dictated by *nomos*, which, according to Pindar, is the lord of all (Hdt. 3.38).

If we were to set aside the inspired picture introduced by the *Phaedrus*, it would be reasonable to claim that those implications of having a body are precisely the natural foundations of human life. We, as humans, are rooted in this natural world, that is, the world of the body. However, Plato by his genius tries to convince his readers that all the natural foundations of our life are not in the 'nature' of the soul, but only its sufferings and unfortunate fate! Plato has us convinced that, to return to its divine origin, we must transform our natural life entirely and uproot ourselves from our natural foundations: whatever the natural life lives on, whether propriety (*nomima*) or good taste (*euskhēmona*, 252a4–5), are nothing but opinions (*doxai*), and opinions only *appear* to nourish the soul (248b4–5), without being its true nourishment (248b5–c2). These opinions must be brought to the trial of reason, in the light of true value – the value of the world beyond (*huperouranios*).[21]

---

[21] This conversion of life, so to speak, is the achievement of love. That is why erotic passion is critical, if not central, to Plato's philosophy. Nussbaum's famous interpretation of the *Phaedrus* (1986, 200–34) depends on the presumption that love is merely a non-intellectual element of the soul, standing either in opposition to, or in cooperation with, the intellectual element. On the basis of this presumption, she arrives at her conclusion that the *Phaedrus* makes a claim about the value of the non-intellectual element of the soul. But we cannot agree with this presumption. Rather, in Plato, the overall pattern of life is at stake when it comes to the object of love. For the same reason, Rowe's (1990) criticism of Nussbaum's interpretation misses the point, too; Rowe, despite his criticism,

Therefore, a life deeply engaged with human affairs can be a flight from the human condition, as long as its natural foundations give way to the order of transcendent reality. With a vision of that transcendent reality, even a practical life could be seen as a flight, that is, an exercise for the soul's departure from the physical world towards the world beyond; without such a vision, on the other hand, one's reflections on one's life, along with one's arrangement of that life, however seemingly 'rational', indicate nothing but what Socrates calls 'mortal prudence' (*sōphrosunē thnētē*): a pseudo-virtue which has no value for the salvation of the soul (256e3–257a2).

From what we have seen in the *Phaedrus* and in other Platonic dialogues, it is evident that Plato understands fleeing from this world not as fleeing into theoretical activity without engaging in practical life, but as transforming one's natural life in light of 'the truth' (*Phdr.* 247c5). To be sure, the supreme position in this transformed life will be reserved for philosophical contemplation; yet the transformed life also consists of all sorts of non-theoretical or, broadly speaking, practical activities: just as the gods take care of the physical world as well as gazing on super-heavenly reality, the godlike life has both theoretical and practical components. The question of whether one engages in *theōria* or in *praxis* is secondary; the primary question concerns the foundations of one's life: whether one's life is rooted in the natural world, in accordance with natural standards and principles, or rooted in divine reality, in the light of what is truly valuable. For Plato, the best life for a man is definitely of the latter kind.

In effect, Plato's conception of godlikeness changes our understanding of our nature. According to the philosopher, our nature is not given by what naturally belongs to a human life, but by that divine part in us that links us to the divine order (*Phdr.* 248c8–d2, 249e4–250a1). Let me conclude with a powerful simile from Plato's *Timaeus*, which illustrates the philosopher's revolutionary understanding of our nature (90a5–b1):

> [The most sovereign part of our soul] raises us up away from the earth and towards what is akin to us in heaven, as though we were plants grown not from the earth but from heaven. In saying this, we speak absolutely correctly. For it is from heaven, the place from which our souls were originally born, that the divine part suspends our head (i.e. our root), and so keeps our whole body erect.

agrees with Nussbaum in taking love as one side of the antinomy of rationality-irrationality. We particularly disagree with his subsequent assertion that erotic passion is a stepping stone to philosophic contemplation, a stepping stone which must ultimately be left behind.

PART III

Emotions, Reason, and the Natural World
(Aristotle)

CHAPTER 6

Human and Animal Emotions in Aristotle

Jamie Dow

[The] sensitive, desiderative and emotional part of the human soul is not strictly rational; but Aristotle insists that it is not simply nonrational either. Its function, he says, is to 'listen to reason'. Thus it 'partakes of reason in a sense' (1102b13–14) . . . . He means that in human beings the functioning of the desiderative part is to be defined by reference to its relation to the strictly rational function. In this respect it differs from the human soul's nutritive part, and also from the desiderative part of nonrational animals. The human nutritive faculty is human only in the sense of being essential to all life, and therefore to human life. But it is not defined by its relation to any specifically human faculty, and so it may be said to be formally the same in human and subhuman organisms. Now in a sense desire, too, is common to a wider class of creatures than man, for according to Aristotle's biological classification, sense perception and desire are universal in animals. But according to the division of the *Ethics*, the fact that dogs, fishes and human beings may all be described as desiderative creatures does not entail that they share something formally the same. For the essence of human desideration is different, it being defined in terms of a functional relationship possible only for creatures rational in the strict sense.

Sarah Broadie, *Ethics with Aristotle*, 62

Introduction

Thinkers in antiquity were not so constrained by the disciplinary boundaries that in more recent generations have tended to separate empirical scientific disciplines from those with normative and evaluative content. The erosion of such boundaries and the attempt to traverse them are welcome features of academic and scholarly life in these last few decades, and alongside that has come a resurgence of interest in the complex array of connections that ancient thinkers saw between what they studied in nature and their accounts of how humans should live, think, feel, and collaborate.

These connections cover cosmology, physics, theology, geometry, biology, history, psychology and beyond, and have been studied by an array of outstanding scholars. The passage above from Sarah Broadie's landmark work on Aristotle's ethical thinking indicates one strand of her contribution to making these connections. It highlights that human appetites and passions, the focus of this essay, are *both* closely connected to the corresponding responses in non-human animals *and also* significantly different from them. It has been fashionable at different times to emphasise either their similarities or their differences. Following the lead of Sarah Broadie and others, I will attempt to chart the middle course, and offer an integrated account of how human and animal emotions are related that neglects neither emphasis.

Aristotle's Comparative Framework

In the opening chapter of *History of Animals* 8, Aristotle sets out a range of ways in which the parts, activities, ways of life, and characters of different types of animals can be compared. In considering the relationship between the passions and passion-related character states of humans compared to non-human animals, we should expect to be able to use Aristotle's own framework:

> In the great majority of animals there are traces of psychical qualities which are more markedly differentiated in the case of human beings. For just as we pointed out resemblances in the physical organs, so in a number of animals we observe gentleness or fierceness, mildness or cross temper, courage or timidity, fear or confidence, high spirit or low cunning, and, with regard to intelligence, something equivalent to sagacity. Some of these qualities in man, as compared with the corresponding qualities in animals, differ only quantitatively: that is to say, a man has more of this quality, and an animal has more of some other; other qualities in man are represented by analogous qualities: for instance, just as in man we find knowledge, wisdom, and sagacity, so in certain animals there exists some other natural capacity akin to these. The truth of this statement will be the more clearly apprehended if we have regard to the phenomena of childhood; for in children may be observed the traces and seeds of what will one day be settled habits, though psychologically a child hardly differs for the time being from an animal; so that one is quite justified in saying that, as regards man and animals, certain psychical qualities are identical with one another, whilst others resemble, and others are analogous to, each other. (*Hist. an.* 8.1, 588a16–b3)[1]

---

[1] Translations are from Barnes 1984.

On the face of things, this gives us a neat division, and – although it is not stated explicitly – it is reasonably clear where the passions and passion-related dispositions fit in. In Aristotle's list of animal psychological features that have similar counterparts in humans, it seems as though it is only the feature similar to 'intelligence in thinking' (τῆς περὶ τὴν διάνοιαν συνέσεως, a23) and the longer list of 'knowledge, wisdom and sagacity' (τέχνη καὶ σοφία καὶ σύνεσις, a29) that are related to their human counterparts 'by analogy'.[2] The other features, including animal counterparts to passions such as fear and confidence, and passion-related states such as courage and cowardice, seem reasonably clearly assigned to the category of animal features that differ by degree from the corresponding human states. Human passions might be thought to be psychologically more complex or more intelligent, and perhaps it is in this respect that we can imagine Aristotle thought they differed from their animal counterparts 'by the more and the less' (a25).

The picture, I will suggest, is not nearly so simple. Some features of this passage should immediately put us on our guard against this simple interpretation. Aristotle's list bears very little resemblance to either his famous 'chart' of the virtues[3] or any of his slightly different lists of the passions.[4] And in the survey of animal activities, lives, and characters that it introduces, through this and the following book, it is striking how rarely Aristotle's focus rests on their emotions or emotional dispositions (such as virtue- or vice-like states). I want to propose that, for Aristotle, animals had a repertoire of types of passions that is substantially different from that of humans. There are many types of human passions that animals simply don't share, including some obvious cases (e.g. emulation, indignation) but also others (e.g. pity and shame) where this may seem more surprising. There are in fact rather few clear-cut cases where Aristotle sees humans and non-human animals as sharing the same type of passion: I defend the assimilation of human and animal passions in the cases of fear and jealousy, resisting a possible objection, and also – albeit more cautiously – in the case of anger/spirit. This emphasis overall on the differences between human and animal passions might seem to reinstate a sharp boundary between the human and non-human realms. But in fact it does no such thing. Rather it

---

[2] It might be more accurate to say 'by analogy alone', since – as Roger White has pointed out – things related by the more and the less are also related by analogy (my hands may be bigger than yours, but it is still the case that as my hands are to me, so yours are to you). Cf. White 2010, ch. 2.

[3] *Eth. Eud.* 2.4, 1220b36–1221a12, with 2.5, 1221a13–b3. Cf. *Eth. Nic.* 2.7, 1107a28–1108b10.

[4] Cf. *De an.* 1.1, 403a16–18; *Eth. Nic.* 2.5, 1105b21–3; *Eth. Eud.* 2.2, 1220b12–14; *Mag. mor.* 1.7, 1186a12–14; *Rh.* 1.1, 1354a16–17; 2.1, 1378a20–3.

locates the continuity between human and animal passions in a different place: that is, in the shared capacity for pleasure and pain. Both human and animal passions are fundamentally exercises of capacities to respond with pleasure and pain to the subject's apparent good or harm. Their functioning well or badly is a matter of both how well or badly they discern the subject's good or harm and also how successfully or otherwise they motivate the subject to actions that will avoid that harm or attain that good. Doubtless in the human case, the subject's good will involve the successful exercise of capacities for reason, and reason will play a vital role in guiding pleasure and pain to discern and respond to the various forms that human good and human harm can take. Through their exercise of reason, humans can understand and analyse the world in vastly more complex ways than is possible without reason. As a consequence of this, humans and animals will have quite different repertoires of types of passion, because of widely differing arrays of goods and harms that apply to them, meriting responses of pleasure and pain. But these differences do not imply that the passions collectively are playing a different role for humans and non-human animals in the life of the organism. In both, the passions are pleasures and pains at perceived goods and harms, motivating appropriate pursuit and avoidance, subject to assessment for the accuracy with which those goods and harms are discerned and for the success with which those motivations promote the attainment of the goods and the avoidance of the harms.

Differing 'by the More and the Less' and 'by Analogy'

As we trace the connections and the differences between the passions of humans and non-human animals, it will be helpful to have as clear as possible a view of Aristotle's distinction between things differing by degree (or 'by the more and the less', as he puts it) and being related only 'by analogy'. It is too rarely noted how one of these categories falls within the other. Parts, character traits, and other features of animals that in different species are identical or differ by degree are *also* related by analogy (as my blood is to me, so your blood is to you; as the larger lungs of the bison are to it, so my daughter's smaller lungs are to her). So, we have two questions. One is what is required for the features of living things to be related by analogy. And the other is what kinds of similarities between features in distinct species are required if those features are to fall within the narrower subcategory of things that differ by degree (i.e. if they are to be variants of essentially the same feature, with differences in the degree to which some attribute applies to them). The most helpful passage is in *Part. an.* 1.5:

Many groups, as already noticed, present common attributes, that is to say, in some cases absolutely identical – feet, feathers, scales, and the like; while in other groups the affections and organs are analogous. For instance, some groups have lungs, others have no lung, but an organ analogous to a lung in its place (τοῖς δὲ πλεύμων μὲν οὔ, ὃ δὲ τοῖς ἔχουσι πλεύμονα, ἐκείνοις ἕτερον ἀντὶ τούτου); some have blood, others have no blood, but a fluid analogous to blood, and with the same capacity (τοῖς δὲ τὸ ἀνάλογον τὴν αὐτὴν ἔχον δύναμιν ἥνπερ τοῖς ἐναίμοις τὸ αἷμα). To treat of the common attributes separately in connexion with each individual group would involve, as already suggested, useless iteration. For many groups have common attributes. So much for this topic. As every instrument and every bodily member is for the sake of something, viz. some action (τὸ δ' οὗ ἕνεκα πρᾶξίς τις), so the whole body must evidently be for the sake of some complex action (πράξεώς τινος ἕνεκα πολυμεροῦς). Thus the saw is made for sawing, for sawing is a function (χρῆσις), and not sawing for the saw. Similarly, the body too must somehow or other be made for the soul, and each part of it for some function (καὶ τὰ μόρια τῶν ἔργων), to which it is adapted. (645b3–20; trans. Ogle in Barnes 1984, modified)

For Aristotle, analogous parts provide the organism with the same *capacity* as each other, as Leunissen insists, against those who see the 'by analogy' relation as resting on shared *function*.[5] But it is also clear that parts are for the sake of something, and here what they are for are activities (πράξεις). The whole body is for the sake of a complex activity, named here as 'the soul', which is presumably a way of referring to the animal's whole life. Aristotle then refers to the goal of each part in a different way: as its 'function' (ἔργον), with the likely implication that the function of the whole animal is its life (as Aristotle, of course, explicitly says in *Eth. Nic.* 1.7). Here, then, the 'function' of parts is their actually achieving their contribution to the animal's life.[6] The parts are for the sake of this in the sense that they provide the capacity for making such a contribution. That is to say that their 'function' is simply the (successful) activation of the capacity they supply to the animal. If this is correct, not much (for our purposes here, at the very least) turns on whether it is the same capacity or the same function[7] in the life of the animal that those analogous features must share.

There is a trickier debate about what is required for differences between features to be 'by the more and the less'. Devin Henry argues that this

---

[5] Leunissen 2014, 172.
[6] The interpretation here is thus compatible with (although it does not require) the understanding of ἔργον as achievement defended in Baker 2015.
[7] Cf. e.g. White 2010, ch. 2; Henry 2014.

requires that the features be instantiated by 'the same underlying material substratum'.[8] Mariska Leunissen rejects this view in favour of saying that the kinds of similarity that ground classifying animals and parts together as differing only by degree are similarities of shape or form that are available (in principle) to observation.[9] A key text is Aristotle's assertion that animals in the same kind (whose differences, he will go on to say, are only by the more and the less (b15)) 'have a common nature and contain closely allied subordinate forms' (ἔχει τε μίαν φύσιν κοινὴν καὶ εἴδη ἐν αὐτῷ μὴ πολὺ διεστῶτα, *Part. An.* 1.4, 644b3–4). Although the debate is hard to adjudicate, one of Aristotle's examples of parts related only by analogy, and thus whose differences extend beyond the bounds of 'the more and the less', is bone in human and spine in fish (b12–13). It seems far from obvious that Aristotle would have thought those differences were observable differences of shape and form, whereas it seems much clearer that he knew that human bones and fish bones were composed of different underlying material. To that extent, my sympathies on this point lie with Henry. But the point may matter little for our purposes. When it comes to the passions, they all tend to involve the temperature of the body in general and the blood in particular; and all of the animals under discussion will be blooded animals. The material substratum for the passions seems to be shared. Conversely, the observable differences in (shape or) form relevant to the passions all seem to be either very small (so as to suggest either that the states involved are identical between species or differ only by degree) or so large as to rule out their being related by analogy. The task now is to investigate in more detail how this will apply to particular kinds of passions as experienced by humans and non-human animals.

Humans' and Animals' Differing Repertoire of Passions

The key claim in this section, then, is that there are very significant differences in how humans and animals subdivide the realm of the pleasant and particularly the painful, and hence in the *types* of passions they can experience.

---

[8] Henry 2014, 163.

[9] Leunissen 2014, 178–80. The use of the disagreement between Henry and Leunissen is complicated by (1) the fact that issues of Aristotle's classification of animals into species and genera are at issue for them in this debate; and (2) the fact that the debate is for them, as for others, framed as being about the conditions for parts being related by analogy, rather than (as I would prefer) the issue of when, among analogously related parts, those parts are similar enough to differ only by the more and the less.

It has been recognised in a number of discussions of the passions in Aristotle that many of the human passions he explores in the *Rhetoric* and the ethical works involve recognising their objects in ways that are possible for humans but not for animals.[10] Pity, indignation, and emulation, for example, involve discriminating between the deserved and the undeserved; it is a matter of some controversy whether there are distinctive passions involved in the virtue of justice, but if there are, they would seem to involve conceptual abilities (discernment of what is just, lawful, equal, and the like) that are beyond non-human animals.[11] This fits with how Aristotle contrasts the cognitive (and expressive) capacities of humans and animals near the start of the *Politics*:

> It is also clear why a human being is more of a political animal than a bee or any other gregarious animal. Nature makes nothing pointlessly, as we say, and no animal has speech except a human being. A voice (φωνή) is a signifier of what is pleasant or painful (τοῦ λυπηροῦ καὶ ἡδέος), which is why it is also possessed by the other animals (for their nature goes this far: they not only perceive what is pleasant or painful but signify it to each other). But speech (λόγος) is for making clear what is beneficial or harmful (τὸ συμφέρον καὶ τὸ βλαβερόν), and hence also what is just and unjust. For it is peculiar to human beings, in comparison to the other animals, that they alone have perception of what is good and bad, just or unjust (ἀγαθοῦ καὶ κακοῦ καὶ δικαίου καὶ ἀδίκου), and the rest. (*Politics* 1.2, 1253a7–18)

The absence of a capacity for reason limits the conceptual reach of animals, and it is uncontroversial that the undeservedness of good or bad fortune can be painful to humans in a way that is not possible for animals. For this reason, and following Aristotle's own cues, we should be cautious about ascribing pity to non-human animals. He comes close to ascribing pity to dolphins in *Hist. an.* 9.48, describing the behaviour of some adult dolphins in bearing up a dead juvenile to prevent it being eaten by predators 'as though out of pity' (οἷον κατελεοῦντες, 631a20). But it is

---

[10] Cf. Dow 2009, 170–2; Fortenbaugh 1971, 148–50; and differences of this kind are the basis for the conclusion drawn in Fortenbaugh 2002, 69, that animal emotions are merely analogous to human emotions.

[11] Friendship is a more complex case because of the varieties of friendship in Aristotle. Certainly the kinds of friendly feelings that involve the recognition of goodness and virtue, and wishing one's friend good for their own sake, will be beyond animals. The same will apply to friendship based on recognition of usefulness. Perhaps friendly feelings of the type based on pleasure are a possibility for animals. But in any event, in Aristotle's use of 'friend' (*philos*) and 'enemy' (*polemios*) terminology in the *HA*, esp. 9.1–2, he gives no trace of interest in the *feelings* associated with friendship. He is concerned solely with perceptions among animals of threats and cooperation, and especially with tracing patterns of cooperation and conflict between species. We should be very cautious about drawing any conclusions from these passages about animal passions in Aristotle.

not actually pity, presumably because it does not involve the recognition of the undeservedness of suffering that pity requires (*Rh.* 2.8, 1385b13–14). Likewise, Aristotle does not seem to ascribe shame to animals, and this seems most naturally explained by the fact that reputation-affecting badness is not something they are capable as perceiving as painful (*Rh.* 2.6, 1383b12–14).[12] Aristotle relays without comment stories of male horses' distress at realising they have mated with their own mother: the horse in one story bites its keeper to death, that in another throws itself off a precipice (*Hist. an.* 9.47). But in neither case is this labelled with any passion-related term (such as αἰσχύνη), nor does Aristotle even refer to shame-like behaviour in the presence of other horses, and it is easy to see why he would be reluctant to do so, given the sophisticated kind of recognition with which he associates shame in his own analysis of it. We should conclude that for Aristotle, non-human animals do not feel pity or shame.

On the other hand, we can be reasonably confident that Aristotle thought that animals experienced real fear and jealousy, the differences between these and their human counterparts being somehow differences 'of degree' in how a state with essentially the same functional role was instantiated. Aristotle cites the peacock (*Hist. an.* 1.1, 488b23–4) as representative of animals that tend to jealousy (φθονερά), within his catalogue of animal states of character. His discussion of eyebrows in animals generally includes the remark that eyebrows pointing down indicate jealousy (*Hist. an.* 1.9, 491b17–18). These general remarks suggest he is happy to attribute jealousy to a reasonably wide variety of animals. He comments specifically on the jealousy of the eagle, grabbing its food in large chunks and ejecting and attacking its young as they approach maturity (*Hist. an.* 9.34, 619b26–34), as contrasted with the eagle known as the 'black eagle' (μελανάετος) or 'hare-killer' (λαγωφόνος, *Hist. an.* 9.32, 618b29–31). Jealousy among animals seems to be a matter of having the kind of awareness of competitors, for good things such as food or territory, that involves a distress at the competitor's possible acquisition of those things, and that generates a motivation to competitive or aggressive behaviour to prevent the competitor from doing so. This is very close to how Aristotle describes human jealousy in the *Rhetoric*, as 'a certain kind of distress felt in connection with

---

[12] The remark about animals such as geese being 'modest' (αἰσχυντηλά) in *Hist. an.* 1.1, 488b22–3 is probably best interpreted as proneness to caution – Aristotle does not use 'shame' terminology in his discussions of specific animals elsewhere in the biological works; so if we are to see this remark as developed elsewhere, it would have to be in the discussions of various animals' cowardice and proneness to fear.

those similar to us, at their apparent success with respect to the goods previously discussed [in the preceding section on indignation, e.g. wealth, power], not to get those things for oneself, but because they have them' (2.10, 1387b23–5). Of course, the goods for which different creatures compete differ, and there are complexities for humans about whether jealousy (φθόνος) is something that humans *should* feel, but these do not count against our supposing that the human and animal passions are essentially versions of the same thing.

Likewise, it is clear that Aristotle thinks animals experience fear, and that this passion and human fear are alike. We have seen already how fear features prominently in Aristotle's survey of human and animal passions and character states at the start of *Hist. an.* 8.1. There is an earlier survey of animal character traits at *Hist. an.* 1.1 (488b12–26) in which he mentions fear- and confidence-related dispositions such as being cowardly (δειλά, b15), courageous (b17), and watchful (φυλακτικά, b23). In the introductory chapter to *Hist. an.* 9, Aristotle discusses how differences in character traits among animals are correlated with the distinction between male and female. Among the passion-related dispositions mentioned is courage (i.e. in relation to fear). But there is an interesting passage which suggests that when Aristotle in various places discusses the 'spiritedness' (τὸ θυμῶδες) of animals, he has in view their proneness to fear and confidence as much as to anything like anger:

> In all cases, excepting those of the bear and leopard, the female is less spirited (ἀθυμότερα) than the male; in regard to the two exceptional cases, the superiority in courage (ἀνδρειοτέρα) rests with the female. With all other animals the female is softer in disposition, is more mischievous, less simple, more impulsive, and more attentive to the nurture of the young; the male, on the other hand, is more spirited (θυμωδέστερα), more savage (ἀγριώτερα), more simple and less cunning. (*Hist. an.* 9.1, 608a33–b4)

It is clear that courage stands in contrast to being 'less spirited', with the clear implication that the courageous female bear and leopard, being less prone to fear than the male, is *ipso facto* more spirited. Spirit must be, at least in part, a disposition to fearlessness, which makes relevant to fear in animals the various passages about 'spiritedness' discussed below. Various creatures are noted as being prone to fear. The cuckoo is 'cowardly' (*Hist. an.* 9.29, 618a29). Other birds fear eagles (9.34, 620a8–10). Little birds are frightened of the hawks used by hunters (9.36, 620a33–b4). Cephalopods discharge their ink due to fear (9.37, 621b28–31). Lions vary, as other animals do, regarding how courageous or cowardly they are (9.44, 629b5–7, b33–5), but are afraid of fire (629b21–3). In all of this, there seems to be no trace of any reservation about attributing fear to animals. Aristotle's description of human fear in the *Rhetoric* as 'a certain kind of pain or disturbance from the appearance of future destructive or painful harm' (2.5, 1382a21–2) may perhaps suggest that humans can discriminate the objects of their fear in more sophisticated ways,[13] but also makes clear that this is substantially the same kind of state as can be felt by animals – a painful recognition of a threat of harm that motivates the animal to avoid it.

The case of anger is more complex. It is at once a very natural candidate for a passion that Aristotle would have seen as common to humans and animals, and a case where the differences between the relevant human and animal passions are significant enough to raise doubts about whether the same kind of passion is involved. When speaking of human anger, Aristotle more often uses the term ὀργή, which he never uses in connection with animals in the biological works. He defines anger in the *Rhetoric* as 'a desire-cum-pain for what one takes to be revenge, on account of what one takes to be a slight against oneself or one's own, when slighting is not fitting' (*Rh.* 2.2, 1378a30–2).[14] And one might worry that it is beyond the cognitive capacities of non-human animals to represent the circumstances of anger as involving 'slights', or to assess things as 'not fitting', or to have 'revenge' as an object of desire. These provide the grounds on which some conclude that Aristotle's considered view was that animals do not share the human passion of anger.[15] But the difficulties can, I think, be resolved. And there are reasons for treating human anger and animal 'spirit' as variants of the same type of passion. One reason is that Aristotle does, in fact, seem to apply both terms on occasions to both humans and animals. In the discussion of calmness in *Rhetoric* 2.3, Aristotle cites the behaviour of

---

[13] One might worry that *De an.* 3.10, 433b5–10 suggests that, for Aristotle, those without the capacity of reason will be unable to register harms as 'future' harms (as I did, in Dow 2009, 171. There is a difficulty here regarding how we understand Aristotle's views on how things can be registered as past or future or possible, without the use of reason. But this must be possible, for at least two kinds of reasons. One is that the fear attributed in the biological works to non-human animals serves to motivate in those animals the avoidance of harms that have not yet occurred and cannot therefore be experienced by the animal as occurrently painful. The other is that any theory of animal locomotion in Aristotle will need to attribute to the animal the ability to discriminate the goal (e.g. eating the stag) for the sake of which it (the lion) moves, where that goal is something that is not the case now (when the animal initiates movement) and that the animal moves to realise. Cf. e.g. Lorenz 2006, ch. 9; Moss 2012, ch. 1.

[14] There is a textual difficulty here, nicely discussed in Trivigno 2011. None of the points made above depends on a particular resolution.

[15] Cf. e.g. Fortenbaugh 1971, esp. 150.

dogs as evidence of his claim that if the object of anger (ὀργή) humbles themself before the angry person, their anger subsides (*Rh.* 2.3, 1380a25–6). Conversely, the discussions of the virtuous disposition in relation to anger in both the *Nicomachean* and *Eudemian Ethics* use both ὀργή and θυμός. The discussion in the *Eudemian Ethics* seems to use language that invites the connection between human ὀργή and animal θυμός:

> In the same way we must ascertain what is gentleness and irascibility (περὶ πραότητος καὶ χαλεπότητος). For we see that the gentle is concerned with the pain that arises from anger (ἀπὸ θυμοῦ), being characterised by a certain attitude towards this. We have given in our list as opposed to the passionate, irascible, and savage (τῷ ὀργίλῳ καὶ χαλεπῷ καὶ ἀγρίῳ) – all such being names for the same state – the slavish and the stupid (τὸν ἀνδραποδώδη καὶ τὸν ἀνόητον). For these are pretty much the names we apply to those who are not moved to anger even when they ought, but take insults easily and are tolerant of contempt. (3.3, 1231b5–13)

Two of the terms used here for excessive proneness to anger, 'irascibility' (χαλεπότης, or 'cross temper') and 'savageness' (ἀγριότης, 'fierceness' or 'wildness'), are regularly applied to non-human animals in the biological works. And 'slavishness' has been shown to have a connection with the kind of lack of spirit that Aristotle associates with colder and thinner blood, and attributes to southerners.[16] The virtue of 'gentleness' described in this passage issues in the correct exercise of the passion that in humans is anger:[17] the incorrect exercise of this passion can constitute states such as 'cross temper' and 'fierceness', which can clearly be possessed by animals such as bulls, and 'slavishness', which in Aristotle's view approximates the character of southerners to that of deer.

This all supports the view that anger and 'spirit' share the same core functional role in humans and in animals, that is, as a 'desire-cum-pain' (ὄρεξις μετὰ λύπης, *Rh.* 2.2, 1378a30) – distress at hostile infractions of the social structure, motivating the animal to take corrective action.[18] Not only that, the similar biological mechanisms (or underlying material substratum, to use Devin Henry's terminology) – particularly hot blood around the heart[19] – by which this role is discharged support the contention that differences between human anger and its animal counterparts are

---

[16] Cf. Leunissen 2012, 520–4.
[17] Aristotle also assigns to *thumos* an indirect role in supporting the virtue of courage in humans *Eth. Nic.* 3.8, 1116b23–1117a9.
[18] Cf. Heath 2008, 255–6.
[19] Cf. *De an.* 1.1, 403a25–b1 with e.g. *Part. an.* 2.4, 650b33–651a4, and discussion of the biological texts in Leunissen 2012, 513–24.

differences of degree (of complexity, of understanding) among varieties of the same passion.

An Objection: Human and Animal Passions Are Functionally Different

There is, however, an objection that might be brought against this assimilation of human and animal passions in the cases of jealousy, fear, and anger. The objection is that, say, human fear plays a different functional role in the life of the organism to animal fear. It rests on the observation made by Sarah Broadie quoted at the start of the chapter. Human fear is subject to regulation by reason, such that humans should fear only 'at the right time, in the right circumstances, at the right objects, with the right motive, and in the right way' (*Eth. Nic.* 2.6, 1106b21–2), as defined by right reason (1107a1–2). Animal fear is not subject to regulation in that way. And if human and animal fear play different functional roles, they cannot be analogous to one another (it would not be the case that as human fear is to the human, so animal fear is to the animal), and *a fortiori* cannot differ only by degree. The functional role of human passions (i.e. their successful functioning) involves their being guided by correct reason. It also involves their being felt in such a way as to help motivate action that is undertaken, 'for the sake of the fine' (e.g. *Eth. Nic.* 3.7, 1115b23–4). This suggests that their purpose is one that cannot be shared by non-human animals.

In order to respond to this objection, we need to distinguish, as Aristotle does, capacities for passionate responses, passionate responses themselves, and dispositions to make those responses in particular ways (*Eth. Nic.* 2.5, 1105b19–28). For Aristotle, the relevant capacity would, in the case of fear, be the capacity to respond to appearances of danger with distress so as to motivate avoidance. The passionate response itself – in this case, fear – would be that distress at apparent danger.[20] The disposition to make responses of fear in the right way is, in humans, a disposition to respond in ways guided, above all, by the deliverances of correct reason about danger, and about how its painfulness should be set, in an integrated way, alongside the pleasantness and painfulness of other features of the subject's situation. These deliverances are the result of the subject's reasoned deliberations about how to live well.[21] Clearly the disposition to

---

[20] This presupposes the view that in humans as well as in non-human animals, the passions are made at appearances. Cf. Moss, 2012, ch. 4; Dow 2014; and the related discussions of how in humans reason can be a source of such appearances in e.g. Lorenz 2006, ch. 13, esp. 189–90; and Grönroos 2007.

[21] This view is, in its essentials, that of Lennox 1999.

make fear responses in the right way is different in animals: Aristotle does not offer us an account of what it involves, but we might surmise that it is a disposition to identify danger correctly and to motivate the animal to successful avoidance behaviour.[22] No integration with reason is involved for animals, because none is possible. The differences in this regard are set out by Aristotle in his discussion of courage in the *Nicomachean Ethics*:

> Those creatures are not brave, then, which are driven on to danger by pain or spirit (δι᾽ ἀλγηδόνος ἢ θυμοῦ). The 'courage' that is due to spirit seems to be the most natural, and to be courage if choice (προαίρεσιν) and motive (τὸ οὗ ἕνεκα) be added. Humans, then, as well as beasts, suffer pain when they are angry, and are pleased when they exact their revenge; those who fight for these reasons, however, are pugnacious but not courageous; for they do not act for the sake of the fine nor as reason directs, but from strength of feeling (διὰ πάθος); they have, however, something akin to courage. (3.8, 1117a2–9)[23]

It seems plausible to suppose that Aristotle's rationale here will generalise across all the dispositions related to the passions. The motivation for virtuous human actions, to which the dispositions for exercising the passions contribute, involves a distinctive goal – 'the fine' – and a way of determining how to respond – through deliberated 'choice' and 'as reason directs', both of which depend on reason. They are dispositions to exercise the passions in a way that is integrated with the exercise of reason, and are therefore not present in animals. Clearly, then, the optimal dispositions[24] in relation to fear in humans and non-human animals are rather different. Perhaps Aristotle might have thought they were analogous to one another, but there is no evidence that he did.[25] This still leaves open the possibility that in the relevant range of cases (e.g. fear, jealousy, and anger), what

---

[22] Animals can fail to possess such a disposition. The fear of the mullet in *HA* 8.2, 591b3–4, for example, seems to show the absence of an optimal fear-related disposition, since the behaviour motivated by fear (hiding its head, 'as though' hiding its whole body) is ineffective avoidance behaviour.

[23] Translation adapted from Brown 2009.

[24] Animal dispositions are never called 'virtues' (ἀρεταί) in the *History of Animals*, as noted in Lennox 1999, 25, surprisingly perhaps, given that optimal dispositions of the kind I am discussing are excellences of animal capacities. The reason may be that in the *History of Animals*, terms like 'courage' and 'cowardice' seem to be used not to identify animal dispositions as optimal or defective, but simply as a shorthand for dispositions to behave in certain ways: 'cowardice' might in fact be the optimal disposition for deer, given that it will almost always be better for the deer to flee than to fight.

[25] Regarding as analogous optimal dispositions to feel, say, fear in humans and animals would require identifying some common function they discharged (White, 2010, ch. 2; Henry 2014) or capacity they enabled (Leunissen 2014) in both types of animal. But this is not straightforward, even in the case of fear. Disposing the animal to respond with fear to all and only fearsome things, to the extent that they are fearsome (such an account would allow for the difference in cognitive capacities

Aristotle sees as the same between humans and animals is either the *capacity* for making passionate responses of that type or the *responses* themselves, or both. Once the distinction between emotional capacities, responses, and dispositions is applied to it, the objection canvassed above seems most plausibly construed as requiring a clear distinction between animal and human *dispositions* to make passionate responses correctly. Thus construed, it seems to leave untouched the claim argued for in the preceding sections, that human and animal fear, jealousy, and anger are varieties of the same kind of passionate response, issuing from the same kind of capacity of soul.

Human and Animal Passions

Where does that leave the relationship between the passions of humans and of non-human animals? If the above arguments are successful, they establish that there are a few types of passion (e.g. fear, jealousy, and anger) that are common to humans and animals. Even in these cases, though, it is conceded that the dispositions to exercise these passionate responses well are very substantially different in humans from their counterparts in non-human animals. And, in fact, such dispositions will be different in relation to *every* type of passion. Moreover, to set alongside these shared passions, there are many others (e.g. pity, shame, emulation, indignation, *schaden-freude*, plus whatever passions are involved in justice and virtue- or utility-based friendship) that are simply not part of the passionate repertoire of animals at all. As such, the view I am recommending traces some significant but limited lines of continuity between human and animal passion types, whilst stressing how substantial for Aristotle are the differences and discontinuities between human and animal passionate experience (bucking, perhaps, a recent trend to emphasise continuity).

Does this reinstate a sharp boundary between the human and non-human realms? The answer is: no. This answer rests on a view I have canvassed previously that Aristotle's general 'theory' of the passions (in humans) is that they are pleasures and pains.[26] Considered in this way, the human capacities for passionate response are (collectively) exactly the same as those of animals: they are simply these core capacities of the sensitive soul to respond to perceptual (and post-perceptual) inputs with pleasure

between species), might be optimal for animals, but this would not be sufficient for human courage as Aristotle understood it (cf. *Eth. Nic.* 3.7).
[26] See Dow 2011 and Dow 2015, ch. 9.

and pain. The commonalities and the differences between the types of human and animal passions are built on this shared foundation. Both human and non-human animals are able to find things pleasurable and painful, in ways that variously involve the heating (e.g. anger/spirit) and chilling (e.g. fear) of the body and particularly the blood of the animal. The bodily mechanisms for making such responses are common to many species.

The differences stem from the different lives of humans and animals, and from the consequent fact that the human good and the good for other animals therefore diverge. The human good is more complex than animals' good, in ways that are tied to the presence of reason, and the apprehension of this good is correspondingly therefore more complex, requiring the exercise of reason. As a result, humans have a significantly different repertoire of ways in which to find things painful or pleasant, and the ability to distinguish between, say, the painfulness of others' success because of one's own failure to attain similar success (emulation) and the painfulness of others' success because they don't deserve it (indignation). The human good involves the active exercise of reason, including developing an understanding of how exercising the virtues and acting for the sake of the fine contributes to the overall goal of living well. Humans, even those whose understanding of the human good is deeply faulty, find things pleasant and painful because of their connection to (what they take to be) the human good. It should not be at all surprising that the passionate repertoire of humans therefore differs significantly from that of animals.

Conclusion

We set out to trace how human passions were connected to, but also different from, those of non-human animals. Our conclusion is that the capacity for the passions, on which all of the particular types of passions are built, is the same for humans and animals. It consists in the same material conditions (especially the temperature of various parts of the body, and especially of the blood), and the same broad capacity. That is the capacity to respond with pain and pleasure to features of the animal's environment. With some types of passion (such as fear, jealousy, and anger), those responses can be identified as of the same kind in humans and animals, differing, if at all, only in degree (of complexity, perhaps). Other types of passion (e.g. indignation, emulation, pity) can only be experienced by humans – they inherently involve a level of sophistication in how their objects are apprehended that is impossible for creatures that lack reason.

There is thus a considerable difference between the repertoires of types of passion available to humans and to animals. As regards the dispositions to feel the passions that in humans Aristotle calls virtues, these are so closely connected with the regulation of the passions by reason that they cannot be identified with (nor even considered analogous to) states available to non-human animals. Though some of these natural states provide the foundation in young humans for the subsequent development of virtue, and though Aristotle sometimes uses terms such as 'courage' to describe the dispositions of animals, it is clear that he does not think that non-human animals are capable of sharing the optimal passion-related dispositions of humans. Thus, while we have found a number of passions and passion-related features in humans and in animals that are either identical or differ only by degree, we have found none that differ only by analogy, and many that are not shared at all.

CHAPTER 7

Reasonable and Unreasonable Affections and Human Nature

Dorothea Frede

She knew that such affections leave lines on the face as well as in the character, and she meant to take warning by the little creases which her midnight survey had revealed.

Edith Wharton, *The House of Mirth*

Prelude

The somewhat puzzling title of this article is due to the fact that 'rational' and 'non-rational' are not appropriate denominations for the distinction between those affections (*pathē*) that do and those that do not follow the decrees of reason;[1] for Aristotle insists in his ethics that the affections belong to the soul's non-rational part, but can be made to 'participate in a way in reason' by 'listening to and obeying' its advice.[2] This potentially obedient non-rational part of the soul plays an important role in the determination of the human character because it represents the desiderative element in the soul that makes it pursue or avoid what strikes the individual as desirable or undesirable. Those affections that 'listen to reason' are called 'reasonable' here and those that do not, 'unreasonable'.[3]

7.1 The Nature of the Affections

The nature and role attributed to the affections in book II of the *Nicomachean Ethics* are simultaneously important and elusive; for Aristotle does not provide a definition of *pathos*, although there can be

---

[1] Translations of Aristotle are from Sarah Broadie and Christopher Rowe (2002), with the exception, here, of 'virtue' as the translation of *aretē*, rather than 'excellence'.

[2] See *Eth. Nic.* 1.13, 1102b13–1103; virtually the same distinction is found in *Eth. Eud.* 11.1, 1219b26–1220a12.

[3] This chapter further pursues Broadie's suggestion in her magisterial treatment of Aristotle's ethics: 1991, 62.

no doubt about the importance of the *pathē*.[4] The affections are introduced
as essential components of the virtues of character, and they are, at least for
a while, treated as on a par with the actions: 'the virtues have to do with
actions (*praxeis*) and affections (*pathē*), and every affection and every action
is accompanied (*hepetai*) by pleasure and pain' (II.3, 1104b14–16). At one
point the affections are even assigned the leading role in the preparation of
the definition of the virtues of character; for, in his determination of the
genus of these virtues Aristotle treats them as the crucial factors (II.5). As he
explains, there are three candidates for the determination of those virtues in
the soul, namely affections (*pathē*), capacities (*dunameis*), and dispositions
(*hexeis*). Both capacities and dispositions are explicated, here, exclusively in
terms of their relation to the affections (II.5, 1105b23–8):

> while capacities are what people are referring to when they say that we are
> susceptible to the affections, as for example with those capacities in terms of
> which we are said to be capable of becoming angry, or distressed, or feeling
> pity; as for dispositions, it is in terms of these that we are well or badly
> disposed in relation to the affections, as for example in relation to becoming
> angry; if we are violently or sluggishly disposed, we are badly disposed, and if
> in an intermediate way, we are well disposed.

The upshot of these considerations is that, given that the virtues are neither
affections nor capacities, they must be dispositions (*hexeis*) with respect to
the affections, and that, as such, they determine the genus of virtue of
character (II.5, 1106a10–14).

As stated in a famous passage in the *Historia animalium* VIII.1, human
beings and many animals have by and large the same capacities to be
affected – and therefore we find in animals 'traces' of the human character
(*ēthos*) of the kind we also find in young children. The closeness between
humans and animals in that respect has received quite some attention in
recent decades.[5] And that concerns ethics as well; for as Aristotle states with
respect to the 'natural virtues of character' at *Eth. Nic.* VI.13, 1144b4–6,
'Everyone thinks each of the various sorts of character traits belongs to us in
some sense by nature – because we are just, moderate in our appetites,
courageous, and the rest from the moment we are born'. And that seems to
accord well with the claim that man is by nature a political animal, even

---

[4] The lack of a definition was already noted by some ancient commentators (Aspasius *In Eth. Nic.*
44.19–45.16; see Sorabji 1999). They clearly ignored the extensive treatment of the *pathē* in Aristotle's
Rhetoric II.
[5] See the relevant articles in Henry and Nielsen 2015, esp. Lennox. For a more detailed and differentiated treatment of the similarities and distinctions between human and animal affections, the different
kinds of affections, and the psycho-physical background, see Dow's contribution to this volume.

'more political' than bees or other gregarious animals (*Pol.* 1.2, 1253a7–9): It is not only natural for humans to congregate in pairs and families, but it is also natural for families to extend to villages, and for villages to unite and form *poleis* as the condition of the autarkic life, the life in fulfilment of human nature. In addition to the form of life that is by nature best for human beings, Aristotle also envisages the form of the *polis* that is by nature best.

But despite such appeals to nature and the natural, there is a wide gap that separates human beings from the rest of nature, for while development in nature takes place 'necessarily or for the most part', human beings' development depends on their own efforts. While all other animals develop naturally and follow their natural course of life by instinct, human beings are left to their own devices. Not only must they find out what is the best form of life for them, what political constitution suits them best and in what way both can be achieved, they must also acquire the requisite knowledge and the moral virtues by their own efforts. By nature, humans have only the potential to recognise what is best for them, to find the ways and means to achieve it, and to educate each other: 'None of the virtues of character come about in us by nature' (*Eth. Nic.* 11.1, 1103a18–19). The acquisition of virtue is the result of habituation that has to be organised by human beings themselves and such habituation can lead to good as well as bad results. That in Aristotle's eyes optimal conditions have not yet been achieved, either in private or in public life, is indicated at two points: the task of his ethics is not theoretical knowledge, as in his other treatises, but to provide insights that help so 'that we should become good' (11.2, 1103b26–4a11). And in *Politics* VII and VIII Aristotle presents the design of an ideal constitution, of a 'city of our prayers' (*kat' euchēn politeia*) with the rudiments of an educational plan.[6]

Because of the importance Aristotle attributes to the affections in the development of virtues of character, it is necessary to take a closer look at the way he introduces and describes them. So what *are* the *pathē*? At first, Aristotle seems intent on emphasising their 'pathetic' (i.e. passive) character, as in the passage referred to above (11.5, 1105b23–8), for he uses the examples 'being angered, being pained, being moved to pity'.[7] But then he indicates that a *pathos* is not just a passive impression of a pleasant or painful sort, caused by external impacts, but always contains either a kind

---

[6] On Aristotle's self-assigned mission, see Frede 2019.
[7] The frequency of these expressions – *lupēthēnai, orgisthēnai*, etc. – seems designed to emphasise their passive character; see also 11.6, 1106b18–21: *phobēthēnai . . . kai holōs hēsthēnai kai lupēthēnai.*

of 'proversion', as present-day psychology describes the desire to pursue, or an 'aversion', a desire to avoid (II.3, 1104b22: *diōkein kai pheugein*). This suggests that the affections have an important role to play as far as human conduct is concerned.

Aristotle, unfortunately, is less explicit concerning this point than we would wish, for he does not comment on the passive-cum-active character of the *pathē* or on the nature of the relation of the affections to the respective actions. The question pursued here first is therefore whether Aristotle is aware that the functions of the actions and of the affections differ in determining the character virtues' nature, because he speaks as if the virtues concern both actions and passions alike: 'Again, if the virtues have to do with actions and affections, and every affection and every action is accompanied by pleasure and pain, this will be another reason for thinking that virtue has to do with pleasure and pain' (II.3, 1104b13–16).

But, as noted before, in chapter 5, he turns exclusively to the *pathē* in order to determine the genus of virtue of character. Although the affections are not themselves virtues, the virtues are essentially tied to the way people are disposed with respect to them (II.5, 1105b28–1106a1):

> Well then, neither the virtues nor the corresponding vices are affections (*pathē*), because we are not called good or bad people on account of the affections, whereas we are so called on account of virtues and vices, for the frightened person isn't praised, nor is the angry person, nor is the person who is simply angered censured, but the person who is angry in a certain way (*pōs*).

And at this point, Aristotle makes clear that to experience an affection means 'being moved' (II.5, 1106a5: *kata ta pathē kineisthai legometha*). Nothing is said at this point about the actions as the counterparts of the affections.

At the beginning of that discussion Aristotle presents a whole barrage of affections: 'By affections I mean appetite, anger, fear, boldness, malice, joy, friendly feeling, hatred, longing, envy, pity – generally feelings that are accompanied by pleasure and pain' (II.5, 1105b21–3). This enumeration raises the expectation that the virtues and vices of character will be spelled out in terms of the dispositions that people have towards those affections. But this is not how Aristotle proceeds in what follows. In preparation of his further account of virtue of character, he first introduces the conception of the 'right mean' between excess and deficiency and in this discussion he includes the actions (*praxeis*): 'I mean the virtue of character; for this has to do with affections and actions, and it is in these that there is excess and deficiency, and the intermediate' (11.6, 1106b16–18). And he spells out the intermediate in terms of the affections and actions (11.6, 1106b18–24):

> So it is possible to be affected by fear, boldness, appetite, anger, pity, and pleasure and distress both too much and too little, and neither is good; but to be affected when one should be, at the things one should, and in the way one should be, is both intermediate and best … In the same way, with actions, too, there is excess, deficiency, and the intermediate.

But while the parallel treatment of action and affection gives the impression that both sides are on a par, the full, formal definition of virtue of character contains an indication that this is not so. It concerns the importance of 'decision' – *proairesis*: 'Virtue, then, is a disposition issuing in decisions (*hexis proairetikē*), depending on intermediacy of the kind relative to us, this being determined by rational prescription (*logos*) and in the way in which the wise person would determine it' (11.6, 1106b36–1107a2). Although Aristotle in what follows still repeatedly speaks as if his definition of virtue applied equally to actions and to affections, reflection shows why that cannot be so. As he has indicated before, affections do not involve decisions: 'Again, we are angry and afraid without decision (*aproairetōs*), but the virtues are modes of decision or involve decision' (11.5, 1106a2–4).

As will emerge, the fact that affections are not the result of decisions constitutes an important distinction between actions and affections that readers tend to overlook, because Aristotle mentions it only once, in passing, and he neither comments on its importance nor returns to it later in the *Nicomachean Ethics*. Instead, in his discussion of virtues of character he at first continues to treat actions and affections even-handedly. But that even-handedness helps to obfuscate the asymmetry between them with respect to decision. It is therefore necessary to expatiate somewhat on the reasons for denying that affections are a matter of decision and why Aristotle rightly holds that the *pathē* just 'happen to us', because we are 'moved in a certain way' (1106a5: *kineisthai*), while moral actions are determined by deliberation and decision.

7.2 Decision and the Virtues of Character

That there is an asymmetry between actions and affections has been noted before. Kosman has commented on it with admirable clarity:

Moral philosophy, then, should count as an important question that of sentimental education and should recognise the proper cultivation of our feelings as within the domain of our moral concerns. But how could this be? It appears to be a distinction between our actions and our passions that actions are within our control, whereas passions are not; we are the initiating principles of what we do, but not of what is done to us.[8]

Some reflections are necessary on the distinction between actions and 'passions' with respect to decisions. As Aristotle has it, actions are determined by practical reason, by *phronēsis*, because it is the capacity that is at work in deliberation and decision. Because *phronēsis* is officially introduced only in book vi, the fact that deliberation and decision are determined by the soul's rational capacity is less prominent in the early books of the *Nicomachean Ethics* and it is therefore easy to overlook the fact that the affections, as capacities of the non-rational part of the soul, differ in that respect from the actions.

But although the affections themselves are elements of the soul's non-rational part, why should they not be the objects of deliberation and decision? Reflection shows that we neither deliberate about nor make decisions on being angry, afraid, feeling appetite, being envious, and so on.[9] And there is no distinction in that respect between feeling all these things in the right or in the wrong way (i.e. feeling them too much, too little, against the right or wrong people, at the right or wrong occasion). The reason why *pathē* are not a matter of deliberation and decision is not difficult to see: we deliberate and decide on what to do about a given situation and about the appropriate means to do it, but we do not deliberate and decide about how to feel about it. The feeling is, rather, determined by the way the situation affects us, once we recognise it for what it is. Someone who 'decides to be angry' on the basis of deliberation and decision to be angry is not really angry, but merely adopts the attitude of an angry person. Such deliberation and decision must, in fact, rather dilute the affective reaction to a given situation. That diagnosis applies to envy, sadness, and all the other types of affection. Deliberation and decision concern the actions that are to be done on the basis of anger, sadness, or envy, but they do not concern the feelings themselves.

If the affections are not determined by deliberation and decision, there is, nevertheless a certain kind of reasoning involved in their formation. Fear, anger, and the other affections arise once we have understood the

---

[8] Kosman 1980, 106.
[9] See Broadie 1991, 75; 79: 'We deliberate on what to do, not on what to feel about something'.

situation we find ourselves in, whether rightly or wrongly. Fear is the reaction to physical danger, anger is the reaction to an insult, and appetite is, for example, the effect of some delicious food put before us. But once we have registered that situation, we either feel a certain way about it or we do not: affections are reactions to that comprehension, and once people have acquired certain reactive dispositions of 'being moved in certain ways', the affections will arise automatically at the respective occasion. If someone tells herself that she 'ought to be sad, afraid, angry etc.', she is actually not in any of those conditions, she only recognises that such is the normal reaction to that particular situation, a reaction which, for some reason or other, she does not have.

With actions the situation is different. The realisation that I should face up to danger, or get back at the person who insulted me, or refrain from eating a certain kind of food, is the first step towards action for it prompts me to deliberate and to decide how to act. And the way I will act is determined by deliberation and decision, while nothing of that sort will happen as long as I merely feel angry or afraid or experience an appetite. Deliberation and decision therefore present a crucial difference between acting and being affected. While somebody who displays anger on the basis of deliberation and choice, even if it is well-grounded anger, is only pretending to be angry; someone who deliberately returns an insult for an insult is really acting.

It is, of course, possible to influence our affective states by reasoning about them. We only have to recollect Odysseus' famous *paramuthia* in *Odyssey* 20.18: 'Bear up, my heart; you have borne other, even more doggish things'. But such reasoning is only an indirect way of influencing one's affective state. Ever since the rediscovery of the affections and their importance in the twentieth century, strategies have been developed to influence them. 'Anger management' is a favourite topic in psychotherapy and so is the management of other affections that get in a patient's way. Patients learn how to forestall anger, to diffuse it, to limit it, to let go of it, or to act out on account of it in certain ways. And the same applies, *mutatis mutandis*, to pathological fear, jealousy, and all other such affections.[10]

The all-important question is whether Aristotle shares this view, namely that the *pathē*, in contradistinction to *praxeis*, are not a matter of decision. What evidence is there, apart from his brief remark at II.5, 1106a2–3, which may, after all, be only an *obiter dictum*? A confirmation lies in the fact that

---

[10] Aristotle mentions such means of forestalling inappropriate affective reactions by an adequate preparation in his discussion of *akrasia* at VII.7, 1150b22–5.

Aristotle in his discussion of voluntariness, of deliberation, and choice in book III of the *Nicomachean Ethics*, focuses exclusively on actions and never even mentions the *pathē*. Kosman regards this as a symptom that the importance of the feelings 'fades in the context of a theory of deliberation and choice and their place in moral conduct'.[11] While this seems right, as an observation, it does not extend to the reason he adduces for this 'fading'. He denies that 'feelings' for Aristotle are not chosen:

> The reason ... is that choice for him is not a concept having to do with individual moments in an agent's life, or with individual single actions, but with the practices of that life within the larger context of the character and intentions of a moral subject, ultimately within the context of what has become fashionable to call one's life plan.[12]

But Kosman's explanation that choice is not about singular actions at particular moments must be mistaken. This point cannot be properly argued here for *proairesis* is used in more than one way in Aristotle. In some connections he does indeed use it in the more general sense of 'plan', 'intention', or 'purpose', so that one can speak of long-term plans or purposes. But in his explanation of action in III.2–6, Aristotle uses *proairesis* in the narrow sense of 'decision' or 'choice' that results from deliberation about particular courses of action. Deliberation leads to the decision of how to act under those circumstances; decision is the result of deliberation and leads directly to the requisite action.[13] That is why it is important to get all the so-called 'parameters of action' right: that one acts towards the person one should (*dei*), in the way one should, at the time one should. If the affections 'fade' from Aristotle's discussion of the virtues, they do so because the affective responses are not a matter of deliberation and decision.

Kosman rightly assumes, however, that our dispositions towards the affections are *shaped* by the actions in the larger contexts of our lives, by the respective deliberations and decisions. And that may well be the reason why Aristotle in the early books treats actions and affections on a par and does not draw definite lines of separation. The acquisition of the virtues by practice does not concern just the disposition of how to act appropriately in a certain situation, but also the disposition of how to feel in that situation. We not only learn to act in the way we should, when we should, towards whom we should, but we also at the same time adopt the right way of feeling. Aristotle therefore applies the 'shoulds' as much to the affections as

---

[11] Kosman 1980, 115.   [12] Kosman 1980, 115.   [13] *Eth. Nic.* III.3, 1113a9–13: *tōn pros ta telē*.

to the actions: there are right and wrong ways to feel about the person in question, about the occasion, and about the way we have been treated. Not only that, but these feelings are intimately connected with the ensuing actions, because the affections contain the desiderative elements of seeking, or of avoiding, a certain end that make us act. That this is Aristotle's view is witnessed by the fact that he criticises those philosophers who want to do away with the *pathē* altogether (II.3, 1104b24–7):

> This is also why people define the virtues as kinds of impassivity (*apatheia*) and tranquillity (*ēremia*);[14] but they go wrong, because they say what they say without specifying – they don't add 'as one should', 'as one should not' and 'when one should or should not' and all the other specifications.

Aristotle has two reasons for rejecting the position that virtue is freedom from *pathē*.[15] First, the capacity for experiencing affections is part of the natural human endowment that cannot be eradicated. Second, our 'pro-versions' and aversions provide the incentives to act. Reason alone does not do anything, as stated later (VI.2, 1139a35–6). The 'apathetic' person would, therefore, at the same time be 'apractic', and that is not a good condition for a human being at all.

The capacity to be affected in certain ways can be influenced by reason, but the affections do not thereby become fully rational. The question is, then, how the affections become 'reasonable' if in and of themselves they belong to the soul's non-rational part. Aristotle is, unfortunately, not nearly as explicit concerning this question as one would wish, and this is in part due to the 'fading' of the affections in the further discussion of the different virtues of character. He apparently presupposes that human beings become well-tempered with practice. Habituation by repeated exposure to dangerous situations, with instructions and imitation of role models on how to act in response to them, will not only train and modify the habitual way of acting, but also the way of feeling fear and confidence. Habituation of how to behave in dangerous situations will, in the long run, also condition the way one feels fear and confidence – when one should, as one should. This must be what Aristotle has in mind when he says that the non-rational part of the soul 'listens to reason or even agrees with reason, as

---

[14] Speusippus is regarded as the source, in agreement with his position referred to at VII.13, 1153b4–8 that both pleasure and pain are evils, while the middle state, freedom from both pleasure and pain, is good (cf. Broadie and Rowe 2002, 299).

[15] This seems to be the reason behind the claim that different individuals have, by nature, different moral propensities (II.8, 1109a12–19) to be countered in various ways (II.9, 1109a30–b7).

one listens to the advice of a father or a friend' (*Eth. Nic.* 1.13, 1102b28–1103a3).

7.3   Influencing the Affections

It is time to take a closer look at the way habituation works and how it makes the affections 'reasonable'. Again, Aristotle is rather reticent concerning this point, but this much is clear: deliberating, deciding, and acting in specific kinds of situations simultaneously condition the dispositions to be affected, for the agent not only gets to like or dislike acting in this or that way, but she will also respond affectively in the appropriate way to the situation she finds herself in. By doing brave acts, first under instruction and then on their own, people gradually come to judge rightly what is the brave thing to do in this or that situation. But they also develop, at the same time, a 'moral taste': they respond emotionally to the situation in the right way so as to fear or feel confidence in the right way, and to desire to act or to avoid acting in that way. The morally correct or incorrect response to a particular situation is, then, a matter of affection-cum-desire for action.

That this complexity does not emerge more clearly in the *Nicomachean Ethics* is due, in part, to the fact that in his introduction of the virtues of character Aristotle does not resort to examples that concern the acquisition of moral standards, but rather to those of technical proficiencies like playing the kithara or building houses: 'it is from playing the kithara that good and bad players come about. So too both with builders and the rest: good building will result in good builders, bad building in bad ones. If it were not like this, there would be no need at all for anyone to teach them' (II.1, 1103b9–13). This explanation is instructive insofar as it shows that 'habituation' is not the mere acquisition of habits through repetition by a kind of mechanical drill or by routine, but also involves instruction and understanding. But, given that playing music and building houses are *technai*, the training and practice concern the requisite skills to act, while affections and their acquisition are not referred to.[16]

How then, does practising influence the affections and not just the enjoyment or pain taken in the respective actions? If the affections are simultaneously both reactive and desiderative driving forces that lead to action, habituation will affect the individual in a complex way. As in the

---

[16] The kinds of affections that accompany those 'technical' activities, i.e. the right or wrong taste in music and architecture, are not moral but artistic affections.

case of learning how to act in a dangerous situation mentioned above, an understanding of the particular situation will provoke the suitable amount of fear and confidence. And the analogous diagnosis applies to anger: as the person learns, by deliberation and decision, how to act in the face of insults and to refrain from acting on merely apparent insults, she also reacts emotionally in the right way. She will neither flare up in a catastrophic rage at the slightest provocation nor remain unmoved by an insult. She will 'be angered' (*orgisthēnai*) as she should be – and this anger will arise in accordance with the kind of provocation she has received. Thus, the exposure to different situations and the training in the appropriate ways to act will also provide the appropriate sentimental education.[17]

This general characterisation still seems rather vague, because it suggests that somehow, with experience and practice, we will become well-tempered with respect to our affections. But it is possible to be more specific than that: it is deliberation and decision that do the tempering of the affections. This explains why Aristotle assumes that actions and affections must fulfil the same qualifications. Sometimes he mentions them *in tandem*, sometimes only one of them (11.1, 1103b15–24):

> [F]or it is through acting as we do in our dealings with human beings that some of us become just and others unjust, and through acting as we do in frightening situations, and through becoming habituated to fearing or being confident that some of us become courageous and some of us cowardly. A similar thing holds, too, with situations relating to appetites, and with those relating to temper: some people become moderate and even-tempered, others self-indulgent and irascible, the one group as a result of behaving one way in such circumstances, the other as the result of behaving another way. We may sum up by saying that dispositions come about from activities of a similar sort.

In his determination of the nature of virtues of character in *Nicomachean Ethics* 11, Aristotle has not yet formally introduced deliberation and decision. That happens only later, in book 111. But it is clear that making the right adjustments to the circumstances is a matter of deliberation and decision. How this works is a much-debated issue that cannot be adequately discussed here. Thought and deliberate decision can, of course, be dispensed with in routine cases, but they will be resorted to in all cases that deviate from the standard cases. For those cases, Aristotle states, 'the

---

[17] This will not work in the case of pathologically impaired persons, as Aristotle's example of the person who is afraid of every fly shows (VII.6, 1148a4–9), but only with people of naturally malleable dispositions.

agents themselves have to consider (*skopein*) the circumstances relating to the occasion, just as happens in the case of medicine, too, and of navigation' (II.2, 1104a8–10). These considerations concern the question of whether the intended action is in accordance with all the parameters that determine the way that a particular action should be performed, for it is these parameters that need to be considered with respect to the right mean, and that mean concerns both actions and affections. That is what Aristotle has in mind when he characterises the affective part of the soul as non-rational by nature, but as capable of 'listening to reason as to the advice of a father or friend' (I.13, 1102b28–1103a3). In the case of a well-brought up adult, there is no longer any need for an 'advisory voice': the emotive response will conform totally to the judgement of reason (I.13, 1102b27–8: *homophōnein*).

'Unreasonable affections' are, then, the affections of people who have been brought up badly, be they in excess or in deficit of the right mean. Such affections overshoot the mark or fall short of it. That applies to the coward, to the rash person, to the self-indulgent, and to the 'under-appetised' person, as well as to persons given to anger either too much or too little.[18] Their judgement of the situation is wrong, and so is their affective response. And their affective disposition determines in turn, along with their decision, the way they will pursue or avoid what they regard as good or bad.

7.4   Virtues and Affections

It is time to return to Kosman's observation that in Aristotle's discussion of the virtues of character the affections gradually fade away. In his detailed depiction of the virtues of character in books III.7 to V Aristotle does indeed refer to the specific affections only in relation to three of the eleven virtues of character listed in II.7: courage with respect to fear and confidence, moderation with respect to appetite, and even-temperedness concerning anger. In the depiction of all other virtues of character, Aristotle discusses only the actions that are typical of the virtuous and the vicious: in the case of liberality and magnificence, he delineates the ways of spending money on a small and on a large scale; in the case of high-mindedness and ordinary ambition, he delineates the pursuit of honours large or small. And

---

[18] Aristotle is unusually explicit concerning the different kinds of wrong dispositions concerning anger in *Nicomachean Ethics* IV.5: there are people who are irascible, bitter, or resentful, and those conditions lead to different ways of overacting in anger.

in the cases of the three so-called social virtues, truthfulness in the way to present oneself, wittiness in social occasions, and friendliness in everyday encounters, no mention is made of specific affections either.

It may seem therefore as if Aristotle does not regard the affections as important elements of the majority of the virtues, but limits them to the 'physical' affections of fear and appetite, and to anger – affections that he regards as natural, because humans share them with the animals. But if such were Aristotle's position, it would have grave consequences for his conception of the virtues of character. For then only a few of the virtues of character would be anchored in the soul's non-rational part, while the majority would have no such connection. Because it seems highly unlikely that Aristotle simply overlooked that fact, the question is why he does not mention the respective affections in his detailed specification of most virtues and vices of character.

The neglect of the 'pathetic' nature of many of the virtues of character is not the only peculiarity in Aristotle's treatment of the affections. It is also worth noting that many of the *pathē* on Aristotle's list[19] turn out not to be associated with any of the virtues of character. There is, for instance, no discussion of a virtue or vice that deals with hatred, joy, longing, envy, or pity. To be sure, malice or 'grudging ill will' is ruled out explicitly, together with schadenfreude and shamelessness, as an inappropriate affection on the grounds that it is by nature bad, so that it is not possible to attain a right intermediary disposition, just as there cannot be any right intermediary concerning bad actions like adultery, murder, or theft (II.6, 1107a8–12).[20] But this still leaves unexplained why many of the virtues and vices on Aristotle's list in II 7 and in his subsequent detailed discussion in III.7–IV are not associated with any affections.

One reason must be that the affections do not have proper names of their own, a possibility that Aristotle anticipates with his remark that everyone aims for that of which he is a 'lover' (I.8, 1099a7–11):

> For pleasure is a state of the soul, and to each man that which he is said to be a lover of (*philotoioutos*) is pleasant ... but also the same way, just acts are pleasant to the lover of justice (*philodikaios*) and in general virtuous acts to the lover of virtue (*philaretos*).

The *passe-partout* term *philotoioutos*, 'lover of so-and-so', is used again later in the discussion of the particular virtues of character (III.II, 1118b22; IV.4,

---

[19] *Eth. Nic.* II.5, 1105b21–3: 'appetite, anger, fear, boldness, grudging ill will, joy, friendly feeling, hatred, longing, envy, pity – generally feelings attended by pleasure and pain'.
[20] For a more extensive treatment of this question see Frede 2014.

1125b14). It suggests an affective basis for all virtues of character, even if the affections do not have names of their own.[21] That in the case of 'friendliness' supposedly no *pathos* is involved does not show that it is an 'affectless' virtue; the friendly agent, rather, has no *personal* affection for those she happens to encounter, because friendliness is a general positive affective disposition towards one's fellows (IV.6, 1126b22–8).[22] As to the source of all these affections, Aristotle is rather quiet. But it stands to reason that he thinks that in their rudimentary form they are part of the natural human endowment, the 'natural virtues', some of which are common to humans and animals. In their proper sense, they are 'trained tastes' that develop fully only once reason sets in.

In the later books of the *Nicomachean Ethics*, Aristotle does indeed pay much less attention to the affective conditions of the particular virtues than his initial treatment in book II would lead one to expect. '*Pathē* are mentioned later only if agents supposedly act under the influence of uncontrolled desire, rather than in accordance with reason. Thus *pathē* are referred to mostly in a critical sense,[23] with reference to people who either act under the influence of an undue *pathos* or live only in accordance with their *pathē* (VIII.3, 1156a30–6; X.9, 1179b13–31). But why, then, does Aristotle at first give the impression that *pathē* are a definitive feature of all virtues (II.5), and that the *pathē* are equipollent with the *praxeis*? A comparison between the *Eudemian Ethics* and the *Nicomachean Ethics* sheds some light on this question, for the explanation of the character virtues in the *Eudemian Ethics* is based, throughout, on the affections, rather than on the actions *and* affections: 'We must now specify the aspect of the soul in virtue of which character traits possess the qualities they do. They do so in relation to the soul's capacities for affections (*pathēmata*), with respect to which people are termed "liable to affection" (*pathētikoi*)' (II.2, 1220b7–10). In the *Eudemian Ethics*, both the list of triads of virtues and vices and their subsequent brief description treat the *pathē* as the definitive factors (II.3, 1220b36–1221b3). Actions, *praxeis*, are introduced there only as the factors that lead up to the establishment of the virtues or that result from them. Thus, in *Eudemian Ethics* II *praxeis* and *pathē* are not paired off together in the way they often are in *Nicomachean Ethics* II.

---

[21] There are various references to 'loves' both good and bad: II.7, 1107b27–1108a1: *timēs orexis*; b9: *philotimos*; IV.1, 1121b15; *philochrēmatos*; 1122a8 *aischrokerdēs*; IV.7, 1127b4: *philalēthēs*.

[22] Because friendliness is treated as an impersonal emotional attitude towards others, Aristotle seems to have introduced *philēsis* as the emotional attitude towards individual friends (VIII.2, 1155b27–31 and passim).

[23] See V.6, 1134a21; V.8, 1135a21. *Akrasia* is notoriously the disposition to follow one's *pathos* of appetite.

Although in the *Eudemian Ethics* virtue is eventually defined as a disposition lying in a mean that is concerned with choice (II.10, 1227b5–11), throughout the lengthy discussion of the individual virtues Aristotle keeps short the 'active' aspect and emphasises only that virtues are characterised by pleasure and pain, by which he clearly means those of the affective kind.[24]

In the *Nicomachean Ethics*, by contrast, the 'mean' is said to concern both the *pathē* and the actions (II.6, 1107a4). Though this is not the only point of difference between the two versions of Aristotle's ethics, a detailed comparison of *Eudemian Ethics* II and *Nicomachean Ethics* II and III would show that the latter is the result of a major reorganisation of the analysis of the virtues and vices of character, and of their conditions. Though such a comparison is beyond the limits of this chapter, it stands to reason that the central role assigned to the affections in the preparation of the definition of the genus of the virtues of character at the beginning of *Nicomachean Ethics* II.5 reflects the discussion in *Eudemian Ethics* II. If he adopts it at first in the *Nicomachean Ethics*, it must be because Aristotle found it less problematic in the case of *pathē* than in that of actions that there should be an intermediary between excess and deficiency and a right measure on a kind of divisible *continuum* (1106a26–9: *suneches*). It is more natural to conceive of a more and a less in the case of affections than it is with respect to the corresponding actions. But once the genus of virtue is defined in terms of affections, Aristotle immediately turns to their 'active' complements; if he afterwards mentions the affections as the counterparts of the actions, he does so without paying much attention to them.

7.5 The Pleasures and Pains of Acting and Being Affected

The separate treatment of the 'pathetic' and the 'active' aspect of virtues of character in the *Eudemian Ethics* also sheds some light on a further point of importance. It concerns the indications that the pleasures and pains that are related to the affections and to the actions are different in kind. This is a difficult issue, because in the *Nicomachean Ethics* actions and passions are mostly mentioned in one breath, and pleasure and pain are usually attributed to both of them in a summary way: 'Again, if the virtues have to do with actions and affections, and every affection and every action is

---

[24] As Woods 1982, 124 observes: 'The *E.N.* lays much greater stress on the fact that virtues and vices have to do with means in actions as well as affections'.

accompanied by pleasure and pain, this will be another reason for thinking that virtue has to do with pleasures and pains' (II.3, 1104b13–16).

But the text of the *Nicomachean Ethics* also contains a more differentiated explanation of the attitudes of the moderate and the courageous person (II.3, 1104b5–8):

> for someone who holds back from bodily pleasure and does so cheerfully is a moderate person, while someone who is upset at doing so is self-indulgent, and someone who withstands frightening things and does so cheerfully, or at least without distress is a courageous person, while someone who is distressed at them is cowardly.

There are clearly two different kinds of pleasures and pains involved in these cases. One concerns the *pathē* – in the case of the courageous person, the fear of injury or death; in the case of the moderate person, the appetite for food, drink, and sex. The second kind concerns the corresponding *action* – the moderate man enjoys the act of behaving moderately, the courageous man the act of holding out in the face of danger.

That the difference between the active and passive kinds of pleasure and pain does not come more to the fore in the *Nicomachean Ethics* is due in part to the fact that in the detailed discussion of most character virtues Aristotle does not even mention the affections that give rise to the action. Hence it is easy to ignore the fact that there are two different kinds of pleasure and pain involved. The question is, of course, whether Aristotle himself was fully aware of the distinction between the 'active' and the 'passive' types of pleasure and pain. This question is hard to answer, because in neither of the two discussions of pleasure, in *Nicomachean Ethics* VII.11–14 and in X.1–5, does Aristotle as much as hint at such a distinction; in both discussions he focuses exclusively on the pleasures of action. In book VII pleasure is identified with an 'unimpeded natural activity' (VII.12, 1153a12–15; VII.14, 1153b9–12), and in book X pleasure is said to 'supervene' on the activities in a way that supposedly 'completes them like the bloom of youth' (X.4, 1174b14–1175a3). But why should 'activity', *energeia*, not also cover the affections? Are they not activities of the soul as well? That the soul is active when it is affected is undeniable; but Aristotle clearly does not have 'pathetic' pleasures (and pains) in mind in either of the two discussions of pleasure in the *Nicomachean Ethics*, for neither 'unimpededness' nor 'perfection' seems to be apt explanations in the case of affections.

That Aristotle focuses on the pleasures of actions in both books must be due to the fact that this discussion is inspired by a controversy concerning the nature of pleasure that originated in the Academy. It led Aristotle to devote much more time to a critique of those conceptions of pleasure than to the elucidation and justification of his own point of view. The critical character of his discussion is more prominent in VII.11–14 than in X.1–5, where Aristotle starts out with a critical assessment of the pro-hedonist stance of Eudoxus, cuts short his critique of the anti-hedonist positions, and then devotes more time to the explanation of his own account of pleasure that focuses exclusively on pleasures taken in actions.

There are, nevertheless, good reasons to think that Aristotle was aware of the fact that 'pathetic' pleasures and pains are of a different kind than the pleasures and pains taken in action. This assumption is confirmed by the fact that in the discussion of the *pathē* in the *Rhetoric* Aristotle defends a different conception of pleasure and pain, the very 'Platonic' conception that he criticises in *Nicomachean Ethics* VII and X, namely that pleasure is a 'motion' and a 'restoration of the natural equilibrium', while pain is its destruction. As *Rhetoric* I.11, 1369b33–5 has it: 'We may set it down that pleasure is an intensive and notable movement (*kinēsis*) and restoration (*katastasis*) of the soul to its normal state of being and that pain is the opposite'.[25]

Prima facie it seems strange that Aristotle never revised this 'Platonic' element in his account of the affections in the *Rhetoric*, despite the fact that there are clear signs that he repeatedly 'updated' that work, just as he did with his other working manuscripts or 'lecture notes'. But as reflection confirms, the 'Platonic' explanation of pleasure as a kind of restoration, and of pain as a kind of destruction or disturbance, fits the affections well.[26] For *pathē* are impressions of a positive or a negative kind; they are disturbances of a person's equilibrium that give rise to desires or aversions, which in turn give rise to actions. It is precisely this Platonic conception of pleasure (and the largely neglected pain) that Aristotle rejects in *Nicomachean Ethics* VII and X, and he does so in no uncertain terms. Not only does he focus exclusively on actions, but his account of pleasure applies only to perfect activities that contain their *telos* in themselves. This account clearly does not apply to pleasant affections; for they are neither perfect nor do they contain an end in themselves. Pleasures (and pains) depend on the object/state of affairs they are taken in.

---

[25] For a fuller discussion of the *Rhetoric*'s treatment of the affections, see Rapp 2002, II, 543–83, and the extensive discussion in Dow 2014.

[26] Plato first treats pleasure as a filling of a lack in *Gorgias* 491e–492a, a view that he develops further in *Republic* IX 583b–586a and discusses extensively in *Philebus* 31b–55c.

Aristotle's neglect of the affections in the elucidation of pleasure in *Nicomachean Ethics* VII and X should not detract from the fact that there is a positive result concerning the affections. The affections, whether pleasant or unpleasant, are reasonable or unreasonable to the degree to which they have been 'in-formed' by reason: the good person's affections are reasonable because they are geared towards the intermediate, the good, and the fine, while the bad person's affections are unreasonable because they are geared to excess or deficiency. Because all moral actions are prompted by affection-cum-desire they remain tied to the soul's non-rational part. It is a part, however, that in the virtuous person has been so thoroughly trained that it is in total agreement with reason's deliberation and decision about what to do and what to avoid (1.13, 1102b28: *panta homophonei tōi logōi*).

In *Nicomachean Ethics* III.4 Aristotle assigns the assessment of the situation to the wish (*boulēsis*) for the good end: 'for the virtuous person the object of wish is the one that is truly so ... for the good person discriminates correctly in every set of circumstances, and in every set of circumstances what is true is apparent to him' (1113a25–32). That wish is here determined by the virtues of character is made clear in the addition: 'Each disposition has its own range of fine things and pleasant things, and what most distinguishes the good person is his ability to see what is true in every set of circumstances, being like a carpenter's rule or measure for them'.

Although Aristotle does not make it explicit at this point, it is wish that motivates the person to deliberate, to decide and to act, and is either reasonable or unreasonable, depending on the person's character. In book VI Aristotle no longer mentions 'wish' as the capacity to settle the end, but attributes that capacity directly to 'character'. It is 'virtue' that makes the goal correct, while practical reason makes correct what leads up to it. A satisfactory explanation of why 'wish' is no longer mentioned as that capacity would be beyond this chapter.[27] But the attribution of the determination of the *telos* to virtue of character confirms that the affective dispositions are the indispensable starting points of deliberation and choice that lead to action. The well-trained affections cause the right kind of desire, while the ill-trained affections cause desires of the wrong kind. That is the distinction between reasonable and unreasonable affections.

---

[27] Wish (*boulēsis*) is not mentioned in either book VI or VII. In the discussion of friendship in books VIII and IX, *boulēsis* designates the good will friends have for each other.

They require an appropriate training and are not a gift of nature, in contradistinction to the affections and character traits that characterise different kinds of animals and young children; in the case of human beings, they are the natural preconditions of all moral training and education.

PART IV

Action and the Natural World (Aristotle)

CHAPTER 8

Chains That Do Not Bind: Causation and Necessity in Aristotle

Thomas Tuozzo

Aristotle holds that adult human beings are morally responsible for many of their actions. Does he also hold that all events, including human actions, are causally determined? and if causally determined, then necessitated?[1] If so, he implicitly endorses compatibilism: the view that moral responsibility is compatible with (a necessitating) causal determinism.[2] In this essay I shall be concerned with determining Aristotle's position on these questions. As a preliminary matter, it will be useful first to distinguish two different ways in which, in contemporary philosophical debate, causal determinism has been seen as a threat to moral responsibility. On the one hand, moral responsibility may be thought to require that at the time of action there be a plurality of actions genuinely open to the agent (the 'Principle of Alternate Possibilities'); if causal determinism is true, then (it can be argued) there are no such genuine alternatives.[3] On the other hand, moral responsibility may be thought to require only that an action have its ultimate source or causal origin in some sense *in* the agent, so that its causal history cannot be traced back, for example, to events before the agent's birth; and causal determinism (it can be argued) does not allow this weaker condition to be met, either.[4] Scholarship on Aristotle's views on moral responsibility has addressed both of these ways in

It is with great pleasure that I offer this chapter to Sarah Broadie, from whose insights and generosity I have benefited ever since her detailed comments on my dissertation many years ago.

Earlier (and rather different) versions of this paper were presented to colloquia at the University of Kansas and the University of Michigan, whose participants I thank for their comments. I also thank the graduate students with whom I explored Aristotelian efficient causation in my seminars at Kansas (fall 2019) and Michigan (winter 2020).

[1] Generally speaking, contemporary discussions of causal determinism (and its compatibility with moral responsibility) do not distinguish between causal determinism and necessitating causal determinism. The importance of distinguishing these two notions in understanding Aristotle's views was brought to scholarly attention by Sorabji 1980.

[2] For arguments that Aristotle endorses causal determinism and compatibilism, see Everson 1990, Meyer 1994. For arguments against this view, see Mesch 2013.

[3] A vast literature on this issue was called forth by Frankfurt 1971.

[4] Attention was drawn to this sort of incompatibilism by McKenna 2001.

which causal determinism may threaten moral responsibility. Focusing on the first naturally involves an investigation of Aristotle's moral psychology and philosophy of action.[5] Focusing on the second naturally leads to a consideration of causal necessity more broadly, without special reference to psychological determinism. In this chapter I shall be concerned with the second way causal determinism may threaten moral responsibility. In particular, I will be concerned with the question whether Aristotle's theory of causation commits him to the view that all events are causally necessitated. My focus will be on a notion that plays an important role in standard treatments of causal determinism: that of a causal chain. Now while the notion that causal occurrences link together to form causal chains arises naturally in Humean causal theories, that notion is much less at home in Aristotle's causal theory. There are, however, at least two passages in which Aristotle does consider the possibility of something like a causal chain extending from the remote past to the present and beyond: *Physics* VIII.5 and *Metaphysics* VI.3. An examination of these will show that while Aristotle does hold that there is one type of causal chain that is necessary from beginning to end, these chains always *do* have a definite beginning and end. There can be no necessary causal nexus of this type extending from the indefinite past to the indefinite future. These passages also show that Aristotle recognizes a second type of causal chain, and that causal chains of this type are in principle extendible indefinitely towards the past and the future. But the links in this type of causal chain are not necessary; so chains of this sort will not support a universal necessary causal nexus, either. Nonetheless, as we shall see, Aristotle's causal theory does seem to commit him to the claim that, given complete knowledge of the state of the world at a given time, one could predict all subsequent events. It is the way he grounds causal necessity in the working of causal powers that allows him to deny, nonetheless, that all events are causally necessitated. If we take compatibilism to be the thesis that moral responsibility is compatible with all actions being causally *necessitated*, Aristotle's general theory does not, in conjunction with his recognition of moral responsibility, commit him to compatibilism.

8.1   Efficient Causation and Necessity

Do Aristotelian efficient causes necessitate their effects?[6] To answer this question, we need to examine the fundamental features of Aristotle's

---

[5] For recent discussions focusing on moral psychology, see Echeñique 2012 and Bobzien 2014.
[6] Sorabji 1980, 3–44 maintains that outside of *Metaphysics* VI.3, Aristotle holds that *per se* efficient causes do not necessitate their effects. Stein 2012 argues that they do necessitate their effects, though he does not believe that this in itself commits Aristotle to causal determinism.

theory of efficient causation. A central difference between Aristotle's theory and Humean treatments of causation is what they take to be their primary *explanandum*. For the Humean, what is to be explained is why things are different at one time than they were at an earlier time. Aristotle, on the other hand, is primarily concerned to explain the *process* by which things become different from what they were, where this process is not reducible to a simple succession of differing states of affairs.[7] Furthermore, Aristotle conceives of this process as one by which something comes to be actually *F* from a previous state of being only potentially *F*. While attaining the final state is, in some sense, the point of the process, nonetheless it is the process itself that Aristotle considers the primary effect that the cause brings about. This process is (in the standard case) constituted by the joint activation of two powers:[8] the patient power of a thing to undergo that change, and the agent power of something else to bring about that change (typically grounded in the agent's already itself being actually *F*). When the agent power of a thing is exercised on the corresponding patient power in something else, the latter's power to be made *F* is activated. While the exercise of the one is the cause of the activity of the other, the cause and the effect are nonetheless simultaneous. The exercise of the agent power keeps pace, as it were, with the process it brings about; the two start and stop together (*Ph.* 195b16–20). To use an Aristotelian example: the house-builder's exercising of her power to build a house is the cause of the planks and bricks' being built into a house, and coincides with it.

That a cause necessarily brings about its effect follows trivially, then, from Aristotle's un-Humean notion that the primary cause and effect are processes (or features of a single process) that cannot exist apart from each other.[9] A more substantive question arises when we consider the start of such a simultaneous causing-and-being-caused. When something that is a potential cause – i.e. possessing an as yet unactivated agent power – comes into contact with something that may potentially suffer an effect – i.e.

---

[7] An efficient cause is, in the first instance, the first source of *change* or *coming to rest* (*Ph.* 194b29–30). On this see Tuozzo 2014. The centrality of process in Aristotle's theory (and the difference between Aristotle's theory and contemporary causal power theories in this regard) is emphasized by Marmodoro 2018.

[8] For reasons of space, I will here consider only cases of 'transeunt' causation, where the agent is distinct from the patient. Aristotle's analysis of 'immanent' causation, where the agent and the patient are identical, is in large part parallel to his analysis of transeunt causation, since he distinguishes distinct agent and patient parts operative in a thing that changes itself. On the parallels, see Coope 2015.

[9] In *Physics* III.3 Aristotle says that the activities of the agent and patient powers are 'one activity, but not the same in being' (202b8–9). For recent discussions of this passage, see Charles 2015, Marmodoro 2007, and Coope 2005.

possessing the relevant as yet unactivated patient power – does the one necessarily cause, and the other undergo, the process in question?[10]

It has not always been agreed that Aristotle believes they do.[11] Typically in these contexts Aristotle speaks of a sort of conditional necessity: when the two entities with these powers meet, the one must act and the other be acted on, 'if nothing prevents'. This is because Aristotle is keenly aware of possible defeaters: the paper may have the power to be burnt, and the fire the power to burn it, but if the paper is soaking wet when the two meet, no burning will take place. But while Aristotle typically does append the proviso 'if nothing prevents', in *Metaphysics* IX.5 he indicates that this is only needed when we are satisfied with a rough, rather than a precise, understanding of the relevant powers. When we do have a precise under-standing of the relevant powers, we see that their interaction is necessary, full stop.

In *Metaphysics* IX.5 Aristotle distinguishes between non-rational powers (such as fire's power to heat) and powers 'with a rational formula (*meta logou*)', such as the craft of medicine. He discusses the necessity involved in the exercise of each of these two kinds of power as follows:[12]

> That which is powerful (*to dunaton*) has the power to do something, at a certain time, in a certain way, and everything else that must be present in the definition (*en tōi diorismōi*) ... As regards [non-rational] powers, when the agent and the patient come together in the way in which they have their power (*hōs dunantai*), it is necessary (*anankē*) that the one act, the other be affected ...
>
> [But as regards the rational powers, desire is necessary.] Therefore everything whose power is in accordance with a rational formula, when it desires that for which it has the power and in the way that it has it, must act. And it has the power [in that way] when the patient is present and is in such-and-such a condition. If not, it will not be able to act.
>
> To add the qualification 'if nothing external prevents' is not further necessary; for it has the power in the way in which this is a power of acting, and it is this not in all circumstances but in certain ones, among which will be the exclusion of external hindrances; for they will be excluded by some

---

[10] For the distinction between this question of causal necessity and the case where the cause and effect are simultaneous, see Stein 2012.

[11] Kelsey 2004, 130 takes Aristotle's doctrine that sublunary processes occur only 'for the most part' trivially to entail that *per se* causes do not necessitate their effects.

[12] This passage is often cited by philosophers who wish to deny that causes necessitate their effects as an example of the position they oppose. See, for example, Anscombe 1973, 64 and Anjum and Mumford 2018, 33.

of the things present in the definition (*en tōi diorismōi*). (1047b35–1048a21)[13]

Aristotle here first makes the general point that any power is a power not simply to do something, but to do something under certain conditions. Those conditions must be stated in the definition of the power; evidently, they count as part of its essence. Aristotle goes on to apply this general point to both rational and non-rational powers. When things with corresponding non-rational agent and patient powers come together in the way required for the exercise of those powers (as specified in their definitions), those powers are necessarily exercised. The case of rational powers is more complicated: one of the conditions for their exercise is the possessor of the craft's *desiring* to exercise it. But when that condition (along with all the others) is satisfied, the exercise of these powers, too, is necessary. Aristotle concludes by reiterating that, on his view, the essences of powers can be so precisely specified that an account of their causal relations needs no *ceteris paribus* clause, no 'if nothing external prevents' proviso. When precisely matching agent and patient powers meet, the process for which they are the powers necessarily occurs.

8.2 Causal Chains I: Proper or *per se* Causation

We may now ask whether Aristotle's endorsement of causal necessity at this local level leads him to endorse a universal necessitating causal determinism. Do all occurrences of causation link together to form a causal chain or nexus, such that any earlier link on the chain necessitates all that comes after? As mentioned earlier, causal chains are quite at home in a Humean causal framework: if a cause is conceived as an event or state of affairs that gives rise to another, then there is no difficulty in viewing a given state of affairs as a link in a chain that extends far into the past and into the future. But things are very different for Aristotle. When something with the power to cause something to become *F* meets something with the power to be made *F*, the process of the latter's becoming *F* takes place, and it ceases when it has become *F*. The state of affairs of its being *F* is not, taken just by itself, of a sort to give rise to some further process. Nonetheless, there are contexts in which a further process does arise, and we have something like a causal chain. Aristotle discusses two different ways in which such a causal chain can occur in *Physics* VIII.5.

---

[13] All translations (modified when necessary) are taken from the Revised Oxford Translation.

In *Physics* VIII.4 Aristotle argues that everything that moves is caused to move by something. In chapter 5 he mounts a complicated series of arguments to show that everything that moves must ultimately derive its motion from an unmoved mover. Since it is manifest that many things are proximately set in motion by something else that is itself in motion, Aristotle takes his first task to be to argue that this cannot be reiterated infinitely: going backwards, we must eventually find something that causes motion without itself being in motion. Aristotle starts his argument by distinguishing two different ways something in motion can give rise to motion in something else:

> All things that are in motion [are] moved by something. Now this may come about in either of two ways, [A] either not in virtue of the mover itself, but in virtue of something else which the mover moves (*di' heteron ho kinei to kinoun*),[14] or [B] in virtue of itself (*di' auto*). Further, in the latter case, either the mover immediately precedes the last thing, or there may be one or more intermediate links: e.g. the stick moves the stone and is moved by the hand, which again is moved by the person. (256a1–8)

This passage in effect distinguishes two different kinds of link that an Aristotelian causal chain can have. These correspond to what is elsewhere called proper or *per se* (*kath' hauto*) causation (marked 'B') and accidental (*kata sumbebēkos*) causation (marked 'A').[15] *Per se* causation is the sort of causation we have analysed above: something with an agent power brings about a change in something with the corresponding patient power. In the text just quoted, Aristotle points out that sometimes there are intermediaries through which the mover exercises its power to change the other thing. Exactly how we are to understand these intermediaries is an interesting question; sometimes, as in the hand-stick-stone example Aristotle gives here, they seem simply to extend the range of what the initial mover might have done on its own; in other cases, such as the doctor curing a patient by administering wine,[16] intermediaries of some sort or another

---

[14] My translation of 256a5 differs from the usual one; I hope the interpretation that follows will serve as an implicit justification. I provide an explicit justification in Tuozzo 2017. Note also that the passage quoted includes the last line of *Physics* VIII 4.

[15] The presence of these two kinds of causation in the passage quoted has not been generally recognized by scholars, probably because Aristotle does not use the usual terms for these kinds of causation. Instead he uses *di' auto* ('in virtue of itself') and *ou di' auto to kinoun* ('not in virtue of the mover itself'). When Aristotle turns to discuss the second sort of link, he uses the standard term, *kata sumbebēkos* (256b5–6); when he turns to the first, he refers to it as *mē kata sumbebēkos, all' ex anankēs* (256b28). A full discussion of these terms must be postponed to another occasion.

[16] See *Gen. corr.* 1.6, 324a29–30.

seem indispensable.[17] Similarly, sometimes the intermediaries seem to act simultaneously with the initial mover (man-stick-stone), sometimes they continue to act after having been set in motion by it (doctor-wine-patient). But in all of these cases, the agent power of the first mover is exercised on the thing that has the corresponding patient power through the mediation of intervening factors.

We have, then, a causal chain that is, in some cases at least, temporally extended, where the links are governed by proper or *per se* causation. Does Aristotle think that every step in the chain is necessary, so that, when the initial mover exercises its power, the final thing moved will necessarily be moved? Certainly in the case of an extended causal chain, there are many opportunities for something to interfere; hence Aristotle typically adds the proviso, 'if nothing prevents'. Nonetheless, as we saw above, Aristotle thinks that the definition of an agent power specifies the conditions that are sufficient for that power's going into action and bringing about that of which it is the power. There is no reason to think that he has a different view when the exercise of that agent power involves intermediaries.[18] Aristotelian powers are powers to produce a process that terminates in something's being *F*. And that process has a definite shape, which may involve distinct stages in which various instruments transmit the causative influence of the mover. Surely these features of the process are grounded in the essence of the power, and would be specified in its definition. The necessity that Aristotle grants the *per se* exercise of causal powers in *Metaphysics* IX.5 applies to cases with intermediaries, too.

Aristotle does recognize, then, something like a causal chain whose beginning necessitates both the intermediate stages and its final result. But as this formulation itself suggests, these chains seem by their very nature to be of only finite length. For the status of the intermediates as links in a causal chain is conceptually dependent on there being a first mover and a last thing moved. Instead of simply relying on this point (which might seem to beg the question), in our chapter Aristotle offers a different, more complicated metaphysical argument for the claim that causal chains of this sort cannot be of infinite length (256b27–257a14). This argument has not been well regarded by commentators – wrongly, as I think. Key to understanding it properly is keeping in mind that an Aristotelian efficient *per se*

---

[17] On the obscurities in Aristotle's view of the role of instruments in causation, see Coope 2007, 128 n. 26. For some of the ways medieval and early modern Aristotelians addressed these issues, see Menn 2000, 129–33.

[18] Indeed, Aristotle emphasizes that the 'if nothing hinders' proviso is not needed in the case of the exercise of crafts (powers *meta logou*, 1048a3), which certainly often involves instruments.

cause is the cause, not just of a new state of affairs, but of a determinate ordered process leading to that state of affairs.

The hypothesis under consideration here is that every proper cause of a change is itself moved by something else, and that its being moved that way is not accidental to its own causal efficacy, but rather essential to it. That is, when something causes something else to undergo a specific change, its doing so requires that it itself undergo a specific change. In another context, Aristotle provides an illustration of a finite series of this sort: an animal moves its limbs because some of the internal parts change size, and that change of size is itself the result of a qualitative change in their temperature, which is itself the result of some other change.[19] Each stage in this sequence must come about if the next is to do so, and all are oriented towards producing the animal's movement. Now the hypothesis under consideration here is that a causal chain of this sort may extend indefinitely in both directions: there is always something further towards which each change is oriented, and each stage itself is brought about by a process oriented towards it.

Aristotle asks us to consider two possible ways in which one link in such a sequence may be related to its successor:

> The mover, insofar as it is in motion, must be moved either with the same kind of motion [as it causes], or with a different kind – either that which is heating, I mean, is itself becoming hot, [and] that which is making healthy, becoming healthy, . . . or else that which is making healthy is in process of locomotion, and that which is causing locomotion is being increased. (256b31–3)

Aristotle treats the first of these two options as clearly absurd, and spends most of the argument showing how the second option reduces to the first. But understanding his argument against the second option requires a clear understanding of why Aristotle finds the first one absurd. He explains that absurdity as follows:

> But it is evident that this is impossible. For we must apply this to the very lowest species into which motion can be divided: e.g. we must say that if someone is teaching some lesson in geometry, he is also being taught that same lesson in geometry, and that if he is throwing he is also being thrown in just the same manner. (256b34–257a3)

The oddness of Aristotle's examples here might make one suspect that he is stacking the deck. The core of his argument can perhaps be better grasped

[19] See *De motu an.* 701b13–16.

if we return to the example he started with. Why is it absurd that a thing should be heating something else up in virtue of itself being heated up? Surely this happens all the time – the pot heats the water in virtue of the fire's heating *it*. But the hypothesis here is that *all* cases of heating up are like this. So we are to imagine an infinite string of causes, each of which is heating up something in virtue of being itself heated up. But then there is nothing actually hot throughout the entire string of causes; so no heating-up can get under way.[20] As Aristotle puts it:

> But this is of course impossible; for it involves the consequence that one who is teaching is learning whereas teaching necessarily implies *possessing* knowledge, and learning *not* possessing it. (257a12–14)

I suggest that, on its own terms, this argument is a strong one. As we saw earlier, for a thing to have the agent power to bring it about that something else become *F* typically involves its being, itself, already actually *F*.[21] A thing cannot both be only potentially *F* (as it must be if it is being moved) and actually *F* (as it must be if it is causing motion).

Aristotle approaches the second option as follows:

> Or if we reject this assumption we must say that one kind of motion comes from another, e.g. that that which is causing locomotion is being increased, that which is causing this increase is altered by something else, and that which is causing this alteration is suffering some different kind of motion. (257a3–6)

It is important to remember that this sequence is supposed to be a sequence of proper causation, which brings with it the implication of a necessarily ordered process. The hypothesis is that whatever causes locomotion does so in virtue of being increased, and that nothing can cause locomotion without being increased. A hypothesis of this sort, as Aristotle himself later points out, is 'fantastic' (*plasmatōdes*): 'It is absurd that that which can cause alteration should necessarily (*ex anankēs*) be capable of being increased' (257a23–5). Nonetheless, something like this is required if we are to have a sequence of nothing but *per se* causes, and its fantastic nature is

---

[20] To put what I think is the same argument another way: the cause is supposed to explain how something comes to be *F*. If we say that the cause brings it about that something becomes *F* in virtue of itself coming to be *F*, we fall into an infinite regress.

[21] Aristotle does recognize that there are exceptions to what has been called the 'causal synonymy principle', i.e. the principle that a cause possesses in actuality the property that it causes something else to acquire (see *Metaph.* 1034b16–19, *Gen. corr.* 320b17–21). I cannot here discuss whether the current argument depends on the universal applicability of this principle. Coope 2015, 250–5 argues that the parallel argument in connection with self-motion (at 257a31–b17) does not.

not enough to rule it out of court; Aristotle needs to show that it is impossible. He does so by reducing it to the first option. The passage quoted above continues as follows:

> But the series must stop somewhere, since the kinds of motion are limited; and if we say that the series bends back, i.e. that that which is causing alteration is in process of locomotion, we do no more than if we had said at the outset that that which is causing locomotion is in process of locomotion, and that one who is teaching is being taught; for it is clear that everything that is moved is also moved by the mover that is further back in the series – in fact it is more (*mallon*) moved by the earlier of the movers. But this is of course impossible. (257a6–12)

An important premise in this argument is the perhaps enigmatic claim that when something is moved as a result of a series of (proper) causes, the earlier a cause is in this series, the 'more' (or, as the Revised Oxford Translation puts it, the 'more strictly') it causes that thing's motion. Aristotle had established a version of this principle for proper causal series earlier in the chapter, when discussing the sequence person-hand-stick-stone:

> Now we say that the thing is moved both by the last and by the first of the movers, but more (*mallon*) by the first, since the first moves the last, whereas the last does not move the first, and the first will move the thing without the last, but the last will not move it without the first: e.g. the stick will not move anything unless it is itself moved by the person. (256a8–13)

In our present passage Aristotle modifies the principle to speak of the 'earlier' rather than the 'first' mover, since the hypothesis under consideration denies that there is a first mover. But the justification for both versions of the principle is the same: in a sequence connected by proper causation, the causal efficacy of the later members derives from the causal action of the earlier ones, which are, accordingly, more strictly the causes of what the later members cause.

Besides this priority principle, Aristotle's argument also relies on the claim that there are only a finite number of different kinds of change.[22] If we grant this premise, then in the series of *per se* causes extending back from a given change (say, heating), we will eventually find one which is itself undergoing a change of that very sort. This is no different, Aristotle

---

[22] Aristotle does not provide a justification for this claim here. It presumably follows from ontological commitments not specific to his causal theory.

remarks, from positing the same sort of change as the immediate cause of the change in question, which he has already shown to be impossible.

How good is Aristotle's argument? Ross thinks not very; if *A* heats something up, and does so in virtue of itself being moved in some other fashion by *B*, which is moved in yet another fashion by *C*, which is itself heated up by *D*, then while *D* may be a remote cause of *A*'s heating something up, it does not do so *by heating A up*; and that, Ross maintains, is what reducing this scenario to the first option would require.[23] But in fact the reduction does not require that. In a sequence of proper causes, the later can serve as a cause only in virtue of its being moved by the earlier. The hypothesis was that we could explain the efficacy of *A*'s heating something up by assuming (fantastically) that it derived that efficacy from the fact that it is itself undergoing some different change.[24] Aristotle argues that, ultimately, it will have to derive that efficacy from some case of heating; but then that itself will need to derive its efficacy, ultimately, from some yet earlier case of heating. Just as in the first scenario, we are referred ever further backwards for an explanation of how something manages to heat something else up, and never reach a satisfactory answer. Thus neither the first nor the second way of constructing an infinite chain of proper causes turns out to be metaphysically possible.

8.3   Causal Chains II: Accidental Causation

We have considered causal chains linked by proper or *per se* causation; but Aristotle also recognizes causal chains linked by accidental causation. When he distinguishes accidental from proper causation at 256a4–5, he characterizes the former as occurring when a thing is moved 'not on account of the mover itself, but on account of something else that the mover moves'. This rather opaque description can be made clear by an example: a dog's running may be the cause of the house's burning down – not on account of itself, but on account of the candlestick it upset. An accidental cause is something that brings it about that a proper cause is in a position to exercise its power to cause change, but does so by means of

---

[23] See Ross 1998, 700.
[24] This does not entail that all the changes throughout the causal chain occur simultaneously. The *per se* causal process that is an animal's locomotion, or the performance of a craft, comprises temporally successive stages. In fact, one way all the world's changes could constitute an infinite chain connected by *per se* causation would be for all of them to constitute one single exercise of some super-craft that has always been at work and will never reach its end. Change the story so that the world-process will eventually reach its end, and we have something like the Stoic picture. See the conclusion of this chapter.

a motion that is not itself part of a process directed towards that subsequent change. Now in *Physics* VIII.5 Aristotle is concerned to show that no infinite causal chain can account for the world's being eternally in motion. As we have seen, there are metaphysical reasons why there can be no infinite *per se* causal chain. The only other option, then, would be an infinite chain governed by accidental causation, which involves no such metaphysical impossibility. But just because the links in such a chain are accidental, there can be no chain of this sort that *necessarily* continues indefinitely. So such a chain cannot account for the necessarily eternal motion of the cosmos.

Or so Aristotle briskly argues at *Physics* 256b7–13. He gives more detailed attention to causal sequences of this sort in the other major passage where he treats causal chains: *Metaphysics* VI 3. In this latter passage he approaches the question from a different angle: he asks whether there are any cases of accidental causation at all. That is to say, he asks whether all cases of causation are proper or *per se*. He does not here adduce considerations of the sort he used to argue against an infinite chain of *per se* causes in *Physics* VIII.5. Rather, he appeals to the fact that *per se* causes necessitate their effects – a doctrine for which (as we have seen) he argues in *Metaphysics* IX.5. Bringing our earlier analysis of *Metaphysics* IX.5 to bear on *Metaphysics* VI.3 will help us understand why Aristotle denies that accidental causes necessitate their effects.

In *Metaphysics* VI.2 Aristotle argues that accidental being is not the sort of thing that can be known by any science. In one of his arguments he points out that a productive craft brings about many features of its product that are not, strictly speaking, within the purview of that craft. Each craft knows how to work its materials so as to achieve its end. But every product of a craft also ends up with myriad features that were not aimed at by the craft, and which the product either inherits from features of the matter it is made from, or which devolve upon it from the relations in which it comes to stand to other things when it is produced. One of the examples Aristotle gives is that of a pastry chef who, in making something tasty, produces something that is also healthful (1027a3–5). Such accidental features of the product are accidental to the causal process that produces them; so Aristotle remarks that 'of things which are or come to be by accident, the cause also is accidental' (1027a7–8). Aristotle makes the same point a different way when he denies that there is 'coming to be and passing away [of] things that exist accidentally' (1026b22–4). What causes accidental being is in process of bringing something *else* about, while there is no process at all directed towards the accidental being it brings about. Since coming-to-be is a process, accidental beings start existing without coming to be.[25]

This explanation of accidental being assumes that there are accidental causes; in *Metaphysics* VI.3 Aristotle provides an argument that there really are accidental causes. He starts by describing such causes as causes that 'are generable and perishable, without coming to be and passing away' (1027a29–30), which simply reiterates the point that accidental causes are not themselves part of a process leading to what they bring about. If there were no accidental causes, Aristotle continues, then every *per se* cause would itself have a *per se* cause. And this, he argues, would have the unacceptable result that everything happens of necessity (*ex anankēs*).

Aristotle's argument for this result depends crucially on the feature of proper causation I have highlighted throughout this essay: proper causes do not just bring about a new state of affairs, but rather bring about a determinate process that leads to that state of affairs. When there are various intermediate steps in such a process, they are ordered in a definite way, so that the overall process has a relatively fixed structure. Therefore if we know that some event or occurrence is produced by a proper causal sequence, we can in principle deduce the stages of the process that led up to it. If everything that occurs is the product of such a sequence, then we can trace back the causal history of anything that occurs (or will occur) into the distant past. Thus a world in which there is nothing but *per se* causation is one in which all events are linked together in a necessary causal nexus. Aristotle begins with a general statement of this argument:

> For otherwise all things will be of necessity, since that which is being generated or destroyed must have a cause which is not accidentally its cause. Will *A* exist or not? It will if *B* happens; and if not, not. And *B* will exist if *C* happens. And thus if time is constantly subtracted from a limited extent of time, one will obviously come to the present. (1027a30–4)

He proceeds to illustrate this general argument with an example:

> This man, then, will die by violence, if he goes out; and he will do this if he gets thirsty; and he will get thirsty if something else happens; and thus we shall come to that which is now present, or to some past event. For instance, he will go out if he gets thirsty; and he will get thirsty if he is eating spicy

---

[25] Polansky and Kuczewski 1988 point out that this does not mean that accidental beings come to be instantaneously, as the tradition has it. It may well be that the pastry becomes progressively more healthful as the pastry chef adds her ingredients. The point is that this change is accidental to the causal process in play: the making of something tasty. So the pastry's gradually becoming more healthful does not constitute a process towards being healthful.

food; and this is either the case or not; so that he will of necessity die, or of necessity not die. And similarly if one jumps over to past events, the same account will hold good . . . Clearly, then, the process goes back to a certain starting point, but this no longer points to something further. (1027b1–5, 13–14)

If there are no causes other than proper causes, then, if a particular sort of action is to occur at some time in the future, the nature of the process leading up to it from the present is quite determinate. To determine whether the action will take place, we need only check to see if the state of affairs that would be needed to bring it about is now occurring. Such a procedure is not available for things that have accidental causes. To use Aristotle's example from *Physics* ii.5: there are very many causes that could be responsible for my debtor's showing up, luckily for me, at the market-place when I am there. In the present passage it is only because we are assuming that the person's going out has a *per se* cause that we may stipulate that, if it happens at all, it is caused by his getting thirsty. But of course 'going out of the house' is in fact an accidental description of the action, whose causally relevant description here is something like 'going to get water'. And there are indefinitely many different proper causal sequences in which his exiting the house could figure, and in which it would have different causally relevant descriptions. It is only the hypothesis that there are no accidental causes that enables us to assume one particular cause of his going out.

Nor is the argument weakened if it is true that sometimes there are alternative paths which a proper causal process might follow. And surely it is true: it may well be, for example, that the administration of one or the other of two drugs might equally well cure someone suffering from a particular disease. But as long as there are only a finite number of ways the process could go, we could in principle check whether any of them is under way. And I think it is safe to say that Aristotle holds that there can only be a finite number of such alternatives. The nature of the projected effect necessarily determines what can bring it about. And for Aristotle, I venture to say, the number of options so determined will always be finite.[26]

It might be objected that (to take the simplest case) if, for event *B* to occur in the future, event *A* must be occurring now, and event *A* is in fact

---

[26] Aristotle insists that a product would require the same determinate process even when considering impossible hypothetical conditions: 'if a house were one of the things that come about by nature, it would come about *in the same way as it does now* by art' (*Ph.* ii.8, 199a12–13).

occurring now, it does not follow that *B* will occur. Cannot something interfere with the causal process now under way?[27] Such an objection, however, underestimates the radicalness of the hypothetical scenario under consideration. The only thing that could interfere with a proper causal sequence would be another proper causal sequence that intersected with it. But the causal influence that the interfering chain would have on the interfered chain would be a case of accidental causation: it would be an effect towards which the interfering chain was not a process. And our hypothesis is that *nothing* happens without there being a process aiming towards it.

Aristotle has a reasonable argument, then, for the claim that if there were no accidental causes, all things would happen from necessity. But one might wonder whether adding in accidental causes makes things any better. For as we have just noted, accidental causes are always, themselves, part of a proper causal sequence – even though that sequence is not aiming at what it accidentally causes. So let us imagine a Laplacean demon in Aristotle's world, a demon that knows the location, powers, and properties of all substances at a given time *t*. Since the demon knows how all the agent and patient powers in the world are situated with respect to each other at time *t*, it will also know what causal processes are under way then. And since such processes unfold necessarily unless interfered with, the demon will know how each causal sequence will proceed until it crosses another. So the demon will also know when they will cross, and, since it knows all their causal powers (and not just those in play in their original causal sequences), the demon will know what new causal sequences will be initiated when they do cross. It may well take a demonic intelligence to work all this out; but those epistemic demands do not affect the metaphysical necessity (if such it be) of what the demon knows. In a word, since accidental causation is itself dependent on *per se* causation, why does it not inherit the latter's necessity?[28]

We may find an answer to these questions by returning to Aristotle's account of the necessity of proper causal sequences in *Metaphysics* IX.5. There Aristotle argues that in describing the necessity with which

---

[27] This worry is raised by Kelsey 2004, who goes to some lengths to disarm it.

[28] Mesch 2013 seems to maintain that taking the view of the Laplacean demon is somehow un-Aristotelian (123) and is tantamount to rejecting Aristotle's theory of accidental causation (125–6). I do not think that this is so; there would still be a distinction between how a *per se* cause brings about its proper effects and how in doing so it brings together causal powers that are irrelevant to its own causal activity. Aristotle does not ban the non-perspectival view, but thinks that, even from that point of view, accidentally caused events are not necessitated.

something with an agent power acts on something with the corresponding patient power, we need include no *ceteris paribus* clause. The essences of these powers can be finitely specifiable, and those definitions will tell us all we need to know about the conditions under which the powers will be exercised. Many philosophers today, chastened by the failure of contemporary efforts to produce counterfactual analyses of causation, think Aristotle's confidence misplaced.[29] We can, in any case, articulate the grounds of his confidence as follows. A causal process has a definite structure, the nature of which determines the specific ways it could be interfered with. These specific ways are finite in number, and can be ascertained; indeed, ascertaining them is part of what understanding the essence of the causal power is. Once we understand the causal power in this way, we will see that what possesses such a power does indeed always do that which it has the (precise) power to do. Given this reasoning, I suggest, it is understandable that Aristotle thinks sequences involving accidental causes are not necessary. For if one proper causal process is connected with another through accidental causation, the combined changes do not constitute a single process whose enabling conditions could reasonably be thought to be grounded in the nature of the agent power active in the first causal process. If the necessity of a proper causal sequence is rooted in the essence of the causal power that initiates it, then this necessity does not extend to the causal sequences it may accidentally trigger. For they reflect nothing of the essence of the power initiating the first sequence.

8.4   Conclusion

Metaphysics IX.5 shows that Aristotelian causal necessity is nothing more nor less than the necessity that agent and patient powers should become activated when the conditions of that activation, set by their essences, are met. In *Physics* VIII.5 Aristotle argues that all the processes that take place in the world cannot constitute a universal causal nexus governed by proper causation of this sort. In *Metaphysics* VI.3 he argues that if all events *were* linked together by this sort of causation, then everything would occur 'of necessity', which conclusion he rejects out of hand. The only way in which

---

[29] As noted above, Anjum and Mumford 2018 cite *Metaphysics* 1048a16–21 to illustrate the (as they see it) mistaken view that statements of causal relations could in principle dispense with *ceteris paribus* clauses. Moline 1975 reflects a very different philosophical climate: he praises the doctrine of 1048a16–21 for eschewing the 'escape clauses' that would 'render dispositional talk beyond refutation' (253). This article appeared just as the project of giving precise counterfactual analyses of causation had been inaugurated by Lewis 1973.

an indefinitely long causal chain is possible is if finite proper causal sequences are linked together by merely accidental causation. And even if a Laplacean demon could predict everything that occurs in such an indefinitely long chain, the links of accidental causation ensure that not every event is causally necessitated. If compatibilism asserts the compatibility of moral responsibility with all events' being causally necessitated, Aristotle's causal theory does not require him to endorse compatibilism.

We may feel uneasy at Aristotle's refusal to ascribe necessity to what is, in principle, predictable. It may be useful in closing to note that the Stoics, who endorse causal determinism and explicitly embrace compatibilism, agree with Aristotle in associating causal necessity with determinate, ordered process. They too recognize that local causal processes intersect, thereby setting off a new causal process of which the triggering event does not itself constitute a part. Unlike Aristotle, however, they view the results of such intersections as necessitated. But that is because they hold that the local processes and their intersections themselves together constitute, at a higher level, a single, ordered causal process: for nature as a whole is a 'craftsmanlike [thing] that proceeds towards generation *along a path* (*via, hodōi*)'.[30]

---

[30] See *Stoicorum veterum fragmenta* 1, 171, 172. For a recent discussion of Stoic views on causation, see Hankinson 2014.

CHAPTER 9

Aristotle on Nature, Deliberation, and Purposiveness

Ursula Coope

In *Physics* II.8, Aristotle draws an analogy between craft (*technē*) and nature: nature, like craft, is the type of cause that is 'for the sake of something' (*heneka tou*, 198b10–11; 199b32–3). He considers – and dismisses – an objection to this analogy. The objection is that craft productions involve deliberation in a way that natural processes do not, and that this undermines the alleged analogy. Perhaps processes of craft production are only 'for the sake of something' because they originate in deliberating agents. If so, then this gives us no reason to think that natural processes will similarly be for the sake of something. In response, Aristotle says that it would be absurd to maintain that a thing cannot have come to be 'for the sake of something unless the mover is seen to have deliberated' (199b26–8). In fact, he claims, even craft does not deliberate (199b28).

Aristotle's response to this imagined objection is puzzling.[1] What does he mean by the claim that craft does not deliberate? How is this claim compatible with the manifest fact that craftsmen, in order to exercise their crafts successfully, often need to think about what to do? Equally puzzling, however, is the fact that Aristotle takes *this* to be the objection that needs answering here. It might seem that there is a more pressing objection he should have considered. This more pressing objection would come from an opponent who claimed that a process could only be end-directed if it originated in desire and cognition (where 'cognition' might include either perception or rational cognition). Such an opponent would agree that nest building and web spinning are end-directed processes, and that when

The earliest version of this chapter was written for a conference at St Andrews in honour of Sarah Broadie's seventieth birthday. I presented later versions at the Humboldt University in Berlin and at University College London. On all these occasions, I benefited a great deal from questions raised by the audience. In particular, I would like to thank Christopher Shields for pressing me to think more about Aristotle's odd counterfactual claim that if the shipbuilding craft were in the wood, it would operate just as nature does. I would also like to thank Barbara Sattler for her comments on the penultimate draft.
[1] This chapter is a response to the thought-provoking discussion of these puzzles in Broadie 2007b.

swallows build their nests and spiders spin their webs, they 'make things not by craft, and without having enquired or deliberated' (199a20–1). But this opponent would dispute Aristotle's claim that *processes of growth* can be end-directed, given that such processes do not stem from desire or from any kind of cognition of the end that is supposedly aimed at. Does Aristotle's answer to the objection from deliberation provide any hints as to how he might respond to this more challenging opponent?

I shall argue that Aristotle's remarks about purposiveness and deliberation hint at an interesting defence of natural teleology. In doing so, however, they suggest a puzzle about the kind of purposiveness we ordinarily take to be less problematic: the purposiveness involved in many ordinary, non-craft-based human intentional actions.

9.1 Craft and Nature: The Context in *Physics* II.8

What exactly does Aristotle mean by the claim that nature is one of the causes that is 'for the sake of something' (198b10–11; 199b32–3)? Earlier in *Physics* II, he says that the type of cause that is 'for the sake of something' (*heneka tou*) is an end (*telos*, II.3, 194b32–5) and that nature is an end (*telos*) and what something is for (*hou heneka*, II.3, 194a28–9). This might suggest that his aim, in II.8, is to defend the view that nature is a final cause. However, there would be something slightly odd in invoking the craft analogy in defence of *this* claim. As he also says earlier in *Physics* II, craft is *not* the final cause of craft production (whereas nature is the final cause of natural processes): 'doctoring is not a process aiming at the craft of medicine, but aiming at health; for it is necessary that doctoring is from the craft of medicine, not towards it' (II.1, 193b14–16). In spite of this difference, there is an important way in which nature and craft are alike: both are efficient causes of processes (and states) that are for the sake of something. I take it that this is the point he is making when he claims in II.8 that nature is like craft in being a cause for the sake of something.

In *Physics* II.8, Aristotle makes two positive claims about the role of purposiveness in nature:

(i)   The 'for something' is present in natural things (i.e. natural things are the way they are, and develop as they do, because being this way, and developing in this way, is good for them) (199a7–8).

(ii) In an end-directed natural process, (a) the earlier stages come about for the sake of the later stages, and (b) these stages come about in this way *by nature* (i.e. the causal role of nature explains the fact that the earlier stages come about for the sake of the later ones) (199a11–12).[2]

He defends (i) with his argument against Empedocles in 198b10–199a8. He defends (ii) by invoking the analogy between nature and craft. Thus, in 199a12–15, he argues that if a process of craft production (such as house-building) were to come about by nature, it would come about in just the way that it does in fact come about by craft, and that if things that come about by nature were to come about also by craft, they would come about just as they do in fact come about by nature.[3] From this, he concludes that the relation of later stages to earlier stages in a natural process is just like the relation of later stages to earlier stages in processes of craft production (199a18–20). In both types of process, the earlier stages occur for the sake of the later ones and, moreover, the causal role of *nature* in explaining why natural processes are structured in this way is analogous to the causal role of *craft* in explaining why processes of craft production are structured in this way.[4]

To claim that a natural thing develops as it does (in such a way that the earlier stages are for the sake of the later stages) *because of that natural thing's nature* is to rule out various other alternative views. One alternative, for instance, would be to hold that natural things develop in this way because they are themselves the products of craftsmanship (perhaps, of a divine craftsman). Another alternative would be to hold that a natural thing develops in this way, not because of its own specific nature, but rather because of some source of change that belongs to the cosmos as a whole.[5] If Aristotle can show that there is an analogy between craft and nature, this

---

[2] There are two respects in which (ii) goes beyond (i). (i) says generally that there is end-directedness in natural things. (iia) makes the claim that there is a *specific type* of end-directedness in natural things: in a natural process, the earlier stages are for the sake of the later stages. (iib) goes still further: it makes a claim about the role of nature in explaining the claim made in (iia).

[3] In support of this latter claim, he points out that certain crafts (such as medicine) attempt to imitate or improve upon what normally happens by nature (199a15–17).

[4] For my understanding of these lines, I am indebted to Kelsey (2011) and Kress (2019). Kelsey argues (against Granger 1993) that Aristotle is not invoking an analogy between natural processes and human actions with his use of the verb *prattein* in 199a8–9 (although obviously Aristotle does draw an analogy between natural processes and actions of craft production in the later lines, 199a18–20). Elsewhere, Aristotle is quite prepared to use the verb *prattein* in describing both what is done by thought and what is done by nature (196b22). Kress (2019) argues that the craft analogy is meant to support the claim that it is *by nature* that earlier stages occur for the sake of later stages in natural processes, and that what this means is that nature acts as an efficient cause of earlier-stages-occurring-for-the-sake-of-later-stages in such processes.

[5] Broadie (2007b) argues that the role of the craft analogy, in the second half of the chapter, is to justify the view that final causality operates on the level of individual natures, rather than on the level of the cosmos as a whole.

will help him to rule out both alternatives. We do not *need* to invoke craft as a cause whenever there is purposiveness, if nature can play an analogous causal role.[6] Moreover, if a particular living thing's nature is analogous to a craft, then that living thing's own nature (rather than some more general cosmic nature) will explain the purposiveness of its behaviour.[7]

9.2   The Claim That Craft Does Not Deliberate

In defending the analogy between craft and nature, Aristotle claims that craft (like nature) does not deliberate. Clearly, individual crafts-men often think about what to do in the course of exercising their craft. What, then, does Aristotle mean by this claim? Two different interpretations have been proposed. According to the first, his point is that the craftsman *qua craftsman* does not deliberate. According to the second, his point is not about the craftsman (even considered qua craftsman), but about the craft itself: *the craft* does not deliberate (even if the craftsman does). In deciding between these interpret-ations, we should bear in mind two criteria of adequacy. A successful interpretation should attribute to Aristotle a view that is consistent with his remarks about deliberation elsewhere; and a successful interpretation should allow us to explain how establishing that 'craft does not deliberate' might contribute to Aristotle's argu-ment that there is an important analogy between nature and craft.

Sarah Broadie has argued that Aristotle's point is that the craftsman, *qua craftsman* does not deliberate.[8] On Broadie's interpretation, Aristotle is saying that the craftsman *par excellence* doesn't have to deliberate, even if the actual craftspeople we encounter often do. Deliberation is the sign of a kind of failure of expertise. A truly skilled craftsman doesn't have to ponder what to do. He just sees straight away that the way to build the

---

[6] Of course, this is not enough to show that it is nature, rather than craft, that plays this causal role in the development of natural things. Perhaps Aristotle could defend that view by appealing to his brief remarks about the priority of nature over craft (199a15–17): if craft imitates and completes nature, that might suggest that the existence of craft presupposes the existence of some non-craft-based natural teleology. In any case, as Sedley points out (2010, 7), Aristotle's views on divinity rule out the possibility of divine craftsmanship.

[7] Note, however, that the analogy with craft might also suggest that there are structural relations between natures, with some being subordinate to (and for the sake of) others, just as some crafts are subordinate to (and for the sake of) others. For example, the craft of bridle making is for the sake of the craft of horse riding, which in turn is for the craft of generalship (*Eth. Nic.* 1.1, 1094a10–14).

[8] Broadie 2007b.

house is to lay the foundations like this. He doesn't have to stop and think and wonder whether to lay them like this or in some other way.⁹

However, this interpretation is difficult to reconcile with Aristotle's remarks about deliberation elsewhere. He discusses deliberation in *Nicomachean Ethics* III.3 and *Eudemian Ethics* II.10. Both passages provide evidence that he takes the craftsman, qua such, to engage in a certain kind of thinking about what to do, and that he is prepared to describe such thinking as deliberation. In both passages, he says that one deliberates not about the end, but rather about how best to achieve the end, and in both passages he illustrates this point with examples from craft production. At *Eudemian Ethics* II.10, he says that the doctor would deliberate whether to administer some drug (1227a19–20). At *Nicomachean Ethics* III.3, he says that the doctor does not deliberate about whether to heal, nor does the orator deliberate about whether to persuade; instead, having set the end, they enquire how and by what means it is to be attained (1112b12–16). This latter passage is, I think, especially revealing for our purposes. When Aristotle says that the doctor does not deliberate about whether to heal, he must mean that the doctor *qua doctor* does not deliberate about this. After all, it would clearly be false to insist that the people who are doctors never engage in such deliberation. He goes on to contrast this with a kind of enquiry in which doctors (and other craftsmen) do engage: working out how to achieve their end. The point of the contrast must be that the doctor, qua doctor, *does* engage in *this* kind of thinking, and that in doing so he is engaging in craft-deliberation. If Aristotle meant to deny that the doctor qua doctor engages in any kind of deliberation, then it would be very odd for him to emphasise here just that the doctor qua doctor does not deliberate about the end. Aristotle is here invoking as an example the kind of deliberation engaged in by a craftsman (when acting qua craftsman) and is doing so in order to illustrate a more general point about deliberation: the point that deliberation is not about ends, but about how to achieve those ends.¹⁰

---

⁹ A more radical version of this thought (also suggested by some of Broadie's remarks): certain skilled craftsmen do not have to think at all, but instead operate by a kind of muscle memory (e.g. a skilled musician or dancer). However, as we shall see, in the *Nicomachean Ethics* Aristotle takes the kind of craft that does involve thought/deliberation as a paradigm of craft. And even the activity of the skilled musician is, in a sense, thought-guided: the process by which such a skill is acquired necessarily involves thinking, and the exercise of such a skill requires a kind of intelligent responsiveness (a responsiveness that need not be manifested in episodes of thinking).

¹⁰ This also tells against Müller's claim that Aristotle does not count productive thinking as deliberation. Müller (2018) argues that there are certain important differences between productive thinking and practical thinking. But even if Müller is right about this, Aristotle's remarks in *Nicomachean*

Admittedly, Aristotle does distinguish between kinds of expertise that involve deliberation and kinds that do not. At *Eudemian Ethics* II.10, he asks 'why do doctors deliberate about matters within their science, but not grammarians?' (1226a34–5). At *Nicomachean Ethics* III.3, he says that there is no deliberation in the sciences (*epistēmai*) that are 'exact and self-contained', such as grammar; rather we deliberate about things that can be brought about by our efforts, but not always in the same way, for example about medicine or moneymaking (1112a34–b4). We deliberate more about navigation than about gymnastics, since the former has been less exactly worked out; generally, we deliberate about crafts more than about sciences, as we are more in doubt about the former (1112b5–8).

These remarks might be invoked in support of Broadie's suggestion that a perfect craftsman would not need to deliberate. After all, Aristotle says here that crafts only depend on deliberation *to the extent that they are less fully worked out.* However, it is not obvious that he means this to imply that a craftsman *par excellence* would have no need of deliberation. For that to follow, Aristotle would need to think that each craft could in principle be developed into a perfected form, which left no room for deliberation. The fact that doctors and navigators need to deliberate would then simply be a sign of the relatively undeveloped state of the crafts of medicine and navigation. But Aristotle gives no indication that this is his view, and there is some reason to think the opposite. Medicine and navigation are crafts that must deal with particular circumstances, liable to changing in unpredictable ways. This suggests that it is in the nature of such crafts to depend upon deliberation, and that when Aristotle says that they are less fully worked out, he means that they are the kinds of crafts in which it is impossible to work out everything in advance.[11] Of course, Aristotle does say, in *Nicomachean Ethics* III.3, that certain types of expertise are not like this. If grammatical expertise (*epistēmē*) counts as a craft, then this implies that a certain *kind* of craft can be exercised without deliberation. But this is unlikely to be the point Aristotle is making in *Physics* II.8. The claim he makes there is quite general ('craft does not deliberate'), and the example of a craft he goes on to invoke in support of this claim is shipbuilding

---

Ethics III.3 suggest that he is prepared to describe both kinds of thought as deliberation. Moreover, if 'craft does not deliberate' (in *Ph.* II.8) meant merely that the craftsman's thinking is productive (not practical) and hence does not *count* as deliberation, then Aristotle's opponent would have an obvious reply: he could claim instead that for there to be purposiveness, the moving cause must engage in thought (either productive or practical).

11 In Coope 2021, I argue that Aristotle has reason to suppose that crafts (or at least, crafts of this sort) depend on deliberation, in a way that theoretical understanding does not depend on enquiry.

(199b28–9).[12] Shipbuilders are presumably just the kind of craftsmen who need to make use of deliberation, adjusting what they do to account for variable materials or for unexpected circumstances.

David Sedley has recently defended an alternative interpretation.[13] On this view, when Aristotle says that 'craft does not deliberate' he means not that the craftsman, ideally, does not deliberate but rather that the *craft itself* does not deliberate. Aristotle's point is that the cause of the movement in the case of craft production is not, strictly speaking, the craftsman but rather the *craft itself*. And the craft itself is not the kind of thing that deliberates (even if the craftsman does). This interpretation makes it possible to reconcile the claim 'craft does not deliberate' with the passages in which Aristotle implies that craftsmen, qua craftsmen, do deliberate.

However, any defence of Sedley's interpretation needs to answer the following challenge. On this interpretation, Aristotle's opponent seems to be left with an obvious reply. The opponent can simply point out that the fact that craftsmen deliberate is itself an important difference between processes of craft production and the kinds of natural processes that occur in plants (or indeed in non-human animals). Even if Aristotle thinks that the craft is the primary or ultimate efficient cause of a process of craft production,[14] he certainly thinks that craftsmen (and, more generally, deliberators) count as efficient causes *in some sense*. At II.3, 194b30, the man who has deliberated is Aristotle's first example of an efficient cause; at 195a30–1, the doctor is said to be the cause of health; at 195a21–3, 'the seed and the doctor and the one who has deliberated, and generally the maker' are said to be efficient causes (sources whence the change or rest originates). Why, then, is it relevant to point out that in craft production the *primary* cause is not the kind of thing that deliberates? If craft production necessarily involves a deliberating craftsman, why isn't *this* enough to show that craft production is importantly disanalogous to a natural process (such as the growth of leaves)? Aristotle's opponent could claim that processes of craft production are only purposive because they are brought about by an agent who deliberates, even if the primary cause of such processes is not the deliberating agent but rather the craft this agent possesses.

---

[12] Earlier in the chapter, he mentioned housebuilding (199a12–13), and (in discussing the fact that craftsmen can make mistakes) both grammatical expertise and medicine (199a33–5).
[13] Sedley 2010.
[14] At 195a6, the art of sculpture is cited as an efficient cause of the statue. At 195b5–6, Aristotle says that the housebuilder (or the housebuilder building) is the cause of the house, but he later adds that the housebuilder builds 'in virtue of' (*kata*) the craft of building, so this cause (the craft of building) is prior (195b21–5).

In what follows, I suggest a way to meet this challenge, and hence to defend (a version of) Sedley's interpretation. My suggestion will be that Aristotle is assuming a general view about causation: the primary cause of a purposive process must be what gives that process its purposive character. If the primary cause of craft production is the craft itself (not the craftsman), then what gives a process of craft production its purposive character is something (namely, the craft) that does not deliberate. If this is so, then in pointing out that craft does not deliberate, Aristotle is implying that craft production does not get its purposive character from any process of thought or deliberation. In Section 3, I ask how Aristotle might defend this claim about the source of purposiveness.

9.3   Craft, Deliberation, and the Purposiveness of Craft Production

Aristotle imagines an opponent who claims that processes of craft production are only purposive because of the deliberation of the agent. Presumably, the imagined opponent would argue as follows. Consider an example of craft production, such as cobbling. The cobbler moistens the leather *for the sake of softening it*. This action of moistening is for the sake of softening, just because of the way in which it (the action) is caused by the cobbler's thought processes: by the cobbler's thinking that moistening the leather is a good way to soften it. From this the opponent concludes that, in the case of craft production, the source of purposiveness is deliberation. When *x* happens for the sake of *y*, in craft production, this is because *x* is brought about by a thought process of this kind. Finally, the opponent generalises this to all cases in which one thing occurs for the sake of another, concluding that the source of purposiveness, in any individual case, must be deliberation.

There are two points Aristotle might make in reply. The first is that deliberation itself is a purposive process, and that the opponent cannot explain *its* purposiveness. I shall argue that any attempt to explain *this* purposiveness threatens to embroil the opponent in an infinite regress of explanations. The second point is that, once we understand deliberation's role in processes of craft production, we shall see that its role is not to explain the *purposiveness* of such processes. Aristotle hints at the role of deliberation in craft production when he says that it would not be needed if craft were (like nature) an internal origin of change. I shall argue that, for Aristotle, deliberation is needed in craft production just because of this crucial way in which craft differs from nature.

Aristotle brings out the purposive nature of the deliberative process in some remarks in *Eudemian Ethics* II.10:

[T]he one deliberating always deliberates for the sake of some end, and he who deliberates has always an aim by reference to which he judges what is beneficial. (1227a6–7)

Deliberation is a kind of enquiry (a process of working out what to do), and enquiry is an end-directed process (*Eth. Nic.* III.3, 1112b22–3). If you find out the answer to some question as a result of enquiring into it, then you must have been aiming to find out the answer to that question. That is the difference between discovering something through enquiry and merely happening upon some new knowledge. Moreover, deliberation is end-directed in a further way. When we deliberate, we are not merely aiming to answer some question ('given my circumstances, what would be the best way for me to achieve such-and-such a goal?'); we deliberate for the sake of acting. Mere idle reflection on the best way to bring about some goal would not count as deliberation. That is why we only deliberate about things in our power (as Aristotle emphasises in *Eth. Nic.* III.3), and we stop deliberating when we realise that it is impossible for us to achieve the goal we have set ourselves (*Eth. Nic.* III.3, 1112b24–6). When we engage in *craft-deliberation*, we deliberate in order to produce something: the shipbuilder deliberates for the sake of producing a ship.

If this is right, then Aristotle has an answer to the opponent who assumes that a process can only be purposive if it is caused by prior deliberation. If deliberation is itself a purposive process, then such an opponent would be committed to an infinite regress: any deliberative process would need to be caused by a prior deliberative process.[15] As Aristotle himself says in the *Eudemian Ethics*, deliberation cannot presuppose prior deliberation: 'For one does not deliberate after previous deliberation which itself presupposed deliberation, but there is some starting point; nor does one think after prior thinking and so on *ad infinitum*' (VIII.2, 1248a18–22).

What, then, is the role of deliberation in craft production? If originating in deliberation is not required for purposiveness, why is deliberation needed in craft production? Aristotle hints at an interesting answer to

[15] Of course, this only answers *an opponent who assumes that a process can only be purposive if caused by prior deliberation*. A different opponent might claim only that *actions of craft production* must be preceded by deliberation if they are to be purposive (allowing that the purposiveness of *the deliberative process itself* need not be explained in the same way). But this second opponent would be on much weaker ground in claiming that natural processes cannot be purposive, since she would have conceded that there *can* be purposive processes that do not originate in deliberation. This would leave open the possibility that natural processes are like *processes of craft deliberation* in being purposive without themselves originating in deliberation.

this question in *Physics* 11.8. Immediately after saying that craft does not deliberate, he goes on to make a peculiar counterfactual claim: if the craft of shipbuilding were present in the wood, it would act in the same way as nature (199b28–9).[16] This suggests that craft production differs from a natural process (and depends upon deliberation in a way that a natural process does not) just because craft differs from nature in being an external cause.

Earlier in *Physics* 11, Aristotle has explained the sense in which nature (unlike craft) is an internal cause of the processes that occur in a natural thing: nature is 'a sort of source and cause of change and of remaining at rest in that to which it belongs primarily and of itself, that is, not by virtue of concurrence' (11.1, 192b20–3). By contrast, the craft of housebuilding operates on something external to the housebuilder (the bricks) to produce a house (192b28–30). Even when a doctor cures himself, using the craft of medicine, he is only accidentally both doctor and patient: he is healed *because he is acted upon by someone who possesses the craft of medicine* (someone who happens to be identical to himself), he is not healed *in virtue of possessing the craft of medicine*. As Aristotle says, 'it is not insofar as he is healed that he possesses the craft of medicine, but being a doctor and being healed merely concur in the same person' (192b25–6)

This difference between craft and nature has two implications, both important for our purposes. First, a craft differs from a nature in being accidental to whatever possesses it. When we consider the shipbuilder qua shipbuilder, we are engaging in a kind of fiction: we are considering the shipbuilder as if he were essentially a shipbuilder. In fact, any shipbuilder is only accidentally a shipbuilder; what he is essentially is a human being. By contrast, when we consider a natural thing, *qua* the natural thing it is, no fiction is involved. How a thing is by nature is how it is essentially. Second, the relation between nature and the matter on which it operates is different from the relation between craft and the matter on which it operates (for example, the relation between an oak's nature and the wood that is the oak's matter is different from the relation between the craft of shipbuilding and the wood that is used in making a ship). This is because of the way in which craft, unlike nature, is an external source of change. I shall argue that both of these differences between craft and nature are relevant to our question about deliberation.

---

[16] In fact, as we saw above, Aristotle has already made a similar claim earlier in the chapter: if a house were one of the things that comes to be due to nature, it would come to be just as it does in fact come about by craft (199a12–13).

Aristotle tells us that if the shipbuilding craft were present in the wood, the wood's development into a ship would be just like a natural process. I take it that this counterfactual is inviting us to imagine a situation in which the craft is not merely present in the wood (in the way that the craft of medicine is present in the doctor when the doctor heals himself), but rather a situation in which the craft is present in *and essential to* the wood (as a nature is present in and essential to a natural thing). When Aristotle says that in that case, the wood's development into a ship would be just like a natural process, he is claiming that this development would still (like ordinary shipbuilding) be end-directed, but it would occur without any need for prior deliberation.

Aristotle's claim, then, is that deliberation is needed in craft production just because craft is unlike nature in these two respects: it is accidental to the thing that possesses it, and it is external to the matter on which it operates. It will help us to understand the role of deliberation in craft production if we look more closely at each of these two ways in which craft differs from nature.

The first difference was that a natural thing's nature is essential to it, whereas no craft is essential to its possessor: nothing is essentially a housebuilder or a doctor. I want to argue that this difference introduces a need for a special kind of flexibility in craft production, a kind of flexibility that is not called for in natural processes. The reason for this is that a process of craft production (unlike a natural process) is always subordinate to some further end. A nature is, in this respect, importantly different from a craft. Since a natural thing is essentially the way it is by nature, a thing's nature is not subordinate to some further end: its nature sets its end. By contrast, when a particular agent engages in craft production, the ultimate end for the sake of which he acts is not determined by the craft itself. A doctor may exercise his craft because he has been ordered to do so by his employer, or because he wants to help a friend, or because he wants to demonstrate his skill, and in exercising his craft he may be aiming to heal, or he may be aiming to make the patient just well enough for some particular purpose (for instance, well enough to do his job), or he may even be aiming to make the patient ill.[17]

---

[17] As Aristotle says, rational powers such as crafts are powers for opposites (*Metaph.* IX.2). Of course, health is the proper end of the craft of medicine, so if there could be an agent who was essentially a doctor, that agent would exercise his craft only to heal. But in fact, no agent is essentially a doctor. Anyone who is a doctor is essentially a human being. Thus, any actual doctor will have other, further ends that influence the ways in which he uses his skill at doctoring.

Because of this, a craftsman is often called upon to exercise his craft in circumstances that are not well-suited to the exercise of that craft. A shoemaker may be called upon to make shoes from leather that is unsuitable (*Eth. Nic.* I.10, 1101a3–6); a doctor may be called upon to treat someone who cannot be fully cured (*Rh.* I.I, 1355b12–14), or to treat someone in circumstances in which suitable drugs are not available. Moreover, a craftsman may need to exercise the craft for some non-standard purpose: the shoemaker who is a prisoner of war may use his craft to make faulty shoes for enemy soldiers, a doctor may use his craft to harm his enemies. Both these points help to explain the need for deliberation: an excellent craftsman needs to be able to exercise his craft in a range of unpredictable circumstances, and for a great variety of ends. Being a good doctor requires more than the ability to heal potentially curable patients in circumstances in which all the appropriate drugs and instruments are available.

The second difference between nature and craft is related to the first. Crafts and natures are differently related to the matter on which they operate. Aristotle hints at this difference between craft and nature earlier in *Physics* II. The crafts, he says, 'make their matter, some make it *simpliciter*, others make it good to work with' (II.2, 194a33–4). The same is not true of nature: 'In the case of artefacts, we make the matter for the work to be done, whereas in the case of natural objects, it is there already' (II.2, 194b7–8).[18]

One reason for this difference is that, in many cases, a natural thing's nature operates on matter that is internal to the natural thing – matter that is already potentially in the state that will be brought about by the operation of this nature. By contrast, a craft operates on matter that is external: matter that could equally well be made into a variety of different things. When dog-form is operative in the coming-to-be of a dog, it is already in material suitable for becoming a dog (material that is not, in the same sense, suitable for becoming anything else). Although the dog's form does explain the development of its material parts (and *in that sense*, nature does make the matter), it does so by operating on matter that is, from the start, such-as-to-be-a-dog. By contrast, the craft of shipbuilding is external to the wood it operates on. The wood could equally well be made into a number of different things. Moreover, often a shipbuilder is required to operate in circumstances where the ideal matter is not available. Shipbuilding can still be well exercised in such circumstances. Indeed,

---

[18] On the importance of this distinction between craft and nature, see Connell 2016, 123ff.

a shipbuilder might show his skill in producing a well-constructed ship out of the unsuitable material that is available.[19]

Of course, natural processes do sometimes involve interacting with external materials. Aristotle cites nest building as an example of a natural process (*Ph.* II.8, 199a26–7).[20] Nest building is not the exercise of a craft, but when birds build nests, they clearly act on material that is external to them, and this is material (twigs and mud) they have to seek out. In the *Historia animalium*, Aristotle even points out that birds sometimes make use of alternative materials, when the most suitable are not available: the swallow 'mixes mud with the stalks [of straw]. And if she lacks mud, she moistens herself and rolls her feathers into the dust' (IX.7, 612b23–5).[21] However, I want to argue that even in this kind of case, the way in which the nature is related to the material it operates on differs from the way in which a craft is related to its materials. This is because of the way in which a nature is related to a natural habitat.

Living things are, by nature, such as to live in a certain habitat, a habitat that provides them with the materials needed for engaging in natural activities such as nest building. For instance, marsh-dwelling birds lead their lives (by nature) in a way that is suitable to the habitat of marshes; riverbank-dwelling birds live their lives (by nature) in a way that is suitable to the habitat of riverbanks.[22] Of course, this does not guarantee that any particular bird will in fact be living in its natural habitat. Any particular bird might be living in captivity. Nevertheless, *if it is to engage in its natural activity*, the bird must be living in its natural habitat. The nest-building capacity that is natural to a certain kind of bird just is the capacity to build nests *in the habitat that is natural to it*. Thus, a marsh-dwelling bird will have a natural ability to build nests from materials found in marshes, while a riverbank-dwelling bird will have a natural ability to build nests from materials found on riverbanks. If this is right, then there is some reason to

---

[19] The craft of medicine is an interesting intermediate case. The body is, in a certain sense, material that is such-as-to-be-healthy. (As Aristotle says, there is a sense in which the craft of medicine is just imitating what nature would do if it were operating successfully.) Here my earlier point becomes important. Because the end for the sake of which the craft is exercised is set by something external to the craft, the craft can be used for many different purposes: a doctor might be required to display his skill even when the patient is in fact incurable, or a doctor might be required to use his skill to make the patient ill.

[20] This does not imply that the product of this process (a nest) has a nature. Nests have no internal principle of change. But Aristotle is committed to the view that birds engage in nest-building behaviour by nature.

[21] Aristotle takes this to show that there is a kind of thought (*dianoia*) that guides the behaviour of swallows. Nest building is thus quite similar to housebuilding, except that it is not guided by craft.

[22] For a much fuller defence of this claim than I can give here, see Gelber 2015.

think that a natural thing, when acting by nature, will typically have readily available to it the external objects with which it needs to interact. There is no similar reason for thinking that a craftsman, when exercising his craft, will have readily available to him the external objects he needs to use. Circumstances can, of course, be more or less conducive to the exercise of a particular craft, but the circumstances are not specified by the craft itself, and indeed they could not be specified by the craft, given that the craft itself does not set the ultimate end for the sake of which it is employed.

How are these differences between craft and nature relevant to the need for deliberation? The answer is that craft production is (in certain ways) more challenging than natural production. Exercising a craft involves seeking out suitable material, and the most suitable material might not even be available in the circumstances in which the craft is being exercised. My suggestion is that deliberation is needed in craft because craft production involves these extra challenges. Deliberation is needed, not for purposiveness, but for a certain kind of sensitivity to changing and unpredictable circumstances, and for the capacity to adjust one's behaviour accordingly. Successful craft production requires this kind of sensitivity, because the craftsman is often required to seek out matter and make it suitable, or even to make use of matter that is not particularly suitable, when that is all that is available.[23]

9.4 Desire and Animal End-Directedness

I have argued that, although deliberation has an important role in craft, its role is not to explain the purposiveness of processes of craft production. Deliberation gives the craftsman a certain kind of flexibility: a flexibility that is needed both because craft production is subordinate to some further end and because of the way in which a craft is related to the matter on which it operates. But even in craft production, deliberation does not explain the purposiveness of the process. If so, then Aristotle has an answer to the opponent who objects that deliberation is needed for purposiveness.

---

[23] Aristotle does allow that something superficially similar happens in nature. Nature often makes use of residues, just because they are what is available (see *Gen. an.* 11.6, 744b15–16). But such residues are reliably available and are suitable for the purposes for which they are used. A nature operates within a specific habitat, where the appropriate kinds of matter will typically be available. Nature is not called upon (as craft is) to operate in an indefinite variety of possible circumstances. By contrast, the general must be able to use whatever army is available and the shoemaker must be able to make use of whatever leather is provided (*Eth. Nic.* 1.10, 1101a3–6).

However, as I pointed out earlier, it might seem that, in responding to this opponent, Aristotle is overlooking a potentially more challenging objection. What would Aristotle say to an opponent who claimed that desire (or, perhaps, desire plus cognition) is needed for purposiveness? Such an opponent would agree that the bird's nest building and the spider's web spinning are purposive, but would object to Aristotle's claim that trees put out leaves for the sake of sheltering their fruit or, more generally, that natural processes such as growth, that do not stem from desire, are purposive. I want to suggest that Aristotle could respond to this opponent in a similar way.

In the last section, I argued that deliberation is itself a purposive process, and hence that it cannot be what ultimately explains purposiveness. Similarly, I suggest, ordinary animal desires (though not processes) are themselves purposive. The sparrow does not *just happen* to be beset by the desire to build a nest. Rather, it has this desire *because building a nest is good for it*. Thus, a general explanation of the bird's purposiveness (of how it is that a bird can act and be a certain way for the sake of some good) needs to explain not only the purposiveness of its nest building but also the purposiveness of its *having the desire* for nest building. Aristotle's claim is that both of these kinds of purposiveness are explained by the bird's nature: it is *because of the bird's nature* that it desires to build (and builds) a nest for the sake of its good.

I have argued that deliberation is needed in crafts because craft production demands a kind of flexibility in responding to particular circumstances. Desire and cognition also make possible a certain (though lesser) kind of flexibility. Although animals are by nature such as to live in a certain habitat, they differ from plants in that they move around within this habitat. For instance, birds need to seek out nest-building materials. Because of this, animals need a certain kind of flexibility in their end-directed behaviour, beyond that required by plants. Although their natural habitat will be such as to provide them with the right kind of food and shelter, they still need the ability to seek out food and shelter within that habitat. Desire enables an animal to adjust its aims in response to changing circumstances: desiring now food, now warmth, now a hiding place, in accordance with what at any moment seems good. Perceptual cognition enables an animal to notice, within its environment, opportunities for satisfying such desires. If this is right, then desire and cognition (like deliberation) are important in explaining a certain kind of flexible end-directedness, but (like deliberation) they are not what explains end-directedness as such.

9.5   The Explanation of End-Directedness: A Puzzle about Human Intentional Action

What, then, does explain the purposiveness of end-directed processes? In the case of natural processes, Aristotle's answer is clear. The *nature* of a natural thing explains the end-directedness of its natural processes. For example, a particular apple tree's processes of leaf production *occur for the sake of some end* because of the apple tree's nature. This particular apple tree puts out leaves for the sake of protecting its fruit because, in the nature of apple trees, leaf development serves the purpose of fruit protection. *Physics* II.8's analogy between craft and nature suggests that we should be able to give a similar account of the purposiveness of processes of craft production. For example, a particular cobbler's leather-moistening is *for the sake of some end* because of the structure of the craft of cobbling. This particular cobbler moistens the leather for the sake of softening it because, within the craft of cobbling, leather-moistening serves the purpose of leather-softening.

   In this final section of my chapter, I raise some puzzles for this way of appealing to the analogy between craft and nature in the explanation of purposiveness. The first puzzle is about the role of craft in explaining the purposiveness of craft production. Can craft really be the ultimate explanation for such purposiveness? As we saw earlier, the end of craft production is always subordinate to some further end. I want to suggest that this gives us reason to doubt both the ultimacy and the generality of explanations of purposiveness that appeal to craft. It gives us reason to doubt the ultimacy of such explanations, because we can always ask of any craft: why does that craft exist and, in particular, what is the good that it serves? In Section 4, I argued that desire could not be the ultimate explanation of the purposiveness of animal movement, since the existence of animal desire is itself explained teleologically. An analogous argument suggests that a craft cannot provide the ultimate explanation of the purposiveness of craft production: the existence of the craft itself stands in need of teleological explanation.

   The worry about generality arises because of the way in which methods of craft production are often employed for non-standard ends, or modified to take account of unusual circumstances.[24] The appeal to craft above relies upon the fact that, within the craft of cobbling, moistening is a *standard method* for softening leather. This kind of craft-explanation is thus

---

[24] As we saw above, these features of craft production help to explain why it often requires the exercise of deliberation.

analogous to nature-explanation, in the way it invokes generality. However, many particular processes of craft production will depart from the use of such standard methods. As we saw in Section 3, such departures may be caused by the particular circumstances in which the craft is exercised (e.g. if the most appropriate materials or instruments are unavailable), or they may be caused by the peculiar purposes for which the craft is being exercised (e.g. if the employer wants a house made of glass, or if the doctor is being employed to make someone ill). These non-standard processes of craft production are still purposive, but it is not very clear how the structure of the craft itself could explain such purposiveness.

In fact, this suggests a further, more general, puzzle. There are many purposive activities that are neither natural processes nor exercises of some craft. Examples are ordinary human intentional actions that are not instances of craft production.[25] But the model of explanation suggested by *Physics* 11.8 seems to leave a puzzle as to how the purposiveness of such actions is to be explained. Is there anything that plays a role analogous to nature (or indeed craft) in the explanation of these actions? In the special case of *virtuous* actions, perhaps virtue might play such a role. For example, when the soldier volunteers for a dangerous mission in order to save the city, we could explain the purposiveness of this action by appealing to the virtue of courage: it belongs to the virtue of courage to act in such ways for the sake of the city. But whatever the merits of this explanation, it is hard to see how it could serve as the model for a *general* account of purposiveness. After all, there are many human intentional actions that are neither virtuous nor the exercise of some craft.

In this chapter, I have attempted to shed light on Aristotle's account of the purposiveness of natural processes. In particular, I have suggested how he might defend the claim that a thing's *nature* is what explains the purposiveness of its natural activities. I have asked whether any analogous explanation could be given for the purposiveness of other processes and activities. Aristotle's analogy between craft and nature might lead us to expect such an explanation. However, I have argued that, for many human intentional activities, it is hard to see what such an explanation would be. That leaves us with a puzzle about explaining the purposiveness of such activities. Should

---

[25] At *Nicomachean Ethics* 11.1, Aristotle argues that the ethical virtues do not arise in us by nature (1103a18–26). His argument is that nothing that is by nature a certain way can be habituated to be otherwise than it is by nature (by contrast, a stone falls downwards by nature, and cannot be habituated to fall in some other way). The same argument seems to imply that when human beings engage in particular intentional actions, they do not do so 'by nature'. For a human being can be habituated to act otherwise than she would have acted had she not been so habituated.

we accept that there are simply two very different kinds of explanation of purposiveness, the first appropriate for natural processes (and possibly for virtuous actions and certain standard instances of craft production) and the second appropriate for the other kinds of intentional actions engaged in by an adult human being? Can an explanation of the second kind in some way be derived from or based upon an explanation of the first kind? The real puzzle we are left with by *Physics* 11.8 is not that of explaining the purposiveness of natural processes; it is, rather, that of explaining the purposiveness of those processes that are purposive but are *not* natural.

PART V

The Naturalness of Goodness

CHAPTER 10

Eudoxus' Hedonism

Joachim Aufderheide

10.1 Introduction

Eudoxus of Cnidus (391–336 BC) maintained thesis T: pleasure is the good. He is rightly regarded as a hedonist, but interpreters struggle to go beyond this very general characterisation because Eudoxus does not provide a theory of pleasure or of the good. All of his contemporaries assume that a successful life centres on the good and that 'the good' refers to a single entity.[1] Since Eudoxus does not provide any arguments against the prevalent view, he probably shares the uniqueness assumption. Within this broad framework, T states that a good life, or living well, crucially depends on having pleasure.

We can approach Eudoxus' hedonism by clarifying what T does not mean. Endorsing T is not a matter of endorsing a life of consumption (*bios apolaustikos*, *Eth. Nic.* 1.5, 1095b17). Aristotle gives short shrift to this kind of life because it belongs to grazing cattle (b19–20). Thus understood, pleasure cannot be the good, at least not for humans. And yet, Aristotle returns to discussing hedonism, in both books VII and X. The attention devoted to Eudoxus in book X – about one and a half OCT pages – indicates that his hedonism does not advocate a life of consumption. On the contrary, 'he was reputed to be exceptionally moderate; hence, he was not thought to say these things as a lover of pleasure, but rather that things

It is a privilege and pleasure to be able to honour Sarah in this volume. She has been an inspiration for me in almost everything I do, philosophically. The beginnings of my tribute to her go back more than ten years, when Sarah first got me excited about Eudoxus.

I learnt much from presenting earlier versions at the Notts Philosophy Research Seminar, the King's philosophy staff seminar, and the Stanford Ancient Ethical Psychology Conference. I thank the audiences, especially my commentator at Stanford, Thomas Slabon. I took the opportunity to rethink my entire approach in the wake of the searching criticism at Stanford – for which I am grateful. For help and advice, I thank Voula Tsouna, Dorothea Frede, and Ursula Coope. I would not have been able to complete the paper without the generosity of Inés de Asis.

[1] The opening moves of Aristotle's *Nicomachean Ethics* (1.1–4) and Plato's *Philebus* (11a–12a) are especially telling.

are truly as he said' (x.2, 1172b16–18).[2] But if, as the context suggests, Eudoxus lives in harmony with his doctrine – how could Eudoxus' lifestyle possibly express *T*?

To understand Eudoxus' hedonism, we must turn to the arguments supporting *T*. But in doing so, we face two difficulties. The first arises because the *Nicomachean Ethics* is our only real source for Eudoxus' ethical views. The absence of a theory of pleasure means that Eudoxus' position cannot be rejected on the grounds of a defective account of pleasure (like Plato's). So, Aristotle can (and does) use Eudoxan material to further his own enquiry – which does not lighten the task of discerning *Eudoxus'* position.[3] Second, just after presenting the key argument, Aristotle states that 'his words (*logoi*) carried conviction more because of his virtue of character than because of themselves' (1172b15–16). We need not take the tribute to Eudoxus' character 'as a device for belittling Eudoxus' argument'.[4] In contrast to other academic philosophers interested in the topic of pleasure, he does not seem to have written anything on pleasure (or on any other philosophical topic).[5] Eudoxus may simply have volunteered his views in the discussions about pleasure, and how one could support them – without trying to put forward philosophically compelling arguments. Given this evidence, we cannot be sure that a coherent theory motivates *T*.[6] Nevertheless, I shall argue that special attention to the role of nature and choice in Eudoxus' key argument points towards a defensible hedonist position.

10.2   The Basics

Key to understanding Eudoxus' hedonism is the argument from universal pursuit, to which Aristotle rightly allocates pride of place:

Εὔδοξος μὲν οὖν τὴν ἡδονὴν τἀγαθὸν ᾤετ' εἶναι διὰ τὸ
πάνθ' ὁρᾶν ἐφιέμενα αὐτῆς, καὶ ἔλλογα καὶ ἄλογα, ἐν πᾶσι   (10)
δ' εἶναι τὸ αἱρετὸν [τὸ] ἐπιεικές, καὶ τὸ μάλιστα κράτιστον·
τὸ δὲ [/δὴ] πάντ' ἐπὶ ταὐτὸ φέρεσθαι μηνύειν ὡς πᾶσι τοῦτο ἄρι-
στον ὄν·ἕκαστον γὰρ τὸ αὑτῷ ἀγαθὸν εὑρίσκειν, ὥσπερ καὶ
τροφήν·τὸ δὴ [/δὲ] πᾶσιν ἀγαθόν, καὶ οὗ πάντ' ἐφίεται, τἀγα-
θὸν εἶναι.   (*Eth. Nic.* x.2, 1172b9–15)[7]

---

[2] My translations follow those in Aufderheide 2020. The interpretation advanced here, however, is not found in the commentary.
[3] This point is argued persuasively by Warren 2009.   [4] As does Weiss 1979, 215.
[5] Lasserre 1966, 148.   [6] So Frede 1997, 391–3.
[7] The text differs in three places (and punctuation) from Bywater's OCT. In b11 and b12 Bywater follows K^b, and in b14, he follows the paraphrast. I have indicated his choices by the square brackets; '/' signifies that the bracketed word replaces the preceding one. My text follows most MSS on all

Now Eudoxus thought that <u>pleasure is the good</u> because <u>he saw all things seeking it</u>, both rational and irrational, and that in all cases the object (to be) chosen is [what is] fitting, and that which is most so is strongest; and [/hence] the fact that all things move towards the same indicates that this is best for all; for each thing finds what is good for itself, just as with food; hence [/and] what is good for all, and <u>what everything seeks, is the good</u>.

At the basic level, Eudoxus' argument for *T* consists of two points, namely the claim that (1) all animals pursue pleasure, and (2) what everything seeks is the good. Instead of jumping right into questions of the argument's cogency, I propose to step back and start with the supplementary argument (i.e. the parts that are not underlined), to find some firm ground on which to place the various moving parts of Eudoxus' hedonism.[8]

10.2.1 The Supplementary Argument

A careful reading of b11–14 should begin with the text. Bywater's OCT, I think, obscures Eudoxus' thought, because the inferential particle *dē* in b12 presents 'the fact that all things move towards the same indicates that this is best for all' as a kind of inference or conclusion, supported by the *gar* clause ('each thing finds what is good for itself') and the further claim (introduced by *de* in the OCT), possibly within the scope of the *gar*, that 'what is good for all, and what everything seeks, is the good'. But this reading seems to have the argument the wrong way round because it musters (2) in support of the weaker claim that the object of universal pursuit is best for all. The text of most manuscripts presents the proper order. The *dē* in b14 suggests that the focus is on establishing something like (2), except that the clause 'and what everything seeks' seems to be an apposition or explication, but not the main point. Eudoxus concludes *T* instead on the strength of 'what is good for all . . . is the good'.

While this reading reduces the pressure on premise (1), we may now wonder what role universal pursuit in fact plays. Interpreters have noted that 'in all cases the object (to be) chosen (*haireton*) is [what is] fitting, and that which is most so is strongest' (b10–11) connects (1) and (2) insofar as *haireton* picks up on the factual claim of (1), but also bears a normative

three occasions. Unlike Bywater, who puts ἕκαστον γὰρ τὸ αὑτῷ ἀγαθὸν εὑρίσκειν, ὥσπερ καὶ τροφήν in parentheses, I take this part to be central to Eudoxus' argument.

[8] My discussion here owes debt to Warren 2009, who, however, takes the supplementary argument to encompasses only 1172b10–11.

dimension – what should be chosen – as required for the transition in (2). More specifically, Eudoxus connects the object of choice with what is fitting for the animal (i.e. with what is good for the animal).[9] So, what the animal *in fact* chooses is *to be* chosen, and what is most of all (to be) chosen and most of all fitting is what is strongest, where 'strongest' (*kratiston*) seems to point both backwards and forwards. Reading on from (1), *kratiston* evokes the strength of psychological pull – pleasure is the strongest element! – but looking back from (2), it sets up the search for the best good (*ariston*, b12–13). Lines b12–13 bring these two strands of thought together. Eudoxus reminds us that all animals move towards the same, but then claims that the object of universal pursuit is best for all. We can expand the compressed reasoning as follows, with square brackets indicating the expansions:

(i) Each finds (*heuriskein*) what is good for itself;
[so: (ii) all find what is good for themselves.] (from (i))
(iii) There is an *X* towards which all move (*pheresthai*);
[so: (iv) the *X* towards which all move is good for all.] (from (ii) and (iii))
So: (v) what is good for all (i.e. what all seek, *ephiēmi*), is the good.

This line of thought does not represent a formally valid argument. In particular, the different verbs in (i), (iii), and (v) blur how the conclusion should follow from the premises. However, if – and this is a big if – we take all the verbs to be roughly equivalent (seeking or choosing), then at least (iv) follows from (ii) and (iii). For (i) illuminates the strength of *haireton* in b11, insofar as Eudoxus' argument turns not on the claim that animals *should* choose what is fitting, but that they *do* choose what is fitting when they make a choice. So, if an animal only chooses things that are good for it, as b11 would suggest on this reading, then the *X* chosen by all will also be good for all.

10.2.2   Eudoxus' Naturalism

The analysis of the supplementary argument highlights the key role of (i), a claim anticipated in line b11. But allocating such a prominent role to this claim raises two questions. On what basis does Eudoxus assert that animals find what is good and fitting for themselves? And why should it be true? Given the setup of the whole argument (1172b9–10), the answer to the first

---

[9] I follow Warren 2009, 258 in translating *epieikēs* as fitting rather than 'good' or 'good for' to capture the circumstantial aspect of an animal's choice (on which see Broadie 1991, 354–5).

question must be observation, as the example of each finding their proper food suggests. But if (i) rests on observation, Eudoxus does not seem to be a good observer: animals are sometimes poisoned by what they eat, and young animals do not survive when their parents do not look out for them. So, for the argument to retain its empirical credibility, (i) must be true not universally, but only for the most part. Presumably, Eudoxus restricts the scope of (i) to well-developed, healthy, sufficiently mature animals. *They* generally find what is good for themselves, just as they generally find the right food.

Restricting the scope of (i) prepares an answer to the next question. We can observe *that* animals generally find what is fitting and good for themselves, but not *why*. Eudoxus does not cite any reasons that would explain (i), perhaps because the answer is both common and obvious: it is simply in the nature of all animals to seek what is good for them. Invoking nature in the explanation of (i) points towards a helpful intermediate between each animal and all animals (cf. the supplementary argument). Although all seek what is good for them, the specific goods sought differ with the animals' natures, as the example of food illustrates. Because each animal shares its nature with others of its kind, attributing a certain nature to an animal amounts to placing it in a system of kind-specific norms that specify what is good and appropriate for the animal. So, moving up from the individual animal to its kind enables us to move beyond the truism that an animal does what it does, and offers an explanation of its behaviour.

We need not worry that invoking nature *eo ipso* gives us an account of the good. True, what is good for each animal is natural to it, and hence the good must also be natural. But 'doing what is natural' constitutes only a framework assumption, not a substantial account of the good life, because it leaves completely open what an animal's choices are *good for*. Assuming different 'goals' will likely result in different natural norms, so that we must not prejudge the good towards which nature aims, if we are to interpret Eudoxus' argument. Instead, he suggests, by observing the behaviour of paradigmatic animals we gain insight into their natures, and thus learn what they should, ultimately, aim at. So when Eudoxus observes that animals tend to find what is good for them and that all animals seek pleasure, Eudoxus can *argue* for the claim that, ultimately, pleasure is the good. So, the notion of 'nature' that underlies his argument does not present a substantial account of the good, but instead helps to facilitate the transition from observation to normative claim.

10.2.3 Eudoxus' Argument from Universal Pursuit

Ignoring the supplementary argument (as does the basic argument in §10.2) oversimplifies Eudoxus' approach. First, it conceals how Eudoxus in fact argues for T (§10.2.1), and second, it plays down the importance of both observation and nature in Eudoxus' argument from universal pursuit (§10.2.2). A better initial characterisation should highlight the inference from the observation that all animals seek pleasure to the claim that pleasure is good for all. Each animal, by nature, successfully chooses what is good for itself (*heuriskein*, b13), and it does so in all situations (*en pasi*, b10). If what an animal seeks or chooses and what is good for it coincide, then there is no clear distinction between choice and choiceworthiness: 'in all cases the object (to be) chosen is fitting' (b11). Since this is true of all animals, what all seek is good for all. So far, the argument yields a conditional: *if* there is one 'thing' sought or chosen by all animals, then this is good for all – and Eudoxus obviously identifies this thing with pleasure (b9). It is on this basis that Eudoxus concludes: 'what is good for all (i.e. what all seek) is the good' (b14–15).

10.3 Interpreting the Argument from Universal Pursuit: A New Approach

Having examined the framework within which Eudoxus asserts thesis T, we can now turn to the more philosophical questions. Both the supplementary argument and the argument from universal pursuit raise the question on what grounds Eudoxus concludes T. Universal pursuit may show that the object so pursued is good for all, but not that it is *the* good (cf. 1172b35–1173a1) – at least not without further assumptions. There are two prominent ways of spelling out these assumptions. (A) As a matter of psychological fact, animals do not seek or choose anything but pleasure. If Eudoxus held (A), he would have strong reasons for believing that the universal pursuit of pleasure shows T. The alternative interpretation leaves the mental states to one side and focuses on the extension of animal choices. (B) Because pleasure is the only good chosen by *all* animals, pleasure has a special role among the other goods, so that *it* must be the good. Both interpretations, although ultimately amiss, make salient points that should inform a more satisfactory interpretation. I propose such an interpretation by diagnosing, and removing, a misleading assumption shared by (A) and (B).

10.3.1 The Psychological Reading

The psychological reading claims that animals in fact seek and choose nothing but pleasure. This reading can draw support from the first two lines of the argument from universal pursuit. Instead of aligning *kratiston* in 1172b11 with *ariston* in b12–13, we can read *kratiston* psychologically: what is *kratiston* has the strongest pull (this use is common in discussions of *akrasia*). Since Eudoxus makes the object of choice something fitting, what is most fitting has the strongest psychological pull and is therefore what is chosen (*haireton*, b11). So, in all cases (*en pasi*, b10) all animals seek and choose pleasure because it exerts the strongest psychological pull. Thus interpreted, Eudoxus would come very close to maintaining what we call 'psychological hedonism' (i.e. the claim that pleasure is the only object desired). But psychological hedonism might seem to entail normative hedonism, the claim that nothing other than pleasure *should* the sought. For if animals can choose pleasure only, proposing that some other object should be sought would be practically irrelevant because we could not possibly act accordingly (cf. *Eth. Nic.* III.4, 1111b22–6). The observation that all animals seek pleasure, understood as 'all animals seek only pleasure' would thus point towards the normative thesis that pleasure is the only object to be chosen – which entails *T*.

There are two problems with this interpretation. The first questions the observational basis of his argument. The problem is not that *we* do not take the pursuit of pleasure to be observable. After all, if we want to characterise *Eudoxus'* hedonism, we must handle the principle of charity carefully. Other philosophers around Eudoxus do not share our worry and unquestioningly assert that animals (and children) seek pleasure. So, we should set our conception of observation aside and grant that Eudoxus can *see* that animals pursue pleasure. But can we observe that animals choose pleasure only? Let us distinguish between pleasure, the agent's (subjective) enjoyment (cf. *hēdetai*, 1172b22–3), and its source, the (objective) event/activity/object that gives rise to pleasure. Now, the pursuit of pleasure and the pursuit of its sources seem to be observationally equivalent. Whenever an animal pursues the 'things' that tend to give rise to pleasure, such as food (*trophē*, b13–14), it can also be said to pursue pleasure – and vice versa. So why assume that animals pursue only the enjoyment of certain goods rather than also certain goods which they enjoy? In order to find out what it is that they pursue, we could rely on the bridge principle that animals (only) pursue what is good for themselves – if we had a prior account of what is good for the animal. But this would be putting the cart before the horse.

The argument from universal pursuit is designed to inform us about the good, and therefore cannot presuppose a substantial account of what is good. So, we cannot observe that animals seek only pleasure.

Second, *T* does not follow even if all animals can choose nothing but pleasure, because the psychological reading fails to flesh out the crucial inference, from 'an animal seeks or chooses *X*' to '*X* is good for the animal'. Animals may find what is good for themselves *because* they choose pleasure, but it does not follow that pleasure is good, let alone the good. In 1172b13 Eudoxus mentions food as an example of something good that each animal finds (*heuriskein*). But if there are other goods than pleasure, the psychological reading (or psychological hedonism) does not rule out the possibility that pleasure merely helps the animals finding what is (really) good for them. By seeking and choosing pleasure (and nothing but pleasure) the animal in fact finds what is good for itself (what, when, for how long), because what is good is subvenient to pleasure.[10] So, the alleged fact that animals seek only pleasure may be no more than the expression of a natural mechanism to ensure that the animal attains these goods.[11] If this were Eudoxus' argument, he could establish *T* only in an attenuated sense: if any universally pursued good is thereby the good, then pleasure would be the good. But the supplementary argument shows that Eudoxus aims for a thicker conception of the highest good, one that the psychological reading cannot secure because pleasure may not in fact be good for the animal (except instrumentally). If there are better interpretations available, it would be uncharitable to attribute psychological hedonism and an unsuccessful argument to Eudoxus.[12]

10.3.2   *The Extensional Reading*

The extensional reading originates with Alexander of Aphrodisias: 'Eudoxus, too, showed pleasure to be the highest good from the fact that all animals choose it, and that none of the other goods admits of choice that is common in this way'.[13] According to Alexander, Eudoxus maintains that

---

[10] Presupposing that only pleasure is good would beg the question.

[11] Broadie 1991, 354 provides a helpful Aristotelian perspective on the 'hedonic guidance system'.

[12] I could not find any ancient Greek writer who attributes psychological hedonism to Eudoxus. Many recent interpreters read the *ephiēmi* ('seek') in b10 psychologically as 'desire' (e.g. Broadie in Broadie and Rowe 2002, 262), but do not read him as a psychological hedonist (clearly stated by Warren 2009, 253).

[13] ἀλλὰ καὶ Εὔδοξος ἐδείκνυε τὴν ἡδονὴν τὸ μέγιστον τῶν ἀγαθῶν ἀπὸ τοῦ πάντα μὲν τὰ ζῷα ταύτην αἱρεῖσθαι, μηδὲν δὲ τῶν ἄλλων ἀγαθῶν κοινὴν οὕτως ἔχειν τὴν αἵρεσιν. (Lasserre D5 = *In Top.* 226.16–19 Wallies, commenting on Aristotle's *Topics* III.I, 116a14–22.)

goods other than pleasure are chosen – thus rejecting the psychological reading – but that pleasure stands out because no other good is chosen uniformly by all animals. We can explain this again through Eudoxus' naturalism. Each kind of animal pursues a set of goods that consists of various subsets, such as food, shelter, etc., suited to its nature. However, the different sets of kind-specific goods intersect: each kind of animal pursues pleasure. We should take the intersection of the kind-specific goods to be the good, because it alone is good for all, and what is good for all is *the* good (1172b14–15). Hence, *T*.

Is the universal pursuit of X both necessary and sufficient for X to be the good, as claimed by the extensional reading? By considering both directions, we can elicit the assumptions to which the extensional reading commits Eudoxus. First, is universal pursuit of X really necessary for X to be the good? Consider: humans seek and choose moral virtue, but no other animal does so. On the extensional reading, we must conclude that moral virtue cannot be the human good because it is not universally pursued. *We* take this argument to be clearly fallacious, because we share at least some of Aristotle's intuition that we should look to what is peculiarly human in order to determine the human good. Given his view of nature, Eudoxus would acknowledge that what is good for each kind should somehow reflect their different natures. But he would struggle to recognise such differences in the good, because it would undermine pleasure as the unique object of universal pursuit, as becomes clear from considering the other direction.

Is universal pursuit of X sufficient for X to be the good? Initially, the answer might seem to be 'no'. Take again the example of food: all animals seek food, but food is not the good. Now, on the extensional account one might try to drive a wedge between other goods and pleasure. Different kinds of animals seek vastly different kinds of commonly pursued goods such as food, shelter, or mates. In order to avoid concluding that the same move applies to pleasure, Eudoxus would have to commit himself to a highly unified view of pleasure. One way of giving such an account would be to allow variety in pleasure and then to focus on what is common to all pleasures, an abstraction.[14] But this move would not repair the argument because one could equally abstract food to make *it* a common object of pursuit. Alternatively, one could deny the variety of pleasure. In this case, the extensional reading saddles Eudoxus with the view that rolling in mud gives pigs the very same pleasure that doing mathematics

---

[14] Discussed by Broadie in Broadie and Rowe 2002, 430.

gives to humans. While this is a possible view, we should not attribute it lightly to Eudoxus, especially if we can interpret the argument from universal pursuit in a way that does not require this view of pleasure.[15]

10.3.3   The Choice Reading

Both interpretations considered so far rely on a view of choice alien to Eudoxus. This view of choice has two components: (a) an animal can choose only one thing at a time, and (b) pleasure is a detachable object of choice, on the same level as other possible objects of choice with which it competes. To derive T from universal pursuit, the psychological reading makes pleasure the only object of choice, whereas the extensional reading claims that none of the other goods is chosen by all animals. But if, as I shall argue, Eudoxus does not subscribe to (a) and (b), he seems to have a more interesting account, one that the other interpretations capture only partially. I propose that Eudoxus maintains T because pleasure features in every good choice as a good. And if, as Eudoxus plausibly assumes, pleasure is the only thing that features in every good choice as a good, it must be the good for each animal and hence the good without qualification (cf. 1172b14–15). I shall develop my interpretation in the remainder of the chapter.

   Let us begin with Eudoxus' view of choice. The Greek fuels assumption (a) because the singular *to haireton* naturally suggests a single object of choice. Since Eudoxus says explicitly a little later that pain in itself is (to be) avoided (*pheukton*, 1172b19), and that we do in fact choose pleasure (*hairoumetha*, b21–2), pleasure seems to be just an ordinary object of choice. If we add the quest for the strongest (*kratiston* b11) or best object of choice (*ariston*, b12–13), (b) seems to be a natural assumption. However, this view of choice goes against the grain of Eudoxus' naturalism as found in the supplementary argument. As we have seen, each animal finds what is good for itself, such as food (b13) and chooses what is fitting in every situation (b11). But he also maintains that pleasure is universally pursued (b10). Without (a) and (b), Eudoxus can connect the universal pursuit of pleasure and b13 by endorsing the much weaker claim that an animal chooses a good such as food only if it normally enjoys it, probably *because* it normally enjoys it. Thus, the psychological reading rightly stresses that pleasure

[15] If the *Philebus* represented Eudoxus' position, Socrates' objection against the unity of pleasure (12c–d) would support interpreting Eudoxus this way. But despite the valiant effort by Gosling 1975, scholars now tend to be more sceptical about using the *Philebus* as a source for Eudoxus hedonism. See especially Frede 1997, 390–4.

features in every choice, but overstates the point by making pleasure the only object of choice.

But how does pleasure feature in the choice? Because of the complexity of choice, there is no simple answer other than: pleasure belongs to the 'package' that animals choose. In some cases, as suggested earlier, the animal makes the correct choice because of pleasure. This does not entail, but is compatible with, the claim that the animal acts out of pleasure or for the sake of pleasure. That is, while pleasure may explain the choice – the animal would not choose *X* unless it normally enjoys *X* – it can, but need not, feature in the justification of the choice. But choosing a good for the sake of pleasure or choosing a good out of pleasure (cf. the indicator view in §10.3.1) does not exhaust the package view. The text supports a broader view of choice in an argument mentioned shortly after our passage (1172b23–5), which I shall call 'the argument from addition'. There, Eudoxus argues that pleasure makes any of the goods more choiceworthy. While it looks as if the goods could be chosen without pleasure, Eudoxus has already stated that an animal chooses what is most choiceworthy in each situation (b11). Therefore, he may reasonably assume that animals tend to choose what they enjoy. That is, they choose a combination of a certain good and pleasure. Given the close connection between pleasure and its source, it may be futile to attempt to separate the different elements of the package to identify their unique contribution.[16] Nevertheless, the package view of choice neutralises the force of the question whether the animal chooses pleasure or its source: the animal chooses the package consisting of both. Instead of competition between pleasure and other goods, as per (b), there is combination.

By reconsidering Eudoxus' view of choice, we can make headway in understanding the argument from universal pursuit. Returning to the question of observability, the package view seems empirically much more plausible than making either component the sole object of choice: we *can* observe that animals seek both. If so, we need not reject off-hand Eudoxus' observation that all animals seek pleasure. As I have interpreted the claim, he means that every natural and fitting choice features pleasure. This is no doubt still a bold claim, but a much more interesting and defensible one than ordinary psychological hedonism. Indeed, Aristotle's account of pleasure may be compatible with this aspect of Eudoxus' thought.[17]

---

[16] Aristotle throws up his hands over a closely related question at x.4, 1175a19–21. I shall expand on Eudoxus' reasoning and the argument from addition more generally in §§10.4.2–3.

[17] Gosling and Taylor 1982, 258–60 further explore the proximity between Eudoxus and Aristotle in this respect.

However, the two definitely part company insofar as only Eudoxus, but
not Aristotle, adopts T.[18] Two further assumptions, to be taken up seri-
atim, drive Eudoxus towards T, namely the uniqueness assumption that
pleasure is the *only* good that makes all choices better and the broader
universalist assumption that pleasure as *the* good is good for all.

10.4   The Choice Reading Expanded

The choice reading builds on Eudoxus' naturalism. Animals choose what is
good for them, and their universal pursuit of pleasure suggests that (i)
pleasure features in all natural and good choices.[19] But does the naturalist
framework also suggest that (ii) pleasure is itself a good? As we shall see,
Eudoxus thinks so, but a positive answer would come near establishing
T only if (iii) no other good features in all choices. If, as (iii) claims,
pleasure turns out to be the only good that features in all choices, Eudoxus
would be justified in maintaining T because our commitment to the good
shows in all our choices (as Plato and Aristotle would agree), and pleasure is
the only substantial good to which we would be committed in all our
choices.

10.4.1   *All Good Choices Are Choices of Pleasure*

We can come to understand the choice reading better by considering an
objection. Animals engage in territorial fights, run away from predators, or
wait their turn in the baking sun near the waterhole despite their thirst. We
cannot dismiss these choices as unnatural, but animals certainly do not do
these things because they feel pleasant: they are manifestly painful! So,
sometimes animals seem to prefer a package of a good with pain to a (lesser)
good with pleasure. Hence, contrary to the choice reading, not all choices
are also choices of pleasure.

Eudoxus provides material for a response in the argument from opposites. In order to establish T, he focuses on pain: 'pain in itself is (to be)
avoided by everything, so that, correspondingly, its opposite is (to be)
chosen' (1172b18–20).[20] Contrasting the choice of X 'in itself' (*kath' hauto*,

---

[18] Aristotle flirts with adopting a thesis similar to T at *Eth. Nic.* VII.13, 1153b7–14, because his definition
  of the good as virtuous activity aligns with his definition of pleasure as unimpeded activity of
  a natural state. Rapp 2009 provides a judicious account of Aristotle's affinity to hedonism.
[19] Henceforth, 'choice' means natural and fitting choice.
[20] οὐχ ἧττον δ' ᾤετ' εἶναι φανερὸν ἐκ τοῦ ἐναντίου· τὴν γὰρ λύπην καθ' αὑτὸ πᾶσι φευκτὸν εἶναι,
  ὁμοίως δὴ τοὐναντίον αἱρετόν. In the interest of space, I set aside two moot points. (a) Most scholars

b19) with avoiding or choosing *X* for the sake of something else, Eudoxus maintains that animals do not choose pain itself, but choose it because of or for the sake of something else (*di' heteron* or *heterou charin*, b20–1). This distinction expands on his view of choice, either setting up (A) a distinction between kinds of choices, or (B) broadening the conception of pleasure featuring in the choice. According to (A), he distinguishes between two levels of choice: instrumental choices and choices that are in themselves good for the animal. Although it does not strictly follow from the fact that pain is chosen for the sake of something else, his naturalism inclines Eudoxus to suppose that a painfully chosen package does not in itself contribute to flourishing, even if the choice is natural.[21] Rabbits that never have to flee foxes and foxes that never have to fight for their territory may still live well! Eudoxus would thus restrict the scope of the thesis that all choices feature pleasure to choices of goods that contribute in themselves to flourishing.

However tempting, the text of the argument from universal pursuit hardly sustains (A). The combination of the universal pursuit of pleasure in 1172b10 and the claim that animals choose what is fitting in all situations (b10–11) rather supports (B), which broadens Eudoxus' conception of the pleasure and/or pain featuring in the choice. If we understand the affective component as overall pain or pleasure, Eudoxus can maintain that every good and fitting choice is a choice of pleasure, even if some episodes of the action are painful. So, the 'package' that is chosen may include not only goods and pleasure, but also some pain where the pleasure always outweighs the pain in a fitting choice.[22] Although this view of choice seems to be cognitively quite demanding, it need not go over the animals' heads. Of course, for many kinds of animals, preferring the overall more pleasant action over the less pleasant must be learnt. But Eudoxus' paradigms, well-developed and mature animals, have learnt to make the correct choices, whatever the cognitive resources required for it. So, by becoming attuned

take 1172b18–20 to be a distinct argument, only to complain that, at best, it shows pleasure to be *a* good, but not *the* good. However, if read in conjunction with the next lines, the argument may at least have a chance of establishing the goal stated at 1172b18, *T* (cf. Aufderheide 2020, 65–8). (b) Pleasure as the opposite of pain may not itself be good but could also be bad or neutral (1173a5–13). This dialectical exchange has been the focus of some excellent recent studies to which I refer the reader: Cheng, 2020, Fronterotta 2018, and Warren 2009.

[21] Plato seems to air a similar view in the division of goods at the beginning of *Republic* 11.

[22] I refrain from casting the view in terms of short-term and long-term pleasures because Gosling and Taylor 1982, 162 have rightly noted that we can ask ourselves for the sake of what are we enjoying any short-term pleasure. But Eudoxus maintains that we do not ask this question because pleasure is end-like, 1172b22–3.

to finding pleasure and avoiding pain overall, the animal cultivates 'a natural element of goodness better than themselves which seeks their own proper good' (1173a4–5).[23]

10.4.2   Pleasure Is a Good

Eudoxus' naturalism, together with his view of choice, suggests that all choices are choices also of pleasure. But in order to move further in the direction of *T*, he must also have held that pleasure itself is a good, not merely an instrument to finding what is really good. He espouses this claim in the argument from addition, to which I have alluded briefly in support of the package view of choice: 'Moreover, he thought that pleasure, when added to any one of the goods, makes it more choiceworthy, such as doing what is just or moderate; hence [/and] the good (*to agathon*) is increased by itself' (Arist. *Eth. Nic.* x.2, 1172b23–5).[24]

I shall postpone the discussion of the ordinary reading to consider, briefly, a deflationary reading first. According to the latter, *to agathon* does not mean *the* good, but only 'what is good' (as it often does). This reading gives us a clear and intelligible argument. Adding pleasure to other goods makes them more choiceworthy; hence (*dè*) what is good is increased by itself. We can unpack the reasoning by invoking the widely accepted principle that if *a* makes *b* more *F*, then *a* must also be *F* (*Top.* II.II, 115a29–31). So, if pleasure makes *b* more choiceworthy, then pleasure must also be choiceworthy. But in this case, one good is improved by another good – summed up pithily by the claim that what is good is improved by itself. Putting the point in this way helps to silence the lingering doubt that pleasure may be merely an instrument: choosing a good and the instrument that furthers it is not better than this good alone (cf. *Top.* III.2, 117a18–21). So, Eudoxus would have a neat argument to the effect that pleasure is a good.

---

[23] This section poses, in my view, the strongest challenge to the choice interpretation. In order to maintain that all choices are choices of pleasure, it must either invoke overall pleasure or make a distinction between short-term and long-term pleasure, or between important and not so important choices. The extensional reading only requires that all animals sometimes choose pleasure, and can thus acknowledge that animals sometimes choose a good when doing so is painful. I do not take this to be a sufficiently strong reason to go back to the extensional reading because it cannot explain why the intersection of goods should be the good, whereas the choice reading plausibly maintains that the good chosen in every choice is *the* good.
[24] προστιθεμένην τε ότῳοῦν τῶν ἀγαθῶν αἱρετώτερον ποιεῖν, οἷον τῷ δικαιοπραγεῖν καὶ σωφρονεῖν, αὔξεσθαι δὴ [/δὲ] τὸ ἀγαθὸν αὐτῷ. I read *dè* with the MSS instead of Heliodorus' *de*, adopted by Bywater.

10.4.3 Pleasure Is the Good

The deflationary reading does not seem to exhaust Eudoxus' thought here, however, unless we radically reconfigure his arguments.[25] The ordinary reading, which originates with our only source, Aristotle, has the argument revolve around *T*. Aristotle cites Plato to show that Eudoxus' argument falls short of establishing *T* (*tagathon*, 1172b29), and then goes on to specify certain conditions for the good (*tagathon*, b31–3). In contrast to the deflationary reading, 'the good' would not have to change meaning between 1172b9 and b24. Although we cannot always trust Aristotle's testimonia, the ordinary reading seems right in this case.

But what could Eudoxus' argument possibly be on this reading? One interpretation applies Eudoxus' view of immanent forms (Arist. *Metaph.* 1.9.991a13–17) to the good.[26] In this case, all goods are good because the form of the good is present in them, so that any good can be made better only by adding more of (the form of) the good. But since pleasure makes other things better, pleasure must be (the form of) the good. Hence (*dē*), the good is improved by itself. This interpretation, note, entails that all goods, such as doing what is just, would be good either instrumentally or because of the pleasure in them. While many hedonists espouse this kind of value monism, Eudoxus does not. The crux of his argument relies on pluralism: pleasure makes any good thing even better and therefore counts as the good![27]

Since he does not offer an explicit theory of the good, we might take Eudoxus' assumptions about the good to come to the fore here: whatever has the magic power to make any good even better must be the good. Instead of pursuing this interesting suggestion further, I shall address the worry that pleasure may not uniquely improve the other goods.[28] Indeed, Aristotle maintains that any two goods together are more choiceworthy than each on its own (1172b27–8), without considering how these two goods relate to each other (he commits the same mistake at *Top.* III.2, 117a16–18). But Eudoxus' examples are deliberately chosen. Doing what is moderate and just is good for humans. Mature and well-developed

---

[25] Weiss 1979 contends that the argument from addition needs only to establish pleasure as a good, because it forms part of a long, cumulative argument – which we discover if we reverse Aristotle's order of presentation.

[26] Tentatively suggested by Broadie in Broadie and Rowe 2002, 430–1.

[27] Eudoxus' view that pleasure stands beyond other goods because, unlike other goods, we do not praise pleasure (cited approvingly at *Eth. Nic.* 1.12.1101b27–31) likewise seems to require a plurality of goods.

[28] A problem also noted by Broadie 2007a, 142–4, who proposes this interpretation.

humans, such as Eudoxus himself, will enjoy these actions, if we are to judge from his lifestyle (cf. §10.1). For these paradigms, the choices mentioned are natural, good, and feature pleasure – and thus illustrate Eudoxus' position. If Eudoxus held that pleasure is the only feature of every choice that improves any of the other goods chosen, we can see why he diverged from Aristotle in maintaining *T*, and not merely making the claim that pleasure is *a* good.

Unfortunately, Eudoxus does not provide an argument for the uniqueness assumption. He probably thought that there is no other good that features in all choices of all animals. There is no *a priori* argument to show that there could be no other good than pleasure. But by sketching how Eudoxus could have thought about three plausible candidates, *philia* (friendship or love), intelligence, and knowledge, I hope to outline his reasons. First, most animals, at some point, pursue *philia*. And indeed, in actions that have to do with others, doing them with *philoi* or in the spirit of *philia* makes those actions more choiceworthy. But not all animal choices have to do with others, and it would be implausible to relegate these choices to the instrumental or conceive of them as choices of *philia* (following the model suggested in §10.4.1). Next, taking a cue from the *Philebus* argument to which Aristotle alludes at 1172b28–32, we could stress that intelligence (*phronēsis*) also features in all choices, and that it, too, makes all choices better. So, either both would be the good – ruled out by the uniqueness assumption about the good – or neither, as the *Philebus* maintains.[29] Eudoxus can push back by pointing out the different levels at which intelligence and pleasure operate. Both good and bad choices necessarily feature intelligence, where intelligence does not improve the bad choices. While bad choices can feature pleasure, only good choices *necessarily* feature pleasure. One may use these differences to argue that intelligence seems to be just part of the mechanism belonging to choice, but not itself a good. In support, one could point to the end-like character of pleasure (cf. 1172b20–3), which intelligence lacks – except when combined with pleasure.[30]

This last point also helps with the final candidate, knowledge. If we understand 'knowledge' as something that only humans can have, Eudoxus would not have to take this candidate seriously because it is not universally

---

[29] *Phlb.* 20b6–9 suggests a rather wide understanding of *phronēsis*, close to cognition. Aristotle probably picks up this sense here.

[30] If asserting that pleasure is most choiceworthy (*malista haireton*) in 1172b20–2 sets up the claim that pleasure makes other goods more choiceworthy (*hairetōteron*) in b24, then we should read these two arguments together. I thank Rhodes Pinto for this suggestion.

pursued. But for the sake of the argument, does choosing with knowledge make any other good better for us? Here we must distinguish between practical and theoretical knowledge. Eudoxus could take practical knowledge to be good insofar as it tends to result in successful choices. In any case, this kind of knowledge *can* be valued instrumentally rather than for its own sake. Pleasure, Eudoxus argues, differs in this respect. While we can enjoy instrumentally valuable things, such as having money, the pleasure we take in money is not, therefore, instrumentally valuable. He supports this point by observing that 'no one asks to what end he is enjoying himself, as if pleasure in itself is (to be) chosen' (b22–3). Finally, does theoretical understanding of, say, the soul improve the choices we make in respect to ensouled things? One could possibly argue that it does. But in comparison to the claim that pleasure makes every choice better, this position seems rather feeble. Pleasure is end-like in all choices and makes all good choices that involve it better. In the absence of other goods that play the same role, Eudoxus can reasonably conclude that pleasure is *the* good.

10.5 Conclusion

To bring out a more general point about Eudoxus' approach, I shall end by considering one last objection: the pleasures that feature in different choices are too different to be classed together as one (cf. *Phlb* 12c–d). Hence, pleasure is not the good for any kind of animal or absolutely. Whether Eudoxus would have been impressed depends on his conception of pleasure – of which we know too little. He may indeed have held the position that Socrates attacks, namely that the sources of pleasure differ, but not the pleasure. But, given his broader naturalist framework, Eudoxus could easily acknowledge that the pleasures a pig takes in eating and in mating differ. However, this does not preclude him (or Arist. *Eth. Nic.* x.5.1176a3–5) from classing a pig's pleasures together – precisely because they are natural for a flourishing pig. Aristotle would urge Eudoxus to stay at the level of kinds because he maintains that what is good and what is healthy differs according to kind (vi.7.1141a23–34) and objects to a universal good anyway (in *Eth. Nic.* i.6). But from a scientific perspective, we can meaningfully speak about health without qualification. The sentence 'health is the good of the body' can be both informative and true, even if the determinants of health differ vastly across different kinds of animal. Likewise, 'food is good for all animals' is true, even if different animals seek different kinds of food. Of course, no animal seeks food or health in the abstract: they seek what is nutritious or healthy for their kind, or something even more specific (cf. 1.6.1097a11–13). Similarly, each seeks only the pleasures congenial to its kind, or those available in a given situation. But if we can class the different pleasures of each kind of animal together as their kind-specific pleasure, then we can also class together the different pleasures of different kinds of animals. The point of doing so is to bring out the commonly shared basis of a good life. A philosopher who believes that all animals, rational or irrational, listen to the voice of nature would find it important to stress that nature sings of pleasure.

In the course of discussing Eudoxus' arguments, I have suggested that he is not a value, psychological, or normative hedonist. There are other things that are by nature good for us, and we can, do, and should desire them for their own sake. Instead of setting Eudoxus aside because he is not a proper hedonist by our standards, we should embrace his (to my mind) unique position. If the choice reading reflects Eudoxus' thought, he proffers the interesting proposal that pleasure features in all our good choices as a good that we also choose. Thus, in pleasure we have a unique good for which we care in everything we do – and this position clearly qualifies as hedonism.

CHAPTER 11

Aristotle and Socrates in the Eudemian Ethics on the Naturalness of Goodness

Christopher Rowe

Socrates appears in Aristotle's *Eudemian Ethics* (*Eth. Eud.*) more prominently than anyone else, being named explicitly six times in the five undisputed books – and six times is a high number, given Aristotle's general practice of discussing ideas without tying them to their authors.[1] But Socrates' presence extends way beyond this: Socrates is surely one of the starting points in the first chapter of the first book;[2] he and his ideas surface both explicitly and implicitly in each of books 11, 111, and V11, while the three chapters of the fragmentary book V111[3] – the first two of which, but especially the second, will be my main focus in this chapter – represent a kind of extended conversation with him.[4] All of this suggests that in the *Eth. Eud.*, whatever may be true of the *Nicomachean Ethics* (*Eth. Nic.*),

---

For Sarah.

[1] 'Socrates' stands here both for Socrates the historical figure – 'old Socrates': Σωκράτης ὁ πρεσβύτης, 1.5, 1216b2–3; Σωκράτης ὁ γέρων, V11.1, 1235a37 – and for Socrates in Plato. That there are references to 'old Socrates', rather than just 'Socrates', may suggest a measure of interest in distinguishing the two, but for the purposes of this chapter it will be sufficient if 'Socrates' in all cases is that Socrates, composite or otherwise, to whom Aristotle responds in the *Eudemian Ethics*.

[2] I.e. when Aristotle asks how happiness is acquired (1.1, 1214a14–25): the list of possibilities not only includes what looks like a reference to Socrates' 'divine voice' as described in Plato's *Apology* and *Phaedrus*, but bears an uncanny resemblance to the list of possible answers to the parallel question about goodness (i.e. ἀρετή, 'virtue', central to Aristotle's own account of happiness) in the conversation between Meno and Socrates in Plato's *Meno*. See further below.

[3] I shall adhere to the traditional numbering of the books of the *Eth. Eud.*, without implying any particular stance on the question of the (so-called) 'common' books (i.e. as to whether they do or do not belong within the *Eth. Eud.*), although such a stance will emerge as my argument proceeds. For the record, *Eth. Nic.* V1 '=' *Eth. Eud.* V names Socrates twice (in a single passage), *Eth. Nic.* V11 '=' *Eth. Eud.* V1 three times (in a single discussion, of 'weakness of will'); the total figure for the *Eth. Nic.* including the 'common' books is seven, for the *Eth. Eud.* including the common books, eleven. These figures tend to bear out my basic intuition that the *Eth. Eud.*, however comprised, is rather more interested in Socrates than is the *Eth. Nic.* – an intuition that is not fundamentally altered by Gabriele Giannantoni's 1990 paper on the *Eth. Nic.*, which 'ha solo lo scopo di dare una prima e provvisoria motivazione alla proposta di considerare anche Socrate tra i punti di riferimento essenziali nella lettura delle pagine aristoteliche' (i.e. the pages of the *Eth. Nic.*, 326).

[4] On V111.3, see Rowe 2013.

Aristotle sees Socrates as perhaps *the* figure against whom he needs to measure his own ideas on ethics.[5] The central feature of Socrates' thinking to which Aristotle takes exception is, notoriously, the identification of goodness with knowledge; goodness, Aristotle insists, includes but is not coextensive with its cognitive element, and this element, as he concludes at the end of *Eth. Eud.* VIII.1, is not knowledge – since after all knowledge can be misapplied – but a different sort of cognition, one he labels *phronēsis* (usually translated as 'practical wisdom'), which is itself a kind of goodness and so not subject to misapplication.

The reason why Aristotle singles out Socrates as the person to disagree with is that he is so close to him. Intellectually, Socrates is his aged grandfather.[6] Like his progenitor, Aristotle thinks we all want our own lives to be happy,[7] thinks goodness is central to that happiness, thinks ordinarily recognised goods can be harmful, and so on; if he diverges from Socrates on major issues, it is important for him to mark these divergences just because the two of them so clearly belong to the same family (whatever one says about Aristotle's relationship to his intellectual father, Plato). Perhaps the most important such divergence is that while both think we all desire the good, Socrates proposes that the good we all desire is what is really good for us, whereas Aristotle says that it is not the real but the apparent good. While Socrates is content to claim that, contrary to the evidence, we never

---

[5] If Aristotle does distinguish between the historical Socrates and the Platonic Socrates (e.g. the reference at VIII.2, 1247b15 must surely be to *Euthydemus* 279d, on good fortune, εὐτυχία), that raises the possibility that when Socrates is not described as 'old Socrates', 'Socrates' is a stand-in for Plato, whom Aristotle typically prefers, for whatever reason, not to mention in person; though that would then raise the question why the name 'Socrates' does not appear more often, since Platonic ideas – and not just Platonic 'ideas' = 'forms' – certainly do. (Note: if 1247b15 does indeed refer to the *Euthydemus*, this is a clear counterexample to what has come to be called 'Fitzgerald's canon', to which Liddell–Scott–Jones subscribes s.v. ὁ, ἡ, τό B.I.c. Maybe Socrates was well-known for saying that the only true good fortune was knowledge – the idea which, I shall argue in the present chapter, is one of the cues for the discussion in VIII.2; or maybe 'canons' allow for exceptions. Or alternatively, this particular canon is no canon at all.)

[6] *Pace* e.g. Guthrie, who (in his *Socrates* of 1971) according to Christopher Moore 'gives excellent expression to Aristotle's uptake of Socrates' when he says that he '"had no personal interest in Socrates," and had "no emotional involvement"' (Moore 2019, 205). Such a judgement gains particular traction (a) from Moore's treatment of the *Magna moralia* (*Mag. mor.*) as a third Aristotelian ethics alongside the *Eth. Eud.* and *Eth. Nic.*, the *Mag. mor.*'s handling of Socrates being markedly blunt and negative – not to say unsubtle – by contrast to those of the *Eth. Eud.* and *Eth. Nic.*; and (b) from Moore's limiting his attention to just those passages where Socrates is mentioned by name. It would not be entirely unfair to remark that if we tried to establish the relationship between Aristotle and Plato on the same basis, we would conclude that the former did not think much of, or even about, the latter at all, except perhaps in the sphere of metaphysics – a conclusion that I take to be patently false. I shall return to the issue of the *Mag. mor.* later.

[7] On the eudaimonism of Plato's Socrates, see Crisp 2003, 55–78 and my reply (Rowe 2003, 79–86).

desire what is actually bad for us,[8] Aristotle is clear that we must: it is desire that causes us to act, reason by itself moves nothing, and so however appalling the consequences of an action we perform may be, even for ourselves, there is no doubt in his mind that it must have been the action we wanted to do (however much we regret it afterwards), since otherwise we would not have done it. But even here Aristotle retains something of Socrates' position, not just in recognising much the same things as good and bad that Socrates did, but because he agrees with Socrates that when we do things that are actually bad we act contrary to our nature: the human being, qua human being, is by nature something good.[9]

The focus of the present chapter will be on one particular manifestation of this shared belief in the naturalness of goodness that results in a surprising appropriation, adaptation, and indeed naturalisation of one of the most notorious aspects of Socrates: his 'divine or demonic something' (θεῖόν τι καὶ δαιμόνιον: Pl. *Ap.* 31c8–d1), the 'voice (as it were)' (φωνή τις: *Ap.* 31d3) that intervenes sometimes to prevent him from doing what he might well otherwise have done. He says that his accuser Meletus made fun of this in his affidavit before the trial, and *prima facie* it does sit uneasily with his otherwise total dedication to the power of reason (Pl. *Ap.* 31d1–2). 'The Socratic saying[10] is right', says Aristotle at *Eth. Eud.* VIII.1, 1246b34, 'that nothing is stronger than *phronēsis*' – except of course, as he immediately admits, he is substituting *phronēsis* in 'the Socratic saying' for Socrates' original 'knowledge' (*epistēmē*). But then he himself immediately goes on, in the next chapter, to introduce something that, while not 'stronger than *phronēsis*' in the sense of being able to overcome it, can make a reasonable pass at substituting for it in its absence, just as Socrates' 'something divine or demonic' can substitute for *epistēmē*; what is more, Aristotle uses the same or similar language of this something, in a way that leaves little doubt that he means the connection with Socrates to be recognised.

---

[8] A claim from which the author of the *Mag. mor.* flat-footedly infers that Socrates said that it is not up to us whether we are good or bad (1.9, 1187a5–13).

[9] I take it that this can legitimately be derived from, e.g. *Eth. Eud.* VII.2, 1237a5–6: 'A human being is well fitted to make progress, those things unqualifiedly good (ἁπλῶς ἀγαθά) being naturally good to/for him', and 1237a16–18: 'Let the human being be among those things good by nature; for the goodness of the one who is good by nature is good unqualifiedly, while that of the one who is not [good by nature] is good for that person [rather than unqualifiedly]' (*sc.* and so not apt for 'virtue'-friendship).

[10] As in *Protagoras*, 352b–c, summed up at 357c2–3.

This is in two closely connected passages. The first is in *Eth. Eud.* 1.1, where Aristotle is raising the question 'in what is good living (i.e. happiness) to be found, and how is it to be acquired?' (1214a15). Do all the people to whom the epithet 'happy' applies become so by nature, or through learning, 'happiness being knowledge of some sort', or through practice of some sort – or rather 'are they like those possessed by the supernatural or divine beside themselves, as it were, through the inspiration of something demonic,[11] or is it through fortune (*tuchē*, 'chance'), since many people say happiness and good fortune (*eutuchia*) are the same thing?' (1214a22–5). These last two possibilities, which as they appear in 1.1 may well look like rank outsiders, are then given a surprisingly full treatment in *Eth. Eud.* VIII.2. This latter chapter has been widely discussed, but little has emerged by way of consensus about its outcomes, no doubt partly because of the poor state of parts of the text;[12] I therefore need to interweave an outline reconstruction[13] of the text with the main argument of the present chapter.[14]

With *Eth. Eud.* VIII.2, the first and overriding question for the interpreter is: what exactly is the phenomenon being discussed? There are, according to Aristotle, some people who enjoy good fortune on a regular basis even though their capacity for practical reasoning is so lacking that they are likely to be better off not using it at all. Who exactly are these fortunate people? The *Eth. Nic.* links good fortune almost exclusively with

---

[11] Three of the four primary MSS of *Eth. Eud.* ('C' = Cantabrigensis 1879, 'B' = Monacensis 635, and 'L' = Laurentianus 81.15) read δαιμονίᾳ, with only 'P' = Vaticanus 1342 giving us δαιμονίου, but δαιμονίᾳ would leave the following τινος orphaned, and δαιμονίᾳ for δαιμονίου after ἐπιπνοίᾳ would be an easy mistake. It is true that there is an obvious etymological motivation for the inclusion of divine or quasi-divine causation in the list. Cf. 1.7, 1217a27–8: 'nor would anything else in the world [be called happy] that did not, as the name [εὐδαιμονία] suggests, partake of something divine (θεῖον = δαιμόνιον)'. But the echo of Socrates' θεῖόν τι καὶ δαιμόνιον, in a context in which Socrates is already present, would still be clear enough. (Note: B has been regarded, if it has been regarded at all, as a copy of C, but my collations demonstrate that this is untrue; it is an independent manuscript, if ultimately – two, three, or four generations back – descended from the same single source as P, C, and L.)

[12] If I refer relatively infrequently to other scholarship on the chapter (e.g. Dirlmeier, von Fragstein, Michael J. Mills, even to van der Eijk 1989 – the most ambitious treatment of VIII.2 until that by Friedemann Buddensiek, which I will briefly discuss below), it is because I am proposing what is in some places a quite radically different text from the one others are starting from.

[13] The reconstruction is an excerpt from a draft of my new critical edition of the *Eudemian Ethics*, to be delivered in 2021, replacing the 1991 Oxford Classical Text of Walzer and Mingay.

[14] Everything begins, of course, with the manuscript evidence; the first question is always about what the manuscripts can offer us. With this in mind, where I offer my reconstructions of critical parts of the text, I shall append a much-abbreviated *apparatus criticus* in the footnotes; the aim is not to give the full justification of my choices as editor in each case, but simply to indicate to the reader just where I or other editors have had to make a leap of imagination – a leap, however, that will usually be quite small, and all the time controlled by the philosophical constraints.

external goods,[15] and this usage is recognised in *Eth. Eud.*, too, as indeed it is in that key passage in 1.1 I referred to at the beginning: 'or [does happiness arise] through fortune, since many people say happiness and good fortune (*eutuchia*) are the same thing?' (1214a24–5). But the fortunate people that interest Aristotle in VIII.2 are actually not those whose 'good fortune' consists in wealth, power, etc., but rather those whose *eutuchia* results from something at least overlapping with the previous item in the original list of possible causes of happiness (i.e. 'through the inspiration of something demonic', etc.): so, for example, they are 'beside themselves',[16] and possess (a sort of?) prophetic capacity.[17] *Eth. Eud.* VIII.2 is actually, and paradoxically, at pains to *exclude* fortune itself (*tuchē*) as a cause of its particular brand of *eutuchia* (the latter being characterised by its regularity, *tuchē* by its lack of it);[18] not only that, but it shows no inclination to limit the outcomes of this *eutuchia* to external goods – rather, as I shall argue, these outcomes seem to be more like the outcomes of ethical goodness.

This second, and crucial, point about the subject of *Eth. Eud.* VIII.2, that it has to do with more than external goods (if it is concerned with these at all), is often missed. It is missed not just because of the appalling state of the text in this part of the *Eth. Eud.*, but also because of a tendency among modern interpreters to interpret the *Eth. Eud.* from the *Magna moralia* (*Mag. mor.*),[19] which for much of its relatively short length seems to shadow the *Eth. Eud.*; for, puzzlingly, *Mag. mor.* II.8, which is its version of *Eth. Eud.* VIII.2, interprets the latter's special *eutuchia* as being concerned with external goods,[20] and external goods alone, even while denying that fortune is the cause. If we take the *Mag. mor.* as our guide, then, the special *eutuchia* of *Eth. Eud.* VIII.2 provides the same benefits on a regular basis, to certain 'well-natured'[21] individuals, that ordinary, fortune-governed, *eutuchia* offers only irregularly, through chance conjunctions. Since Aristotle thinks external goods necessary to the living of a good life, this special good fortune could thus be seen as a kind of adjunct to the good activity required for the best Aristotelian life.[22] But one has to ask whether interpreting *Eth. Eud.* from the *Mag. mor.* is the best policy, given that the

---

[15] At 1.8, 1099b6–8; IV.3, 1124a14; V.1, 1129b1–3; VII.13, 1153b14–25; IX.9, 1169b14, etc. The one exception is X.9, 1179b22–3, where Aristotle refers, somewhat mysteriously, to 'the *truly* fortunate'. I shall return to these two tantalising lines in X.9 in the last paragraphs of the present chapter.

[16] I.e. subject to ἐνθουσιασμός (VIII.2, 1248a33); cf. 1.1, 1214a24: ὥσπερ ἐνθουσιάζοντες.

[17] VIII.2, 1248a35: μαντική.   [18] VIII.2, 1247b10, 1247b28–1248a2, 1248a11–12, a16 ff.

[19] Cf. n. 6 above.   [20] *Mag. mor.* 1.8, 1206b30–6, 1207b16–18.

[21] VIII.2, 1247a38, b22: εὐφυεῖς.

[22] This is the kind of interpretation of VIII.2 offered in Buddensiek 2012 (an essay that deserves much closer attention than I can afford it here).

authorship of *Mag. mor.* is at best disputed,[23] and, unlike the *Eth. Nic.* and *Eth. Eud.*, the *Mag. mor.* 'seems to identify the dependency on external goods and the dependency on *eutuchia*'[24] – thus in my view exemplifying its typical lack of nuance and subtlety. The point here, however, is not about the authenticity and qualities or otherwise of the *Mag. mor.*, but rather whether its take on the subject of *Eth. Eud.* VIII.2 is in any case plausible. Not only is there, as I have said, nothing in the chapter itself that restricts the sphere of the special *eutuchia* in question to external goods; there are actually several indications that no such restriction is intended.

Take, first, the opening clause of the chapter: 'Since not only *phronēsis*, and goodness, bring about well-doing, but we say the fortunate too do well, on the basis that good fortune too brings about well-doing along the same lines as knowledge'.[25] The first three things listed as possible causes of happiness in *Eth. Eud.* I.I – nature, learning/knowledge, practice – have by now all been given a role in happiness-making, as aspects, constituents, or conditions of the combination *phronēsis*/goodness, which leaves the last two, divine inspiration and fortune, represented under the heading εὐτυχία – what about them? The surprising use, here at the beginning of VIII.2, of 'knowledge', *epistēmē* ('along the same lines as knowledge'), in place of *phronēsis* – it's Socrates, after all, who says 'knowledge' when he should be saying *phronēsis*, as Aristotle has said just a moment ago (VIII.I, 1246b34–6) – helps to confirm that reference to *Eth. Eud.* I.I, with the substitution of 'well-doing' for happiness; 'producing well-doing along the same lines as knowledge' then surely makes it more likely than not that what 'we say' is that *eutuchia* (i.e. of the sort to be discussed) can substitute for knowledge/*phronēsis tout court*. And some of the language Aristotle goes on to use is consistent with this. Thus the fortunate in question 'desire . . . as one should and what one should and when' (VIII.2, 1247b24–5; similarly at 1248a6); while these are indeed things that could be said of the good man just in relation to external goods, external goods have not been mentioned specifically, and the formulae 'as one should' etc., are typically used of the good person's actions and decisions as a whole.

This is not, of course, to claim that the fortunate in question are themselves good. They simply behave – somehow – *like* good people, without the reasoning and the dispositions that being good and acting

---

[23] See e.g. Rowe 1975. Buddensiek (2012, 155) 'do[es] not regard the *MM* as authentic in form, but as close to Aristotle in content'.

[24] As Buddensiek 2012, 156 acknowledges.

[25] I omit the textual issues here, as too complex to be dealt with briefly – or at the length they deserve – in the present chapter.

well requires. One big advantage of such an interpretation is that Aristotle would be likely to recognise significant numbers of such people: people who live apparently quite decent lives, even by Aristotelian standards, rather like those happy non-philosophers whom Socrates recognises in the *Phaedo*, 'the people who have practised the common, civic goodness ... that has come about from habit and practice and in the absence of philosophy and intelligence'.[26] By contrast, it is hard to see why Aristotle would give special recognition to those who happen somehow to be good at getting external goods, especially when the course of the argument leads him to bring out some of the very heaviest of his artillery: what is at issue, he says at a crucial point in the argument, is nothing less than 'what is the starting point of movement in the soul?' (VIII.2, 1248a24–5) in general. A big question if ever there was one, to which his answer is god, or the divine in us, which stands above even knowledge. 'What could be above even *epistēmē*? [It can't be goodness,] because goodness is an instrument of intelligence . . .' (1248a24–9). The mention here of goodness, alongside knowledge, intelligence, and god, surely itself constitutes confirmation that the context is about much larger things than the mere acquisition of external goods. Or, *pari passu*, than accommodating Aristotle's position to the *endoxa* (VIII.2, 1246b38–1247a2).

It is around this point, in the climax to the whole chapter, that the worst of the textual difficulties are to be found. The text as I presently propose to reconstruct it runs as follows (Aristotle has just rejected the possibility that fortune, *tuchē*, could be the cause of everything, inclusive of its being the cause of the fortunate person's having the desire, when she should, for what she should, and having it over and over again):

1248a23 ἢ[27] ἔστι τις ἀρχὴ ἧς οὐκ ἔστιν ἄλλη ἔξω, αὕτη δὲ διὰ τὸ τοιαύτη [τὸ] εἶναι τοιοῦτο δύναται ποιεῖν;[28] τὸ δὲ ζητούμενον **a25** τοῦτ᾽ ἐστί, τίς ἡ τῆς κινήσεως ἀρχὴ ἐν τῇ ψυχῇ. δῆλον δὴ ὥσπερ ἐν τῷ ὅλῳ θεός, καὶ πᾶν ἐκεῖ κινεῖ.[29] κινεῖ γάρ πως πάντα τὸ ἐν ἡμῖν θεῖον, λόγου δ᾽ ἀρχὴ οὐ λόγος, ἀλλά τι κρεῖττον. τί οὖν ἂν κρεῖττον καὶ ἐπιστήμης εἴη ποτὲ[30] <καὶ νοῦ>[31] πλὴν θεός; ἡ

---

[26] Pl. *Phd.* 82a11–b8. For more on degrees of goodness, or rather 'goodness', in Plato, see e.g. Rowe 2017.

[27] ἢ Susemihl = *aut BF*; εἰ PCBL ('*BF* = *Liber de bona fortuna*, a Latin combination of *Mag mor.* II.8 and *Eth. Eud.* VIII.2 whose Greek source is probably earlier than our MSS).

[28] διὰ τὸ τοιαύτη [τὸ] εἶναι τοιοῦτο δύναται ποιεῖν *scripsi*: διατί τοιαύτη τὸ εἶναι τὸ τοῦτο δύνασθαι ποιεῖν PCL; διατὶ τοιαύτη τὸ τοῦτο δύνασθαι ποιεῖν B; διὰ τὸ τοιαύτη [τὸ] εἶναι [τὸ] τοιοῦτο δύναται ποιεῖν Walzer; *quod tale secundum esse tale potest facere BF.*

[29] καὶ πᾶν ἐκεῖ κινεῖ Jackson: καὶ πᾶν ἐκείνῳ PCBL; *et omne illud BF.*

[30] εἴη ποτὲ *scripsi*: εἴη Spengel; εἴποι PCBL; [εἴποι] Jackson.

[31] <καὶ νοῦ> Spengel; *et intellectu BF* (following *et scientia*).

γὰρ ἀρετὴ τοῦ νοῦ ὄργανον. καὶ διὰ τοῦτο, **a30** ὃ³² πάλαι ἔλεγον, εὐτυχεῖς
καλοῦνται οἳ ἂν³³ ὁρμήσωσι κατορθοῦσιν³⁴ ἄλογοι ὄντες. καὶ βουλεύεσθαι οὐ
συμφέρει αὐτοῖς, ἔχουσι γὰρ ἀρχὴν τοιαύτην ἢ κρείττων τοῦ νοῦ καὶ³⁵ τῆς
βουλεύσεως,³⁶ οἱ δὲ τὸν λόγον, τοῦτο δ'³⁷ οὐκ ἔχουσι, καὶ ἐνθουσιάζουσι,³⁸
τοῦτο δ' οὐ δύνανται. ἄλογοι γὰρ ὄντες ἐπιτυγχάνουσι³⁹ καὶ τοῦ τῶν⁴⁰ **a35**
φρονίμων καὶ σοφῶν⁴¹ ταχεῖαν εἶναι τὴν μαντικήν, καὶ μόνον⁴² οὐ τὴν ἀπὸ τοῦ
λόγου δεῖ ἀπολαβεῖν⁴³. ἀλλ' οἱ μὲν δι' ἐμπειρίαν οἱ δὲ διὰ συνήθειαν [τε] ἀν<τὶ
τοῦ>⁴⁴ τῷ σκοπεῖν χρῆσθαι, τῷ θεῷ⁴⁵ δὲ αὗται· τοῦτο γὰρ⁴⁶ εὖ ὁρᾷ καὶ τὸ
μέλλον καὶ τὸ ὄν, καὶ ὧν ἀπολύεται ὁ λόγος οὕτως⁴⁷ ... **1248b3** φανερὸν δὴ⁴⁸
ὅτι δύο εἴδη εὐτυχίας, ἡ μὲν θεία, διὸ καὶ δοκεῖ ὁ εὐτυχὴς διὰ θεὸν κατορθοῦν·
οὗτος⁴⁹ **b5** δ' ἐστιν ὁ κατὰ τὴν ὁρμὴν διορθωτικός, ὁ δ' ἕτερος ὁ παρὰ τὴν
ὁρμήν. ἄλογοι δ' ἀμφότεροι, καὶ ἡ μὲν συνεχὴς εὐτυχία μᾶλλον, αὕτη δὲ οὐ
συνεχής.

1248a23 Or is it that there is some starting point that has no other starting
point outside it, and this can do the sort of thing in question because of

---

³² ὃ = *quod* BF: οἱ PCBL.   ³³ οἳ ἂν BL: *qui si* BF; οἵαν PC.
³⁴ κατορθοῦσιν Susemihl = *dirigunt* BF; κατορθοῦν PCBL.
³⁵ τοιαύτην ἢ κρείττων τοῦ νοῦ καὶ *desunt* PCB (which means, interestingly, that PCB, lacking τοῦ νοῦ in
a28–9 too, do not describe the ἀρχή in question as κρείττων τοῦ νοῦ at all; but the presence of τοιαύτην ἢ
κρείττων τοῦ νοῦ καὶ in L shows that the description was originally in the common source of PCBL).
³⁶ τῆς βουλεύσεως: βουλήσεως PCBL; βουλεύσεως Bekker; *consilio* BF.   ³⁷ τοῦτο δ': τοῦτον B.
³⁸ καὶ ἐνθουσιάζουσι *scripsi*: καὶ ἐνθουσιασμοί PCL; missing in B; *neque divinos instinctus* BF (the
whole sentence, as the MSS present it to us, is hopeless, and *BF*'s version is hardly better: *qui autem
racionem* [sc. *habent*] *hoc autem non habent neque divinos instinctus, hoc autem non possunt*. Those
who possess reason must themselves be subject to the same first principle as the fortunate, even if it
operates in a different way in their case [i.e. so far as we have been told, at least as first principle of
their reasoning], and if so it is the fortunate that must be the subject of οὐκ ἔχουσι; in which case the
negative following, i.e. *BF*'s *neque*, must be wrong, and PCL's καὶ must be right. ἐνθουσιάζουσι [cf.
I.I, 1214a14 ὥσπερ ἐνθουσιάζοντες; on the ὥσπερ, see below] seems a good bet to replace
ἐνθουσιασμοί and *BF*'s *divinos instinctus* [= ἐνθουσιασμούς?]).
³⁹ ἐπιτυγχάνουσι Susemihl et al.: *BF adipiscuntur*; ἀποτυγχάνουσι PCL; ἀποτυγχάνουσιν B.
⁴⁰ τοῦ τῶν Sylburg: τούτων PCBL; *horum* BF (without Sylburg's tiny correction there seems no
explanation for the following infinitive).
⁴¹ φρονίμων καὶ σοφῶν: 'ironice', says the OCT, as it would have to be if we retained the impossible
τούτων (as the OCT does), but not otherwise (see below).
⁴² μόνον L: μόνων PCB; *solorum* BF.
⁴³ ὑπολαβεῖν Ross = *suscipere* BF (but why not 'and one should practically take/receive [= ἀπολαβεῖν] it
as that arising from λόγος'? It is actually harder, I think, to make sense of ὑπολαβεῖν).
⁴⁴ [τε] ἀν<τὶ τοῦ> τῷ σκοπεῖν *scripsi*: τε ἐν τῷ σκοπεῖν PCBL; *in considerando BF* (editors generally have
bracketed τε, which has no counterpart in *BF* and is evidently dispensable; ἀν<τὶ τοῦ> is intended *inter
alia* to begin the construction of a story about how τε got there [loss of τοῦ before τῷ; ἀντὶ > ἂν τε > ἔν τε
> τε ἐν?]. But the important question is about the sense. The verb σκοπεῖν would typically be used of
rational enquiry; and if ἐμπειρία and συνήθεια were meant to be aspects of such an enquiry, why τῷ
σκοπεῖν χρῆσθαι and not just σκοπεῖν? More likely, I think, they are examples of *non*-rational processes
[see below]).
⁴⁵ θείῳ Spengel (presumably because of the following τοῦτο; but we had θεός followed by τὸ ἐν ἡμῖν
θεῖον in a26–7; why should we not have it again here?).
⁴⁶ γὰρ von Arnim: *enim BF*; καὶ PCBL.   ⁴⁷ οὕτως Jackson = *sic BF*; οὗτος PCBL.
⁴⁸ δὴ Susemihl = *itaque BF*; δὲ PCBL.   ⁴⁹ οὕτω PCB.

being the sort of thing it is? What we are seeking **a25** is just this, what the starting point of movement in the soul is. Well, it is clear that just as god moves everything in the universe, so he moves everything in the soul, too. For in a way the divine in us moves everything [in us], and the starting point of reasoning is not reasoning but something superior to it. So what could ever be superior even to knowledge <and intelligence> but god? Goodness, for its part, is an instrument of intelligence. And because of this, **a30** as I was saying before, people are called fortunate if they succeed in what they are impelled towards without reasoning. It is of no advantage to them to deliberate, because they have a starting point that is such as to be superior to intelligence and deliberation, while the others have reasoning, and this they [the fortunate] do not have, and they are inspired, but this [reasoning] they are incapable of. Though lacking the reasoning they match even the **a35** speediness of divination achieved by the wise and intellectually accomplished, so that one could almost take it for the divination engendered by reasoning. But some of them [achieve it] through experience, some through habituation, instead of using enquiry, and [the outcomes of] these are thanks to the god [= the divine in us]. For this sees the future well, and the present, even in those whose reasoning capacity is disengaged in this way ... **1248b3** Plainly, then, there are two kinds of good fortune, the one divine, which is why the fortunate are thought to succeed through god (and this kind of fortunate person **b5** is the one who has the capacity to make things right in accordance with impulse), while the other is the one [who succeeds] contrary to impulse; but both lack reasoning. And one of the two kinds of good fortune tends to be continuous, while the second is not continuous.

This remarkable turn in the argument has been prepared for especially by the idea that the relevant *eutuchia* arises 'according to the well-naturedness of appetency and desire' (1247b39–1248a1); the outcome of this 'well-naturedness', despite its not arising from human *logismos* (reasoning), 'is not altogether *alogiston*, given that the desire for it is natural' (1248a7–8).[50] That the (executive) desire is correct is because of two factors, working together: the well-formed nature of the individual, plus 'the divine in us', which as it were makes desire in a particular case into an executive desire. The impulses (*hormai*) in the naturally fortunate are inclined in the right direction:

---

[50] The full text of 1248a5–9 as I propose to restore it runs ἐκείνη δὲ πότερον εὐτυχία ἢ οὐκ ἔστιν; εἰ ἐπεθύμησεν ὧν ἔδει καὶ ὅτε ἔδει, λογισμός <γ'> ἀνθρώπινος οὐκ ἂν τούτου εἴη <αἴτιον>, οὐ γὰρ δὴ πάμπαν ἀλόγιστον τοῦτο οὗ γε φυσική ἐστιν ἡ ἐπιθυμία, ἀλλὰ [*sc.* λογισμὸς ἀνθρώπινος] διαφθείρεται ὑπό τινος. The crucial – and palmary – emendation is Jackson's οὗ γε for οὔτε PCBL = *neque BF*; a negative here, after we have been told that there is 'well-naturedness' of desire in this case, would be intolerable.

for if [the impulse] for the pleasant (i.e. the desire) is by nature, then by nature everything will tend towards the good. If then some people are well-natured, in the way that good singers[51] are born like that[52] even if they don't know how to sing, and impulse takes them <in the direction>[53] natural to them, and they desire what they should, at the time[54] when they should and as they should, such people will be successful[55] even if they are actually mindless and unreasoning. (viii.2, 1247b20–6)

But then what is it that causes them to desire *this particular thing, now* (given that it is something they should desire, in the way they desire it, and it's the right time)? Is it *fortune, tuchē*, after all? (1248a16–17). If so, won't fortune (chance) turn out to be the cause of everything – of our having a particular thought (*noēsai*), or of our going through a particular process of deliberation (*bouleusasthai*, a18–21)? Thinking is not the starting point of thought, nor deliberation of deliberation; so what possible starting point is there, if it is not chance (a21–2)?

Now follows the long passage cited just above, 'Or is it that there is some starting point that has no other starting point outside it, and this can do the sort of thing in question because of being the sort of thing it is? . . .', where Aristotle wheels in his 'demonic something' (i.e. 1248a23 ff). But it is no mere *deus ex machina*,[56] any more, I think, than was the original Socratic model. The 'sort of voice' Socrates 'seems to hear', holding him back from crossing the river Ilissus after his first speech on love in the *Phaedrus*,[57] is surely internal: something inside him is telling him, even though he has not thought it through, that something is wrong (something he would or should have seen was wrong if he had thought more, or had been thinking

---

[51] ᾠδικοί Sylburg; ἄδικοι PCBL; *indocti BF*; ἀδίδακτοι ᾠδικοί Jackson.

[52] εὖ πεφύκασι: εὖ = *bene BF*; οὐ PCBL.   [53] ἧ *suppl.* Jackson = *secundum quod BF*.

[54] καὶ τότε = *et tunc BF*; καὶ πότε PCB; ποτὲ L.

[55] κατορθώσουσι = *dirigent BF*; κατορθοῦσι PCL; κατορθοῦσιν B.

[56] As it might be said to be, for example, according to the interpretation offered by Struck 2016: 'Due to the difficulties with the νοῦς idea [i.e. that 'god' moves things us via νοῦς or τὸ ἐν ἡμῖν θεῖον] that we have already shown, the consensus has settled on the hypothesis of independent divine involvement', which Struck explains as the operation of the Prime Mover through our natural impulses: 'movements from potentiality to act are precipitated via [?] the Prime Mover. While nature sets out the circuits for these movements, the divine provides the voltage that activates them . . . this impetus veers towards the good . . . Without [this] impulse hypothesis, we do not have an explanation for why bare impulses in even rudimentary natures (in this case, ourselves as organisms) vector towards the good. With it, we do. In such a state we are akin to plants sending roots toward water' (152–3). There is much that is admirable in this analysis, but it lays too much weight on a single word, πως, in 1248a27 in order to disarm 'the νοῦς idea', which in some form or other will surely remain central to the passage; the reference to a 'consensus' is puzzling; and the impulses in question in the chapter are not 'bare impulses . . . of ourselves as organisms', but rather the 'well-natured' impulses of a select category of individuals (the fortunate).

[57] He calls it 'the δαιμόνιον, the sign that I'm used to having come to me' (242b8).

more clearly). Aristotle takes over this model and deploys it in a rather more central role, or roles: instead of being something that operates intermittently, the 'demonic something' now becomes, in the guise of the divine in us, originating principle of both (i) the actualisation of the 'well-natured' impulses and desires of the fortunate and (ii) rational processes in human beings in general. In the present context, the latter role of the divine in us is incidental, simply providing part of the dialectical progress to the solution of the problem of good fortune as Aristotle has framed it. What prompts the use of the Socratic model here[58] in the first place is that the cases of the fortunate and of Socrates on the Ilissus both involve what one might call a rational irrationality: in both cases, the right path, and the path that the agent would naturally follow, is actually followed even in the absence of reasoning, thanks to 'the divine in us', operating as first cause in us as god does in the universe – as Aristotle puts it and Socrates might not have been averse to putting it himself.[59]

'The divine in us' is here divine just because it is a first cause.[60] There is nothing about it that is actually supernatural, or outside our natures (even if it is something that allows us – some aspect of us – to be, in some small way, comparable to god). Nor, in the end, is there any magic or mystery about the nature of its operation.[61] The originating principle, *archē*, in this case does not operate in a vacuum. Rather, 'some of [the fortunate] achieve what they achieve through experience, some through habituation, instead of using enquiry, and [the outcomes of] these are thanks to the god' (1226a36–8, cited above). Just as the decisions and actions of reasoning agents are preceded by deliberation, the actions of the fortunate are preceded by the unthinking absorption of data from their lived, habitual experience[62] (cf. Socrates' 'from habit and practice and in the absence of philosophy and intelligence', in the *Phaedo*); and these data, in

---

[58] Or, at least, Aristotle's continuing nods to Socrates, in case 'use of the Socratic model' appears too strong a claim (which it probably is).

[59] That Socrates' δαιμόνιόν τι only acts to stop his doing something, while Aristotle's is cause of positive actions, presumably has something to do with the fact that the actions in Aristotle's case have a basis in the agent's natural impulses and desires; such a basis for positive actions (which would require the best argument(s) available) is lacking in Socrates' case.

[60] To adapt Peter Struck (n. 56 above), 'nature organises the circuits for these movements in the right way, while the divine in us provides the voltage that activates them'.

[61] Nor, perhaps, is there any mystery about the presence of a first cause in us; there has to be something of the sort, if human beings are themselves 'first principles of actions', ἀρχαὶ πράξεων (*Eth. Eud.* II.6, 1223a15, 16).

[62] *Eth. Eud.* II.8, 1224a27–33 suggests that what is said by inspired people who foretell the future is not in their power. I take it that this will apply to our fortunate individuals insofar as they have no idea why they are doing what they are doing, but it does not mean that they are not responsible for their actions; after all, the causes of what they do – on the interpretation proposed – are entirely internal.

confrontation with actual situations, and in combination with the 'well-naturedness' of their desires, are what the demonic/divine in them operates on in order to produce their version of good living.[63]

So why, then, if there is in the end nothing magical or supernatural involved, does Aristotle use the language of religion in the way that he does? In *Eth. Eud.* i.i, he does at least add qualifications, talking about those who might be happy '*like* those possessed by the supernatural or divine, beside themselves, *as it were*, through the inspiration of something demonic'; in viii.2 there are no such qualifications. The fortunate are said straightforwardly to be subject to inspiration, and to be prophetic – as indeed are 'the wise and intellectually accomplished' (i.e. people who use the reasoning the fortunate fail to use); the divine in the fortunate sees well both future and present, as it must if it is – instantaneously? – assessing the situation here and now, '(fore)seeing' what it requires (even if they themselves cannot articulate the reasons why). Here, too, there is a Socratic parallel. Plato's Socrates continually appropriates the language of religion, without apology or qualification, subverting it to his own uses.[64] But the metaphorical use of *mantikē*, '(the art of) prophecy', for example, in this context is hardly different in kind from the treatment of intelligence (*nous*) in *Eth. Nic.* vi '=' *Eth. Eud.* v as perception:

> And intelligence has as its objects what is last in both directions; for both the primary definitions and what is last in practical reasoning are to be grasped by intelligence, not reasoning, the objects of the sort of intelligence that operates in demonstrations being definitions that are unchanging and first, while the object of the sort that operates with practical dispositions is what is

---

[63] The Socratic connections of the *Eth. Eud.* go still deeper, in a way even shaping the whole – if it is a whole (viii is after all a fragment on any analysis); if it is not, it certainly has a beginning, and an end that is connected to the beginning, in a way that is strikingly similar to that of Plato's *Meno*. Aristotle starts by asking how happiness is acquired (i.i, 1214a14–25), whether by nature, by learning ('it being knowledge of some sort'), or practice – or else by divine inspiration, or by chance, and ends by returning, in a way, to include each of the last two alternatives. In the *Meno*, Meno asks Socrates the same question about goodness (ἀρετή, 'virtue', central to Aristotle's own account of happiness): do we acquire it by being taught, by practice, by chance – or in some other way (Plato, *Meno* 70a1–4)? And having supposedly shown in the course of the ensuing conversation that it cannot be taught, Socrates concludes that those who have it, if they do, must have it either through chance (99a) or because they are divinely possessed (99e). And the language in the Aristotelian context shows what looks like more than a coincidental overlap with that of the *Meno*: 'by divine inspiration' in the *Eth. Eud.* is καθάπερ οἱ νυμφόληπτοι καὶ θεόληπτοι … ἐπιπνοίᾳ δαιμονίου τινὸς ὥσπερ ἐνθουσιάζοντες; at *Meno* 99d2–4, people (politicians) who – supposedly – get things right do so because of their being θείους (divine) … καὶ ἐνθουσιάζειν, ἐπίπνους ὄντας καὶ κατεχομένου ἐκ τοῦ θεοῦ (= θεόληπτοι). (If the argument has been correct, then 'goodness would not be by nature, or be something taught, but would come by divine apportionment to whomever it should come': 99e5–100a1. The *Meno* is not serious; the *Eth. Eud.* is.)

[64] See e.g. Morgan 2010.

last and contingent, and belongs to the second premiss. For these are the starting points of that for the sake of which, since things that are universal consist of particulars. So one must have perception of these, and this is intelligence. (*Eth. Nic.* vi.11, 1143a35–b5; trans. Broadie and Rowe, with two minor modifications)

This last passage seems to me key to understanding the operation of 'the divine in us' in the case of the possessors of the special *eutuchia* of *Eth. Eud.* viii.1. Those people capable of reasoning will presumably utilise – what *Eth. Nic.* vi '=' *Eth. Eud.* v calls – 'intelligence', *nous*, 'in both directions' (i.e. at the level of both universals and particulars), while the fortunate have available to them either it or something like it only at the level of particulars. Aristotle is evidently not inclined to call it *nous* at this point in the *Eth. Eud.*, whether in relation to reasoners or to the fortunate, given that he uses *noein* and its cognates in the context freely in a general, non-technical sense (1248a18, 20, 21, 29, 32), and it is an interesting question why, if *Eth. Nic.* vi '=' *Eth. Eud.* v has preceded *Eth. Eud.* viii, why this should be so. My own long-held view[65] is that whatever may hold of the other two 'common' books, what we know as *Eth. Nic.* vi, and are encouraged by much of the tradition to treat as *Eth. Eud.* v, never in fact formed part of the *Eth. Eud.*, and that the fragment we are used to calling *Eth. Eud.* viii is a part of an original Eudemian treatment of some of the same or similar topics; thus in my view the treatment of 'the divine in us' in *Eth. Eud.* viii.2 (and 3) could well be the precursor of that of *nous* in *Eth. Nic.* vi.11. The ending of the *Eth. Eud.* book – though actually, according to the manuscripts, it was not originally the end at all[66] – is much more like that of *Eth. Nic.* vi, despite first appearances, than it is like the ending of *Eth. Nic.* x, and overall the content of viii is more distinctive, more different from the *Eth. Nic.* (with or without the common books), than any other part of the *Eth. Eud.* (its extended engagement with Socrates being a significant part of that difference). But that is another story.

This interpretation of viii.2 helps resolve an apparent inconsistency at the heart of Aristotle's ethics. 'Nature', for Aristotle, is both normative and a matter of what happens always or for the most part. Outside ethics, nature's dual role presents few problems; indeed 'nature' usually serves as

---

[65] First stated in the published version of my 1969 doctoral thesis, Rowe 1971.

[66] The last words of the *Eth. Eud.* as we have it are a kind of summary, with a particle (μέν) that looks forward to a treatment of some new topic.

normative just because it represents what happens always or for the most part. But in ethics the two roles are *prima facie* not so easy to reconcile. On the one hand, a human being is naturally something *spoudaion*, good; on the other, those who are actually and fully *spoudaioi* according to the Aristotelian specification will be relatively few in number (*Eth. Nic.* 1.9 is markedly optimistic about the number of people who might aspire to it; x.9 gives the pessimistic view, writing off the majority of people in fairly uncompromising terms: 1179b7–16). Given Aristotle's dislike for paradox, one would suppose that he would accept approximations to the specification, and indeed this is spelled out in the *Eth. Nic.*, in a passage that also refers, almost in passing, to a type of person that bears a striking resemblance to the *eutucheis* of *Eth. Eud.* VIII.2:

> But perhaps we should be satisfied if, with all the factors in place through which it is thought that we become decent people (*epieikeis*), we were to acquire a portion of excellence. Now some people think we become good by nature, while others think it is by habituation, and others again by teaching. Well, *the natural element clearly does not depend on us, but belongs by divine causes of some kind to the truly fortunate*;[67] while talk and teaching may well not have force under all circumstances, and the soul of the hearer has to have been prepared beforehand through its habits in order to delight in and loathe the right things ... (*Eth. Nic.* x.9, 1179b18–26)

If the italicised words do refer to our special kind of *eutuchia*,[68] and it is hard to think of any alternative candidates,[69] then the passage confirms that the effect, if not the intention, of VIII.2 is to help towards a broadening of the category of those who lead decent lives (i.e. lives – as *Eth. Nic.* upholds as much as the *Eth. Eud.* – of a sort consistent with human nature); it is left open whether or not 'some people' are right in thinking that goodness itself could thus be said to arise by nature (presumably not). The consequence of Aristotle's deployment of divine

[67] τὸ μὲν οὖν τῆς φύσεως δῆλον ὡς οὐκ ἐφ'ἡμῖν ἀλλὰ διά τινας θείας αἰτίας τοῖς ὡς ἀληθῶς εὐτυχέσιν ὑπάρχει: *Eth. Nic.* x.9, 1179b22–3.

[68] Which it seems to sum up quite well: true, in our εὐτυχία it is not 'the natural element' itself that belongs to the fortunate by virtue of the divine, but it is the divine that as it were translates the 'well-natured' element in the fortunate, their εὐφυΐα, into action.

[69] The possibility that happiness arises κατά τινα θείαν μοῖραν is raised in *Eth. Nic.* 1.9, 1099b19, in a passage that is the counterpart of *Eth. Eud.* 1.1, without its being developed or discussed in the *Eth. Nic.* itself. I do not go so far as supposing that the Nicomachean Aristotle ever deliberately intends to refer to his Eudemian self, but that may be the actual effect of *Eth. Nic.* x.9, 1179b22–3, if it is not explicable by reference to any other passage than *Eth. Eud.* VIII.2 – which will represent the kind of ἄλλη ... σκέψις to which *Eth. Nic.* 1099b13–14 devolves the discussion of divine causation in this context.

causation in *Eth. Eud.* VIII.2 is the reverse of Socrates' in the *Apology* and the *Phaedo*: whereas Socrates' 'demonic something' is private to him, or to him plus anyone else who shares his totalising commitment to reason,[70] Aristotle's enables *him* to assign a degree of happiness even to some whose capacity for successful practical reasoning for themselves approaches zero.

---

[70] The extreme exclusiveness of the strict Socratic position is underlined by the marking off of the possessors of demotic/civic goodness in the *Phaedo* as barely even human (if they are to be reborn as 'bees, wasps, or ants, or perhaps even as decent human beings' – where 'decent' renders μέτριοι, which I take in my 1993 Cambridge commentary on the dialogue as a nod towards Herodotus *Histories* 11.32, μέτριοι ἄνδρες: 'men of a decent size', contrasted with pygmies).

Bibliography

Anjum, R. L. and Mumford, S. 2018. *What Tends to Be: The Philosophy of Dispositional Modality*. Abingdon and New York: Routledge.

Annas, J. 1999. *Platonic Ethics, Old and New*. Ithaca, NY: Cornell University Press.

2017. *Virtue and Law in Plato and Beyond*. Oxford: Oxford University Press.

Anscombe, G. E. M. 1973. 'Causality and Determination', pp. 63–81 in E. Sosa (ed.), *Causation and Conditionals*. Oxford: Oxford University Press.

Armstrong, J. M. 2004. 'After the Ascent: Plato on Becoming Like God', *Oxford Studies in Ancient Philosophy* 26: 171–83.

Aufderheide, J. 2020. *Aristotle's* Nicomachean Ethics *Book* x. Cambridge: Cambridge University Press.

Baker, S. H. 2015. 'The Concept of *Ergon*: Towards an Achievement Interpretation of Aristotle's "Function Argument"', *Oxford Studies in Ancient Philosophy* 48: 227–66.

Barnes, J. (ed.) 1984. *The Complete Works of Aristotle: The Revised Oxford Translation*. Princeton: Princeton University Press.

Bartels, M. 2017. *Plato's Pragmatic Project: A Reading of Plato's* Laws. Stuttgart: Franz Steiner Verlag.

Bobonich, C. 2002. *Plato's Utopia Recast: His Later Ethics and Politics*. Oxford: Oxford University Press.

Bobzien, S. 2014. 'Choice and Moral Responsibility in *Nicomachean Ethics* III 1–5', pp. 81–109 in R. Polansky (ed.), *The Cambridge Companion to Aristotle's* Nicomachean Ethics. Cambridge: Cambridge University Press.

Broadie, S. 1991. *Ethics with Aristotle*. Oxford: Oxford University Press.

2001. 'Theodicy and Pseudo-History in the *Timaeus*', *Oxford Studies in Ancient Philosophy* 21: 1–28.

2007a. 'On the Idea of the *Summum Bonum*', pp. 135–52 in *Aristotle and Beyond: Essays on Metaphysics and Ethics*. Cambridge: Cambridge University Press.

2007b. 'Nature and Craft in Aristotelian Teleology', pp. 85–100 in *Aristotle and Beyond: Essays on Metaphysics and Ethics*. Cambridge: Cambridge University Press. (First published as 'Nature, Craft and *Phronesis* in Aristotle', *Philosophical Topics* 15 (1987): 35–50.)

2011. *Nature and Divinity in Plato's* Timaeus. Cambridge: Cambridge University Press.

Broadie, S. and Rowe, C. J. 2002. *Aristotle:* Nicomachean Ethics. Oxford and New York: Oxford University Press.

Brown, L. (ed.) 2009. *The* Nicomachean Ethics, trans. D. Ross, new edition. Oxford: Oxford University Press.

Buddensiek, F. 2012. 'Does Good Fortune Matter? *Eudemian Ethics* VIII.2 on *Eutuchia*', pp. 155–84 in F. Leigh (ed.), *The* Eudemian Ethics *on the Voluntary, Friendship, and Luck* [the sixth S. V. Keeling Colloquium in Ancient Philosophy] = Philosophia Antiqua 132. Leiden: Brill.

Burnet, J. (ed.) 1899–1907. *Platonis Opera*, 5 vols. Oxford: Clarendon Press.

Burnyeat, M. F. 1997. 'First Words: A Valedictory Lecture', *Proceedings of the Cambridge Philological Society* 43: 1–20.

2012. 'The Passion of Reason in Plato's *Phaedrus*', pp. 238–58 in *Explorations in Ancient and Modern Philosophy*, Vol. 2. Cambridge: Cambridge University Press.

Bywater, I. (ed.) 1894. *Ethica Nicomachea*. Oxford: Clarendon Press.

Caluori, D. 2011. 'Reason and Necessity: The Descent of the Philosopher Kings'. *Oxford Studies in Ancient Philosophy* 40: 7–27.

Carone, G. R. 2005. *Plato's Cosmology and its Ethical Dimensions*. Cambridge: Cambridge University Press.

Charles, D. 2011. 'Desire in Action: Aristotle's Move', pp. 75–94 in M. Pakaluk and G. Pearson (eds.), *Moral Psychology and Human Action*. Oxford: Oxford University Press.

2015. 'Aristotle's Processes', pp. 186–205 in M. Leunissen (ed.), *Aristotle's* Physics: *A Critical Guide*. Cambridge: Cambridge University Press.

Cheng, W. (2020) 'Aristotle and Eudoxus on the Argument from Contraries', *Archiv für Geschichte der Philosophie* 102: 588–612.

Connell, S. 2016. *Aristotle on Female Animals*. Cambridge: Cambridge University Press.

Coope, U. 2005. 'Aristotle's Account of Agency in *Physics* III 3', *Proceedings of the Boston Area Colloquium in Ancient Philosophy* 20: 201–21.

2007. 'Aristotle on Action', *Proceedings of the Aristotelian Society, Supplementary Volume* 81: 109–38.

2015. 'Self-Motion as Other-Motion in Aristotle's *Physics*', pp. 245–64 in M. Leunissen (ed.), *Aristotle's* Physics: *A Critical Guide*. Cambridge: Cambridge University Press.

2021. 'Aristotle on Productive Understanding and Completeness', pp. 109–30 in T. K. Johansen (ed.), *Productive Knowledge in Ancient Philosophy: The Concept of* Technē. Cambridge: Cambridge University Press.

Cooper, J. M. 1996. 'An Aristotelian Theory of the Emotions', pp. 238–57 in A. O. Rorty (ed.), *Essays on Aristotle's* Rhetoric. Berkeley: University of California Press.

(ed.) 1997. *Plato Complete Works*. Indianapolis and Cambridge: Hackett.

2013. *Pursuits of Wisdom: Six Ways of Life in Ancient Philosophy from Socrates to Plotinus*. Princeton: Princeton University Press.

Cornford, F. M. 1997. *Plato's Cosmology: The* Timaeus *of Plato*. Indianapolis: Hackett.

Crisp, R. 2003. 'Socrates and Aristotle on Happiness and Virtue', pp. 55–78 in R. Heinaman (ed.), *Plato and Aristotle's Ethics*. London: UCL/Ashgate.

Curd, P. and Graham, D. W. (eds.) 2008. *The Oxford Handbook of Presocratic Philosophy*. Oxford and New York: Oxford University Press.

Denniston, J. D. 1950. *The Greek Particles*, 2nd ed., revised by K. J. Dover. London: Duckworth.

Diels, H. and Kranz, W. 1952. *Die Fragmente der Vorsokratiker*. 6th ed. revised by W. Kranz, 3 vols. Berlin: Weidmann.

Dillon, J. 1993. *Alcinous: The Handbook of Platonism*. Oxford: Clarendon Press.

  1996. *The Middle Platonists, 80 B.C. to A.D. 220*, 2nd ed. Ithaca, NY: Cornell University Press.

Dow, J. 2009. 'Feeling Fantastic? Emotions and Appearances in Aristotle', *Oxford Studies in Ancient Philosophy* 37: 143–75.

  2011. 'Aristotle's Theory of the Emotions – Emotions as Pleasures and Pains', pp. 47–74 in M. Pakaluk and G. Pearson (eds.), *Moral Psychology and Human Action in Aristotle*. Oxford: Oxford University Press.

  2014. 'Feeling Fantastic Again: Passions, Appearances and Beliefs in Aristotle', *Oxford Studies in Ancient Philosophy* 46: 213–51.

  2015. *Passions and Persuasion in Aristotle's* Rhetoric. Oxford: Oxford University Press.

Echeñique, J. 2012. *Aristotle's* Ethics *and Moral Responsibility*. Cambridge: Cambridge University Press.

Eisenstadt, M. 1974. 'Xenophanes' Proposed Reform of Greek Religion', *Hermes* 102: 142–50.

Emilsson, E. K. 2017. *Plotinus*. Abingdon: Routledge.

Everson, S. 1990. 'Aristotle's Compatibilism in the *Nicomachean Ethics*', *Ancient Philosophy* 10: 81–103.

Fantino, E., Muss, U., Schubert, C., and Sier, K. (eds.) 2017. *Heraklit im Kontext*, Studia Praesocratica 8, Berlin and Boston: De Gruyter.

Ferrari, G. R. F. 1987. *Listening to the Cicadas: A Study of Plato's* Phaedrus. Cambridge: Cambridge University Press.

Fine, G. 2003. *Plato on Knowledge and Forms: Selected Essays*. Oxford: Clarendon Press.

Fortenbaugh, W. W. 1971. 'Aristotle: Animals, Emotion and Moral Virtue', *Arethusa* 4: 137–65.

  2002. *Aristotle on Emotion: A Contribution to Philosophical Psychology, Rhetoric, Poetics, Politics and Ethics*, 2nd ed. London: Duckworth.

Frankfurt, H. G. 1971. 'Freedom of the Will and the Concept of a Person', *The Journal of Philosophy* 68.1: 5–20.

Frede, D. 1996. 'Rationality and Concepts in the *Timaeus*', pp. 29–58 in M. Frede and G. Striker (eds.), *Rationality in Greek Thought*. Oxford: Oxford University Press.

  1997. *Platon* Philebos*, Übersetzung und Kommentar*. Göttingen: Vandenhoeck & Ruprecht.

2010. 'Puppets on Strings: Moral Psychology in *Laws* Books 1 and 2', pp. 108–26 in C. Bobonich (ed.), *Plato's Laws: A Critical Guide*. Cambridge: Cambridge University Press.

2014. 'A Swarm of Virtues: On the Unity and Completeness of Aristotle's Scheme of Character-Virtues', pp. 83–103 in M. Lee (ed.), *Strategies of Argument: Essays in Ancient Ethics, Epistemology, and Logic*. Oxford: Oxford University Press.

2019. 'The Deficiency of Human Nature: The Task of a "Philosophy of Human Affairs"', pp. 258–74 in G. Keil and N. Kreft (eds.), *Aristotle's Anthropology*. Cambridge: Cambridge University Press.

Fronterotta, F. 2018. 'Eudoxe et Speusippe sur le plaisir (selon Aristote): un débat dans l'ancienne Académie', *Revue de philosophie ancienne* 36.1: 39–72.

Gelber, J. 2015. 'Aristotle on Essence and Habitat', *Oxford Studies in Ancient Philosophy* 48: 267–93.

Giannantoni, G. 1990. 'Etica Aristotelica e etica Socratica', pp. 303–26 in A. Alberti (ed.), *Studi sull' etica di Aristotele*. Naples: Bibliopolis.

Gill, C., 2003. 'The *Laws* – Is It a Real Dialogue?', pp. 42–7 in S. Scolnicov and L. Brisson (eds.), *Plato's Laws: From Theory into Practice*. Sankt Augustin: Academia Verlag.

Giovannini, A. 1985. 'Peut-on démythifier l'Atlantide?', *Museum Helveticum* 42: 151–56.

Gosling, J. C. B. 1975. Philebus: *Translated with Notes and Commentary*. Oxford: Clarendon Press.

Gosling, J. C. B. and Taylor, C. C. W. 1982. *The Greeks on Pleasure*. Oxford: Oxford University Press.

Graham, Daniel W. 2010. *The Texts of Early Greek Philosophy*, 2. vols. Cambridge: Cambridge University Press.

Granger, H. 1993. 'Aristotle on the Analogy between Action and Nature, *Classical Quarterly* 43: 168–76.

2013. 'Xenophanes' Positive Theology and His Criticism of Greek Popular Religion', *Ancient Philosophy* 33: 235-271.

Graver, M. and Long, A. A. (trans.) 2015. *Seneca: Letters on Ethics*. Chicago: Chicago University Press.

Gray, V. J. 2007. *Xenophon on Government*. Cambridge: Cambridge University Press.

Grönroos, G. 2007. 'Listening to Reason in Aristotle's Moral Psychology', *Oxford Studies in Ancient Philosophy* 32: 251–71.

Guthrie, W. K. C. 1971. *Socrates*. Cambridge: Cambridge University Press.

Hackforth, R. 1952. *Plato's* Phaedrus. Cambridge: Cambridge University Press.

Hankinson, R. J. 2014. 'Efficient Causation in the Stoic Tradition', pp. 54–82 in T. Schmaltz (ed.), *Efficient Causation: A History*. Oxford: Oxford University Press.

Harper, K. 2017. *The Fate of Rome*. Princeton: Princeton University Press.

Harte, V. 2004. 'The *Philebus* on Pleasure: The Good, the Bad and the False', *Proceedings of the Aristotelian Society*, 104: 111–28.

Harvey, G. 2020. 'The Cosmic Purpose of Natural Disasters in Plato's *Laws*', *Ancient Philosophy* 40.1: 157–77.

Heath, M. 2008. 'Aristotle on Natural Slavery', *Phronesis*, 53.3: 243–70.

Heinimann, F. 1945. Nomos *und* Physis: *Herkunft und Bedeutung einer Antithese im griechischen Denken des 5. Jahrhunderts.* Basel: Wissenschaftliche Buchgesellschaft.

Henry, D. 2014. 'The Birds and the Bees: Aristotle on the Biological Concept of ἀνάλογον', *Proceedings of the Boston Area Colloquium in Ancient Philosophy* 29.1: 145–69.

Henry, D. and Nielsen, K. M. (eds.) 2015. *Bridging the Gap between Aristotle's Science and Ethics.* Cambridge: Cambridge University Press.

Hölscher, U. 1993. 'Paradox, Simile, and Gnomic Utterance in Heraclitus', pp. 229–38 in A. Mourelatos (ed.), *The Pre-Socratics: A Collection of Critical Essays*, 2nd ed. with editor's supplement. Princeton: Princeton University Press.

Ierodiakonou, K. and Hasper, P. S. (eds.) 2016. *Logical Analysis and History of Philosophy*, 19 [volume on Ancient Epistemology]. Münster: Mentis.

Inwood, B. 2005. *Reading Seneca: Stoic Philosophy at Rome.* Oxford: Clarendon Press.

Irwin, T. 1995. *Plato's Ethics.* Oxford: Oxford University Press.

Jaeger, W. 1960. 'Praise of Law: The Origin of Legal Philosophy and the Greeks', pp. 319–51 in W. Jaeger (ed.), *Scripta Minora*, Vol. 2. Rome: Edizioni di storia e letteratura.

Johansen, T. 2004. *Plato's Natural Philosophy: A Study of the* Timaeus-Critias. Cambridge: Cambridge University Press.

Kelsey, S. 2004. 'The Argument of *Metaphysics* VI.3', *Ancient Philosophy* 24.1: 119–34.

2011. '*Physics* 199a8–12', *Apeiron* 44: 1–12.

Keyt, D. 2006. 'Plato and the Ship of State', pp. 189–213 in G. Santas (ed.), *The Blackwell Guide to Plato's* Republic. Malden and Oxford: Blackwell.

Konstan, D. 2006. *The Emotions of the Ancient Greeks: Studies in Aristotle and Classical Literature.* Toronto: University of Toronto Press.

Kosman, A. 1980. 'Being Properly Affected: Virtues and Feelings in Aristotle's Ethics', pp. 103–16 in A. O. Rorty (ed.), *Essays on Aristotle's Ethics.* Berkeley: University of California Press.

Kraut, R. 1973. 'Egoism, Love, and Political Office in Plato', *Philosophical Review* 82.3: 330–44.

Kress, E. 2019. 'How Things Happen for the Sake of Something', *Phronesis* 64.3: 321–47.

Lafond, Y. 1998. 'Die Katastrophe von 373 v. Chr. und das Verschwinden der Stadt Helikê in Achaia', pp. 118–23 in E. Olshausen and H. Sonnabend (eds.), *Naturkatastrophen in der Antiken Welt.* Stuttgarter Kolloquium zur Historischen Geographie des Altertums 6, 1996. Stuttgart: J. B. Metzler.

Laks, A. 2000. 'The *Laws*', pp. 258–92 in C. Rowe and M. Schofield (eds.), *The Cambridge History of Greek and Roman Political Thought.* Cambridge: Cambridge University Press.

2005. *Médiation et coercition: pour une lecture des* Lois *de Platon*. Lille: Presses Universitaires du Septentrion.

Laks, A. and Louguet, C. (eds.) 2002. *Qu'est-ce que la philosophie présocratique?* Lille: Presses Universitaires du Septentrion.

Laks, A. and Most, G. W. (eds.) 2016. *Early Greek Philosophy*, 9 vols. Loeb Classical Library 524–32. Cambridge, MA and London: Harvard University Press.

Lännström, A. 2011. 'Socrates, the Philosopher in the *Theaetetus* Digression (172c–177c), and the Ideal of *homoiôsis theôi*', *Apeiron* 44: 111–30.

Lasserre, F. 1966. *Eudoxos von Knidos. Die Fragmente*. Berlin: De Gruyter.

Lebedev, A. V. 2017. 'The Metaphor of *Liber Naturae* and the Alphabet Analogy in Heraclitus' *Logos*-Fragments', pp. 231–67 in E. Fantino, U. Muss, C. Schubert, and K. Sier (eds.), *Heraklit im Kontext*. Studia Praesocratica 8. Berlin and Boston: De Gruyter.

Lee, H. D. P. (trans.) 1952. *Aristotle:* Meteorologica. Cambridge, MA: Harvard University Press.

Leighton, S. 1982. 'Aristotle and the Emotions', *Phronesis* 27: 144–74.

1984. 'Feelings and Emotions', *The Review of Metaphysics* 38: 303–20.

Lennox, J. G. 1999. 'Aristotle on the Biological Roots of Virtue: The Natural History of Natural Virtue', pp. 10–31 in J. Maienschein and M. Ruse (eds.), *Biology and the Foundation of Ethics*. Cambridge: Cambridge University Press.

Leunissen, M. 2012. 'Aristotle on Natural Character and Its Implications for Moral Development', *Journal of the history of philosophy* 50.4: 507–30.

2014. 'Commentary on Henry', *Proceedings of the Boston Area Colloquium in Ancient Philosophy* 29.1: 170–81.

Lewis, D. 1973. 'Causation', *Journal of Philosophy* 70.17: 556–67.

Long, A. A. 1968. 'The Stoic Concept of Evil', *Philosophical Quarterly* 18: 329–43.

1996a. *Stoic Studies*. Cambridge: Cambridge University Press (repr. Berkeley: University of California Press, 2001).

1996b. 'Heraclitus and Stoicism', pp. 35–57 in A. A. Long (ed.), *Stoic Studies*. Cambridge: Cambridge University Press.

1996c. 'Stoic Eudaimonism', pp. 179–201 in A. A. Long (ed.), *Stoic Studies*. Cambridge: Cambridge University Press.

2005. 'Law and Nature in Greek Thought', pp. 412–30 in M. Gagarin and D. Cohen (eds.), *The Cambridge Companion to Ancient Greek Law*. Cambridge: Cambridge University Press.

Long, A. A. and Sedley, D. N. 1987. *The Hellenistic Philosophers*. Cambridge: Cambridge University Press.

Long, A. G. 2017. 'The Ship of State and the Subordination of Socrates', pp. 158–78 in P. Destrée and R. G. Edmonds III (eds.), *Plato and the Power of Images*. Leiden: Brill.

[in press]. 'Nature in Politics and Moral Psychology', in M. M. McCabe (ed.), *Re-Reading Plato's Republic*.

Lorenz, H. 2006. *The Brute Within: Appetitive Desire in Plato and Aristotle.* Oxford: Oxford University Press.

Mahoney, T. A. 2004. 'Is Assimilation to God in the *Theaetetus* Purely Otherworldly?', *Ancient Philosophy* 24: 321–38.

Marmodoro, A. 2007. 'The Union of Cause and Effect in Aristotle: *Physics* 3.3', *Oxford Studies in Ancient Philosophy* 32: 205–32.

 2018. 'Potentiality in Aristotle's *Metaphysics*', pp. 15–43 in K. Engelhard and M. Quante (eds.), *Handbook of Potentiality.* Dordrecht: Springer Netherlands.

Mayhew, R. 2008. *Plato: Laws 10.* Oxford: Oxford University Press.

McKenna, M. 2001. 'Source Incompatibilism, Ultimacy, and the Transfer of Non-Responsibility', *American Philosophical Quarterly* 38.1: 37–51.

McKirahan, R. 2011. *Philosophy before Socrates*, 2nd ed. Indianapolis: Hackett.

Menn, S. 2000. 'On Dennis Des Chene's *Physiologia*', *Perspectives on Science* 8.2: 119–43.

Mesch, W. 2013. 'War Aristoteles ein Determinist?', *Zeitschrift für philosophische Forschung* 67.1: 113–31.

Meyer, S. S. 1994. 'Self-Movement and External Causation', pp. 65–80 in M. L. Gill and J. G. Lennox (eds.), *Self-Motion: From Aristotle to Newton.* Princeton: Princeton University Press.

 2011. 'Legislation as a Tragedy: On Plato's *Laws* VII, 817b-d', pp. 387–402 in P. Destrée and F.-G. Hermann (eds.), *Plato and the Poets.* Leiden: Brill.

 2015. *Plato: Laws 1 & 2.* Oxford: Oxford University Press.

Miller, F. D. Jr. 1991. 'Aristotle on Natural Law and Justice', pp. 279–306 in D. Keyt and F. D. Miller, Jr. (eds.), *A Companion to Aristotle's* Politics. Oxford and Cambridge: Blackwell.

Moline, J. 1975. 'Provided Nothing External Interferes', *Mind* 84: 244–54.

Moore, C. 2019. 'Socrates in Aristotle's History of Philosophy', pp. 173–210 in C. Moore (ed.), *Brill's Companion to the Reception of Socrates.* Leiden: Brill.

Morgan, K. 2010. 'The Voice of Authority: Divination and Plato's *Phaedo*', *Classical Quarterly* 60.1: 63–81.

Morrison, D. R. 2007. 'The Utopian Character of Plato's Ideal City', pp. 232–55 in G. R. F. Ferrari (ed.), *The Cambridge Companion to Plato's* Republic. Cambridge: Cambridge University Press.

Mosely, D. J. 1998. 'Politics, Diplomacy and Disaster in Ancient Greece', pp. 67–77 in E. Olshausen and D. Sonnabend (eds.), *Naturkatastrophen in der Antiken Welt.* Stuttgarter Kolloquium zur Historischen Geographie des Altertums 6, 1996. Stuttgart: J. B. Metzler.

Moss, J. 2012. *Aristotle on the Apparent Good: Perception, Phantasia, Thought, and Desire.* Oxford: Oxford University Press.

Mourelatos, A. P. D. 1965. 'Heraclitus Fr. 114', *American Journal of Philology* 86: 258–66.

 (ed.) 1993. *The Pre-Socratics: A Collection of Critical Essays*, 2nd ed. with editor's supplement. Princeton: Princeton University Press.

2002. 'La Terre et les étoiles dans la cosmologie de Xénophane', pp. 331–5 in A. Laks and C. Louguet (eds.), *Qu'est-ce que la philosophie présocratique?* Lille: Presses Universitaires du Septentrion.

2008a. *The Route of Parmenides*. 2nd ed. Las Vegas: Parmenides Publishing.

2008b. 'The Cloud-Astrophysics of Xenophanes and Ionian Material Monism', pp. 134–68 in P. Curd and D. W. Graham (eds.), *The Oxford Handbook of Presocratic Philosophy*. Oxford and New York: Oxford University Press.

2013. 'Parmenides, Early Greek Astronomy, and Modern Scientific Realism', in J. McCoy (ed.), *Early Greek Philosophy: The Presocratics and the Emergence of Reason*. Studies in Philosophy and the History of Philosophy 57. Washington, DC: Catholic University of America Press.

2016. '"Limitless" and "Limit" in Xenophanes' Cosmology and in His Doctrine of Epistemic "Construction" (*Dokos*)', pp. 16–37 in K. Ierodiakonou and P. S. Hasper (eds.), *Logical Analysis and History of Philosophy*, 19 [volume on *Ancient Epistemology*] Münster: Mentis.

Müller, J. 2018. 'Practical and Productive Thinking in Aristotle', *Phronesis* 63.2: 148–75.

Nightingale, A. W. 1999. 'Historiography and Cosmology in Plato's *Laws*', *Ancient Philosophy* 19.2: 299–327.

Nussbaum, M. C. 1986. *The Fragility of Goodness*. Cambridge: Cambridge University Press.

Olshausen, E. and Sonnabend, D. (eds.) 1998. *Naturkatastrophen in der Antiken Welt*. Stuttgarter Kolloquium zur Historischen Geographie des Altertums 6, 1996. Stuttgart: J. B. Metzler.

O'Meara, D. 1993. *Plotinus: An Introduction to the* Enneads. Oxford: Clarendon Press.

Polansky, R. and Kuczewski, M. 1988. 'Accidents and Processes in Aristotle's *Metaphysics* E 3', *Elenchos* 9: 295–310.

Price, A., 2011. 'Aristotle on the Ends of Deliberation', pp. 135–58 in M. Pakaluk and G. Pearson (eds.), *Moral Psychology and Human Action*. Oxford: Oxford University Press.

Rapp, C. 2002. *Aristoteles:* Rhetorik. *Übersetzt und Erläutert*, 2 vols. Berlin: Akademie Verlag.

2009. '*Nicomachean Ethics* VII.13–14: Pleasure and *Eudaimonia*', pp. 209–35 in Natali, Carlo (ed.), *Aristotle's* Nicomachean Ethics*, Book* VII*: Symposium Aristotelicum*. Oxford: Oxford University Press.

Ross, W. D. 1998. *Aristotle's* Physics: *A Revised Text with Introduction and Commentary*. Oxford: Clarendon Press.

Rowe, C. J. 1971. *The Eudemian and Nicomachean Ethics: A Study in the Development of Aristotle's Thought*. Cambridge: Cambridge Philological Society.

1975. 'A Reply to John Cooper on the *Magna Moralia*', *American Journal of Philosophy* 96.2: 160–72.

1986. *Plato* Phaedrus. Warminster: Aris & Phillips.

1990. 'Philosophy, Love, and Madness', pp. 227–46 in C. Gill (ed.), *The Person and the Human Mind: Issues in Ancient and Modern Philosophy*. Oxford: Oxford University Press.

1993. *The Phaedo*. Cambridge: Cambridge University Press.

2003. 'Reply to Roger Crisp', pp. 79–86 in R. Heinaman (ed.), *Plato and Aristotle's Ethics*. London: UCL/Ashgate.

2013. 'Socrates and His Gods: From the *Euthyphro* to the *Eudemian Ethics*', pp. 313–28 in M. Lane and V. Harte (eds.), Politeia *in Greek and Roman Philosophy*. Cambridge: Cambridge University Press.

2017. 'The Athenians against the Persians: Plato's View (*Laws* III, 699b–d)', pp. 64–81 in J. F. Finamore and S. Klitenic Wear (eds.), *Defining Platonism: Essays in Honor of the 75th Birthday of John M. Dillon*. Steubenville, OH: Franciscan University Press.

Rue, R. 1993. 'The Philosopher in Flight: The Digression (172C–177C) in the *Theaetetus*', *Oxford Studies in Ancient Philosophy* 11: 71–100.

Ryle, G. 1966. *Plato's Progress*. Cambridge: Cambridge University Press.

Sassi, M. M. 2013. 'Where Epistemology and Religion Meet: What Do(es) the God(s) Look Like?', *Rhizomata* 1: 283–307.

Sattler, B. M. 2020. *The Concept of Motion in Ancient Greek Thought: Foundations in Logic, Method, and Mathematics*. Cambridge: Cambridge University Press.

Schofield, M. 2003. 'Religion and Philosophy in the *Laws*', pp. 1–13 in S. Scolnicov and L. Brisson (eds.), *Plato's Laws: From Theory into Practice*. Sankt Augustin: Academia Verlag.

2013. 'Cardinal Virtues: A Contested Socratic Inheritance', pp. 11–28 in A. G. Long (ed.), *Plato and the Stoics*. Cambridge: Cambridge University Press.

2015. 'Heraclitus on Law (Fr. 114 DK)', *Rhizomata* 3: 47–61.

2016. 'Plato's Marionette', *Rhizomata* 4.2: 128–53.

Schofield, M. and Griffith, T. 2016 (trans.) *Plato:* The Laws. Cambridge, Cambridge University Press.

Schopenhauer, A. 1966. *The World as Will and Representation*, trans. E. J. Payne. New York: Dover Publications.

Schöpsdau, K. 1994–2011. *Platon:* Nomoi, 3 vols. Göttingen: Vandenhoeck & Ruprecht.

Sedley, D. 1997. '"Becoming Like God" in the *Timaeus* and in Aristotle', pp. 327–39 in T. Calvo and L. Brisson (eds.), *Interpreting the* Timaeus – Critias, *Proceedings of the* IV *Symposium Platonicum*. Sankt Augustin: Academia Verlag.

1999. 'The Ideal of Godlikeness', pp. 309–28 in G. Fine (ed.), *Plato 2: Ethics, Politics, Religion, and the Soul*. Oxford: Oxford University Press.

2010. 'Teleology, Aristotelian and Platonic', pp. 5–29 in J. G. Lennox and R. Bolton (eds.), *Being, Nature and Life in Aristotle: Essays in Honor of Allan Gotthelf*. Cambridge: Cambridge University Press.

2012. 'The *Theoretikos Bios* in Alcinous', pp. 329–48 in T. Bénatouil and M. Bonazzi (eds.), *Theōria, Praxis and the Contemplative Life after Plato and Aristotle*. Leiden and Boston: Brill.

2013. 'The Atheist Underground', pp. 329–48 in V. Harte and M. Lane (eds.), *Politeia in Greek and Roman Philosophy*. Cambridge: Cambridge University Press.

Segal, C. 1990. *Lucretius on Death and Anxiety*. Princeton: Princeton University Press.

Sihvola, J. 1996. 'Emotional Animals: Do Aristotelian Emotions Require Beliefs?', *Apeiron* 29: 105–44.

Smith, M. F. (trans.) 1975. *Lucretius:* On the Nature of Things. Revision of trans. by W. H. D. Rouse. Loeb Classical Library 181. Cambridge, MA: Harvard University Press.

Solmsen, F. 1951. 'Epicurus and Cosmological Heresies', *American Journal of Philology* 72: 1–23.

1960. *Aristotle's System of the Physical World*. Ithaca, NY: Cornell University Press

Sorabji, R. 1980. *Necessity, Cause, and Blame: Perspectives on Aristotle's Theory*. Ithaca, NY: Cornell University Press.

1993. *Animals Minds and Human Morals: The Origins of the Western Debate*. Ithaca NY: Cornell University Press.

1999. 'Aspasius on Emotion', pp. 96–106 in A. Alberti and R. Sharples (eds.), *Aspasius: The Earliest Extant Commentary on Aristotle's* Ethics. Berlin: De Gruyter.

Stalley, R. F. 1983. *An Introduction to Plato's* Laws. Oxford: Blackwell.

1994. 'Persuasion in Plato's *Laws*', *History of Political Thought* 15: 157–77.

Stein, N. 2012. 'Causal Necessity in Aristotle', *British Journal for the History of Philosophy* 20.5: 855–79.

Striker, G. 1993. 'Emotions in Context', pp. 286–302 in A. O. Rorty (ed.), *Essays on Aristotle's* Rhetoric. Berkeley: University of California Press.

Struck, P. T. 2016. *Divination and Human Nature: A Cognitive History of Intuition in Classical Antiquity*. Princeton: Princeton University Press.

Taylor, A. E. 1928. *A Commentary on Plato's* Timaeus. Oxford: Clarendon Press.

Taylor, C. C. W. 2007. '*Nomos* and *Phusis* in Democritus and Plato', *Social Philosophy and Policy* 24.2: 1–20.

Too, Y. L. 2001. 'Legal Instructions in Classical Athens', pp. 111–32 in *Education in Greek and Roman Antiquity*. Leiden: Brill.

Trivigno, F. 2011. 'Aristotle's Definition of Anger', *The Society for Ancient Greek Philosophy Newsletter* 12.2: 20–7.

Tuozzo, T. 2014. 'Aristotle and the Discovery of Efficient Causation', pp. 23–47 in T. Schmaltz (ed.), *Efficient Causation: A History*. Oxford: Oxford University Press.

2017. 'External Causes of Elemental Motion in Aristotle: Incidental or *Per Se*?' Paper delivered at a meeting of Society for Ancient Greek Philosophy, Baltimore.

van der Eijk, P. 1989. 'Divine Movement and Human Nature in *Eudemian Ethics* 8.2', *Hermes* 117: 24–42.

van Emde Boas, E., Rijksbaron, A., Huitink, L., and de Bakker, M. 2019. *The Cambridge Grammar of Classical Greek*. Cambridge: Cambridge University Press.

Warren, J. 2009. 'Aristotle on Speusippus on Eudoxus on Pleasure', *Oxford Studies in Ancient Philosophy* 36.1: 249–81.

Weiss, R. 1979. 'Aristotle's Criticism of Eudoxan Hedonism', *Classical Philology* 74.3: 214–21.

White, R. M. 2010. *Talking about God: The Concept of Analogy and the Problem of Religious Language*. Transcending Boundaries in Philosophy and Theology. Farnham: Ashgate.

Whittaker, J. (ed.) 1990. *Alcinoos: enseignement des doctrines de Platon*. Paris: Les Belles Lettres.

Williams, G. D. 2012. *The Cosmic Viewpoint: A Study of Seneca's* Natural Questions. Oxford: Oxford University Press.

Wilson, L. G. 1973. 'Uniformitarianism and Catastrophism', pp. 418–23 in P. Wiener (ed.), *Dictionary of the History of Ideas*, Vol. 4. New York: Charles Scriber's Sons.

Woods, M. 1982. *Aristotle's* Eudemian Ethics: *Books* I, II, *and* VIII. Translated with a commentary. Oxford: Clarendon Press.

Zeyl, D. 2000. *Plato:* Timaeus. Translated, with introduction. Indianapolis and Cambridge: Hackett.

Index Locorum

General Index

actions
  gods do not engage in 94
  how they differ from natural processes 40–8, 180–1
  purposiveness of 179–81
  relation to virtues of character 128–42
  whether they are necessitated 147–8, 160–2
affections, *see* emotions
analogy
  being related by 112–14
  between nature and craft 164–7, 179
anger 118–23, 128–9, 131, 135, 136
animals
  characters (dispositions) of 110–11, 120–2, 126, 143
  emotions (affections, passions) of 111–24
  role of desire in purposive behaviour of 178
  seek their own good (pleasure) 188–9, 191–8
animism 75, 85
anthropomorphism
  critiques of 71, 75–85, 88–9
  types of 72–4, *see also* anthropo-*philautia*, epistemic
anthropo-*philautia*, epistemic
  examples of 73–4, 83, 87, 89
  meaning of 71
art, *see* craft
atheists 17, 29–31
Athens, ancient 32–3, 46–7, 56–7, 59–60
Atlantis 32–3, 42, 43, 47, 55–7, 59, 62

Berkeley 73–4
Bible 51, 53

capacity, *see* power
catastrophe
  effects of 48, 57–60
  explanations of 53–4
  meaning of 50
  regularity of 39–40, 46, 53, 57, 62
  responses to 52, 64–8

catastrophism 51, 61
causation, causality
  accidental causation 152, 157–63
  causal chains 148, 151–63
  causal powers 149–51, 153, 162
  efficient cause 148–9, 165, 170
  final cause 165, *see also* teleology
  per se (proper) causation 152–7, 159–62
choice (*hairesis*, Eudoxius' theory of) 194–201
compatibilism 147–8
conflagration 40, 51, 56, 57, 62, 66
contemplation (*theoria*) 94–6, 97, 99–100
cosmogony 72–3, 84–5
cosmology (cosmologists) 33–4, 39, 65–6, 89
craft (art, skill, *technē*)
  accidental features of product of 158
  analogy with nature 164, 165–7, 179
  and deliberation 164, 167–77
  as external cause 173–5
  as rational power 150–1, 174
  gods exist as a result of 17
  relation to legislation 30
creation (of universe) 32, 66, 83, 84–5
culture
  development and destruction of 48, 55, 57, 58, 66
  relation to nature 33–4, 38–40, 43–4

daimonion (Socrates') 205–6, 212–13
death 65, 67, 98
decision (choice, *proairesis*) 129–32, 135–6
degree (more-and-less) 112, 113–14, 116
deliberation 120–1, 130–2, 135–6, 164, 167–77, 212
  as a purposive process 171–2
determinism, causal 147–8, 151
Deucalion 53, 55, 61
divination 80
doctors
  and deliberation 168–9
  free-born 21, 25
  working according to nature 19, 21–2, *see also* medicine

234

9 781108 813723